Murder On the Bluff

THE CAREW POISONING CASE

Molly Whittington-Egan

Neil Wilson Publishing • Glasgow • Scotland

To the memory of Mimi,
at Lyonshall, who was still with me
when I began this book.

Published by Neil Wilson Publishing Ltd
303a The Pentagon Centre
36 Washington Street
GLASGOW
G3 8AZ

Tel: 0141-221 1117
Fax: 0141-221 5363
E-mail: nwp@cqm.co.uk
http://www.nwp.co.uk/

A catalogue record for this book is available
from the British Library.

ISBN 1-897784-52-X

Typeset in 10/13pt Sabon by
The Write Stuff, Glasgow
Tel/fax: 0141-339 8279
E-mail: wilson_i@cqm.co.uk

Printed by WSOY, Finland

CONTENTS

LIST OF PLATES

ACKNOWLEDGMENTS

I am indebted to Glenn Chandler, who so magnanimously supplied me with the rare text of the *Japan Gazette*; to Richard Whittington-Egan, who was always walking beside me; to Maureen Mullaney, for unstinting help with field research; and to Keith Skinner, my wise and indispensable researcher.

I would also wish to thank for their encouragement and special knowledge the following friends and colleagues: the late Betty Abel, Literary Editor of *Contemporary Review*; Hilary Bailey, whose writing continually spurs me on, Dr Marc Hinchliffe, for sound advice on medical issues; Lewis McDonald, Pamela Scott, and Jerry Mullaney for his photographic expertise.

This book would not have been possible without the help of Adrian Blunt, Inner Temple Library; David Bromwich, Somerset Archaeological Society; R.J.E. Bush, Somerset Record Office; Willie George, Gerald Smith and Graham Hitchings of Dinas Cross; R. Gregory, of the Home Office; Paul Guy, the British Library; the Headmaster, Edgarley Hall; Sarah Hetherington, Foreign Office Library; Guy Holborn, Lincoln's Inn Library; S.D. Hookey, Pembrokeshire District Council; Revd R.C. Jones, Newport; Louis Kelly, antiquarian bookseller; Malvern Library; the secretary, Malvernian Society, Malvern College; Christina M. Marley, University of Virginia Library; Yoshitaka Nishimiya, National Diet Library, Tokyo; A. Alan Pace, Parc Gwyn Crematorium, Narberth; the Public Record Office; Simon J. Pulford, City of Swansea; M. Rowe, County Archivist, Devon County Council; Teruko Sekiguchi, Japan Information and Cultural Centre and David Wright Translation Services.

John Loveridge, Glastonbury Antiquarian Society, was a repository of information, and a most reliable guide.

Author's Note: Takao Tokuoka, an elderly Japanese scholar,

published in Tokyo in 1990 a study of the Carew Case, which has not been translated into English. Unfortunately, I have been unable to make contact with him, but would wish to attribute to him, where so indicated, the five family photographs which he had obtained. It would be a shame indeed for these historic photographs to be lost to the English readership.

Molly Whittington-Egan, Malvern, 1996

Chapter 1
A GLASTONBURY ROMANCE

It was mid-afternoon in Yokohama, and a small procession was winding its way along the cliff road known as the Bluff. There, carried on a stretcher, an Englishman lay dying. Walking at his side were his wife, his brother-in-law and a doctor.

Far below in the harbour, beyond the bluish roofs of the Japanese quarter, sails were fluttering, but the regatta days of the Englishman were over. Gaunt and dazed with suffering, his swarthy and once fleshy face was unshaven, and his hands plucked at the blankets which had been ripped in haste from his own bed to wrap him against the November chill.

At last the procession entered the gates of the Royal Naval Hospital. The wife was allowed no further than the office, as her husband was borne away to his death in an inner room. Already perhaps in her mind she was rehearsing the Tennysonian words which were to be graven into his tombstone:

Sunset and evening star
And one clear call for me!
And may there be no moaning of the bar,
When I put out to sea.

Only seven years before this death in Yokohama there had been a fashionable wedding at Glastonbury, in the county of Somerset. In the parish church of the Blessed St John Baptist, on May 4th, 1889, at noon, Edith May Porch had married Walter Raymond Hallowell Carew. There was, naturally, no public acknowledgement that the bride's parents disapproved of her choice. On a continuum of discredit, the bridegroom, a second son, had no money to hand — only expectations — and, being 15 years older than Edith, he had a

past. Only a few present in the rustling, whispering pews knew the extent of that past.

However, as the couple proceeded up the flower-garlanded aisle, while the organist played Handel's *Angels Ever Bright and Fair*, there was every sign that love had conquered all. A full choir led into the first hymn, a favourite epithalamium from John Keble's poem, known popularly then as *The Voice That Breathed o'er Eden.*

The bride was of perfect age, 21, and of correct, medium height, with discreetly brown hair. She had the sweet, candid look of some head girl at Cheltenham Ladies' College, but an aristocratic arrogance — the 'look of eagles' of the Arabian horse — was already apparent in nascent form. It was not a weak face.

She wore a glistening, pearly dress: the bodice and train were of white satin trimmed with orange blossom, the skirt of brocaded silk. A wreath of the same blossom twined a coronal around the veil of lace. The bouquet was of white azaleas.

Two small cousins of the bride, Dorothy and Winnie Porch, carried the train, and four older girls were attendant bridesmaids. Their costume consisted of a Directoire dress of delaine, with a pale sash of eau-de-nil, and they carried baskets of flowers. All the bridesmaids wore a gold brooch, the gift of the bridegroom.

There was no refinement in the features of the groom. It would be inappropriate to describe Walter Carew as distinguished. Sensual and worldly are the epithets that defy any unwillingness to define character by appearance. The large, dark eyes, almost exophthalmic, seem to have mirrored red-shaded parlours of cane and plush. On *his* insouciant lap, at a piano of Rio rosewood, there sits with loosened hair an uneasy mistress, in William Holman Hunt's Pre-Raphaelite painting *The Awakening Conscience.*

The groom's moustache is an obscenity, a growth sported *en avance*, concealing lips like the mouth of a sea-anemone. It is a weak face. And, finally, Walter Carew is remarkably similar to Charles Bravo[1], who died mysteriously at The Priory, Balham, on April 21st, 1876.

The formal words of love and duty were exchanged at the altar, and the reluctant father, John Albert Porch, Justice of the Peace, oftentime Mayor of Glastonbury, gave away his only daughter in the full knowledge that she would be sailing off

within a fortnight to an uncertain future in the Far East.

While the bridal party were signing the register, the organist played Mendelsshon's *Wedding March*. John and Margaret Porch witnessed their daughter's signature. Then out through the doorway under the carved roses which commemorate an old war, and between the lines of children from the bride's own Sunday School class at St John's, who were waiting to strew flowers in her path.

The wedding carriages, supplied by the George and Pilgrims Hotel, trotted off in procession with the burnished horses, on their toes, plunging at the cheers, the peal of bells, and the flags and bunting fluttering in the streets. They made their way through the quiet Somerset lanes, past cottage gardens, then fields with lambs still spared slaughter, nearly one and three-quarter miles to Edgarley House, the bride's home, for the reception.

The arch spanning the road at the entrance, the flags flying at Edgarley Lodge, the shots fired throughout the day by the tenant farmer of Ash Farm on the estate, might be considered an excessive display, but it was in fact quite normal for the social position of the parties concerned.

When later that year, on August 10th, Mary Rocke, of Chalice Hill, Glastonbury, married Douglas Hamilton McLean — whose father had been Treasurer of Queensland — the town was decorated to look as it did for the Jubilee Celebration of 1887. Arches bearing mottoes are a forgotten art form: one was made for Mary Rocke in Venetian style, incongruously adorned with the McLean tartan. Another, composed of evergreens, rosettes, flags and Japanese lanterns, proclaimed *God Bless The Happy Pair*.

At Edgarley House a collection of gifts was laid out for inspection — from pin-cushions to a diamond and pearl bracelet, from Mary Rocke's mother. The recently invented electro-plate ware was much in evidence. Thoughtful presents were cheques, a china and brass writing-set from the indoor servants at Edgarley, and a book of photographs of the neighbourhood. In the afternoon they dressed Edith May Hallowell Carew in a sombre costume — a brown cloth tailor-made dress[2], with a hat and jacket to match — and waved the married couple off to their strange destiny.

Glastonbury had been Edith's home for as long as she had memories. The Tor, a far green hill, rising strangely erratic, mammiform, out of flatlands, old wetlands, had always been on the skyline of her imagination. At twilight, or on a misty day, you could conjure up the shapes of the three gibbets on the summit, upon which King Henry VIII's executioner had, with two other victims, despatched the last, frail Abbot, Richard Whiting. They had dragged him through the streets on a hurdle, and afterwards his head was displayed on the gateway of his Abbey.

The Porch family actually owned the ruined Glastonbury Abbey, which had passed back and forth through many private hands since the Dissolution. They also owned the large Edgarley Estate. In about 1825, John Fry Reeves, Edith's great-grandfather, bought the Abbey. After marrying Maria, the daughter of Thomas Porch, of Wells, Somerset, he had acquired Edgarley with all its land.

Edith was born in fact on May 1st, 1868, in the small market town of Langport — set on a hill by the River Parrett, some 15 miles away — quite probably at her maternal grandparents' home. When she was baptized at St John's, Glastonbury, her father's address was 'Edgarley'.

By the time of the census return of 1871, however, Edith was living with her parents at the Abbey House, Chilkwell Street, Glastonbury, with three servants: Elizabeth Elliott, Edith's nurse, Elizabeth Wood, the cook and Jane Helborne, house and parlour-maid.

The Abbey House, a fine and stately stone residence which is now a Retreat and Conference House of the Diocese of Bath and Wells, held within its bounds at that time the ruined Glastonbury Abbey. Literally at the bottom of the garden, beyond the terraces and cedar of Lebanon, the startlingly vast, crumbled shell lay amid 36 acres of farmland.

Bad luck was supposed to attach to the various secular owners of the dishonoured, ghostly site. Moreover, an ominous legend, not quite received history nor yet quite Tennysonian, relates that King Arthur lies buried there in front of the High Altar, beside Queen Guinevere, repentant of her adultery with Sir Lancelot.

The Porch family were well connected, and their pedigree appears in *Burke's Landed Gentry*. Edith's father, John Albert, born in Glastonbury on April 22nd, 1833, spent nearly all his life in that town, living the life of an English country gentleman of the old

school. He served on Glastonbury Town Council from 1871 to 1901, and was thrice Mayor — in 1879, 1892 and 1897. Edith's mother, Margaret, was the second daughter of Edward Bagehot, a merchant of Langport, and Rachel, born Barnes. Edith's great-uncle Thomas Watson Bagehot, banker and shipowner, a brother of Edward Bagehot, was the father of the world-famous economist, Walter Bagehot (1826-77), author of *The English Constitution* and *Lombard Street*. Walter Bagehot's mother, born Edith Stuckey, a 'lively and fascinating woman, with intellectual vivacity', was subject in later years to frequent attacks of insanity[3]. Her mind was thought to have been unhinged by exogenous factors — personal tragedies.

Joseph Prior Estlin, her first husband, died while she was still a young woman. Only a few years later the eldest son of this marriage died of an illness, and the second died as the result of a coach accident. The third son, Vincent, grew up as an 'imbecile'. Walter Bagehot suffered from 'melancholy' as a young man, and had an abiding fear of actual insanity. He himself, a dashing figure — handsome, witty, one of the best conversationists of his day — was born, and died, at Langport.

The Bagehots can be traced back to the fifteenth century: there was family property at Prestbury, Gloucestershire. Several times allied by marriage, the Bagehots and the Stuckeys had long dominated the life of Langport, where Stuckey's Bank, the largest private bank of issue in England, was founded by Samuel Stuckey in about 1772. Stuckey's later became a part of Westminster Bank. Thomas Porch Porch (sic), Edith's grandfather, was a director of Stuckey's, and his signature appeared on £5 notes. For a final distinction, a cousin of Edith's, Montague Phippen Porch, who lived at Edgarley Lodge, on June 1st, 1918, married Jennie, the widow of Lord Randolph Churchill, and thus became Winston Churchill's stepfather[4]. Jennie was 64, 'Montie' was 41. The marriage was happy, until Jennie died suddenly on June 29th, 1921. Montague Porch remarried on July 1st, 1926. It was another exotic choice — of Donna Guilia Patrizi, only daughter of the Marchese Patrizi della Rocca, of Umbria.

Edith was the first-born child and only daughter of John Albert and Margaret Porch. Albert, born on October 30th, 1869, survived

only until November 18th of that year. Cecil Porch was born on January 25th, 1873, Robert Bagehot on April 3rd, 1875, Reginald Colmore on December 14th, 1876, and, lastly, Edward Albert was born on June 23rd, 1879.

For our purposes, the significance of Edith's exposed position at the top of the family hierarchy, is not so much, as her brothers were born, her demotion from cherished only girl child, with her status vitiated by her gender, as the lack of a sisterly confidante. In turn the boys went off to their public schools, and she grew to be self-reliant, self-preservative, secretive.

By 1881 the entire enlarged and completed family had moved into Edgarley House, with its greater acreage. A 20-year-old footman, George Fisher, had joined the staff. The female servants had been transmogrified into Adah Sharman, Elizabeth White and Emma Lapham. Edgarley House, now Edgarley Hall, the preparatory school for Millfield, and a cheerful, optimistic place, must then have borne a gloomy, Gothic aspect, with its own 'White Lady', but it was home, and here Edith grew up in considerable style. Her upbringing was conventional, with the social round of strict importance, and she did not question it. Not at all shy, she took part in amateur theatricals. Somewhat eulogistically, she was later described as 'One of the most popular young ladies in the town, her general kindness to the poor and the geniality with which she always joined in everything for the public service rendering her beloved by all classes of the community'.

Edith's position in society will not have sheltered her from a lively awareness of the perils and realities of the lanes of rural Somerset. The local newspapers were filled with gory paragraphs. Impalement seems to have been the most frequent risk of stirring from your safe hearthside: on the horns of passing cattle, on the spikes of a level-crossing gate when your horse attempted to jump it, on the pommels of your side-saddle, or on some derrick or detritus of railway *materia*. Throat-cutting — whether your own or someone else's — was scarcely less prevalent, and bullets were liable to ricochet all around the coverts and copses.

There was absolutely no trace in Edith of the swooning Victorian violet. She came from a long-lived family, and she had every intention of living her given life to the hilt. An outdoor girl,

always accompanied by dogs, sporting, athletic and hardy, she played tennis quite well, and learnt to swim at the seaside. When it rained she pined indoors with novels and Tennyson.

An important part of her early training, which was to contribute fundamentally to her adult life, was the horsemanship which was instilled into her at the Edgarley stables. She grew up to be a fearless rider — not to any advanced, fancy standard — and also picked up from the grooms a fair knowledge of horse-management. In fact, she conformed to the familiar English stereotype of the girl who loved horses. Nevertheless, Edith did not, as can happen, stay arrested at that stage of her development (would that she had!) but, while still retaining her hippophilic inclinations, progressed to the erotic, if not quite the social, goal that was expected of the Porch girl. It was no doubt an expression of her sharp, brittle, passionate, but not profound temperament, that the love-match on which she insisted proved to be a mismatch.

It is well established that Walter Hallowell Carew did not have the Porchs' approval. As their only daughter, she was of course special to them, and the admired ornament of Edgarley, over-valued, over-praised. But it was really the Carews, rejoicing at Walter's catch, who should have entertained the misgivings.

Reputedly, the couple met at a ball at Bridport, Dorset. Perhaps it was so. Walter, born on September 12th, 1853, was the second son of Robert Hallowell Carew, an army major, who on July 17th, 1851, had married Anne Rycroft Smythies, a widow, daughter of Oliver Raymond at St Paul's Church, Covent Garden, the 'Actors Church'. In 1889 the family home was Elmsleigh, Exmouth, South Devon; the house was held on a 99-year lease.

Walter too was well connected, with his lineage appearing in *Burke's Landed Gentry*. His grandfather, Robert's father, was a personage of some fame: Admiral Sir Benjamin Hallowell Carew (1760-1834), the son of Benjamin Hallowell, a commissioner of the American Board of Customs. The Admiral was born in Canada, but joined the Royal Navy at an early age, took part in many dangerous engagements, and served with distinction under Nelson. A man of intrepid, unconventional character and great personal strength, he is said to have been of gigantic frame, and to have discouraged a rumbling mutiny on the *Swiftsure*, off Cadiz, by means of his own fists.

Upon the death of his cousin, Mrs Anne Paston Gee, on March 28th, 1828, he succeeded to the estates of the Carews of Beddington near Croydon, in Surrey, and pursuant to her will assumed the name and arms of Carew. He was not in any degree related to the Carew family. The estates had come to Mrs Gee by the will of her husband's brother. The Hallowell Carews were not therefore pukka Carews, but had moved into Beddington by a windfall.

Walter's father, Robert, did not succeed to Beddington in 1838. The heir was Robert's elder brother, Captain Charles Hallowell Carew, R.N., who died in 1849 at the age of 47. *His* heir, Charles Hallowell Hallowell (sic) Carew, inherited at the tender age of 18. Charlie Carew was addicted to betting on racehorses, and was forced into bankruptcy. Within ten years the estates were split up and the manor of Beddington was sold at auction in 1859, when Walter was only six years old.

It is possible that Walter was taken to see the great Tudor Hall, the parkland where once King Henry VIII had hunted deer, and retained a memory of a place that was somehow important, but sad. Ill luck had killed off the original Carew family. Sir Nicholas Carew, one of King Henry's favourites, was condemned for treason, and, on March 3rd, 1539, he was beheaded on Tower Hill. Charlie Carew died miserably at the age of 41 in a London lodging- house. Walter, himself a second son, had been deprived of splendours, and like his father had to earn his own living. A career in the colonial service was quite appropriate for a man in his circumstances, and he took up a number of minor official positions. He was not a high-flier — perhaps he could have achieved more — but, as were many similar officers, he was held back by acquired, not idiopathic, chronic ill-health. Perhaps too he lacked ambition to rise because he felt that he should really have been living the landed life. He was a disappointed man.

They gave him rotten postings, in the back of beyond, in the white man's grave area of the Straits Settlements, that being before 1946 the generic term for the territories of the British Crown Colony, situated in the East Indies on and off the Malay Peninsula, and occupying 1650 square miles. Here he held administrative posts, and also worked for a time in the telegraph service. As early as 1880, the climate had already eroded his constitution, and on one

occasion he had been invalided home *via* Australia, on the SS *Portosi*, suffering from congestion of the liver, jaundice and malaria. By 1883 he was back in Singapore, where he held the position of Sheriff.

Now, as a steady married man Walter could hope for advancement and its consequent pension. He was bound for the posting of Treasurer, with the possibility of making Resident, in Sungei Ujong, which was one of the rather precarious Protected States of Malaya — also, like the Settlements, administered by brave British officials. Malaya did not suit him, but it was where his expertise lay.

The honeymoon in the West Country on which the couple embarked on that May day in 1889 was typically Victorian, with a nice blend of family visiting and a sojourn at a genteel seaside resort. Lynton, in North Devon, high and sylvan above Lynmouth, was a favourite setting for a honeymoon, and here Edith and Walter stayed for eight or nine days. Walter will have been attentive to Edith — his prize — but it would be wrong to imagine that they did not stir from the romantic isolation of their rooms. Walter would certainly have become bored, and they were both restless, active, drawn to outdoor activities. Surprisingly soon, a pair of hacks would have been brought round for a ride along the flowered lanes.

Although he *could* ride, in the natural course of things, boating or sailing off Lynmouth would have been Walter's preference. The blood of the Admiral flowed through his jaundiced veins, and he took to the water at every opportunity: perhaps he persuaded Edith to join him. These were the early days, and separate pursuits would have been incongruous. The time left together in England passed for ever — three days with an uncle of Edith's at Treeborough, on the Brendon Hills in Somerset, one week with Walter's parents at Exmouth, and a last four or five days back at Edgarley.

Finally the Carews sailed for Singapore, and then, after four days' wait, a smaller steamer took them up to Sungei Ujong. It was hot, and it was humid, but Edith easily survived the great adventure, although she did not manage to escape the almost inevitable malaria, which was to stay with her in periodic outbreaks. What she did escape, or avoid, was pregnancy. There was to be none of those frightful Victorian dramas of being carried in agony on a hurdle

over rutted tracks to be delivered in a mud hut without benefit of anaesthesia.

The extent of Walter's chronic ill-health could not be hidden from his young wife. He was never really well, consistently 'liverish' and 'out of sorts'. After soldiering on for three months as Treasurer he was confirmed Acting Resident, which was the height of his career. By June 1890 he was finished, and (there was no option) had to leave the Straits for a more bracing climate. The doctors told Edith that he was suffering from 'nervous depression' — that obsolete portmanteau diagnosis about as useful as 'neurasthenia'. If only he could have lasted eleven more months he would have secured his Government pension.

There was nothing at home for them; abroad was Walter's best hope. They made their way to Singapore, and joined a ship bound for Hong Kong. On board was a forceful English barrister, John Frederic Lowder, who practised in Japan, and the three formed a light friendship which was to have deeper consequences a few years on. From Hong Kong the Carews travelled to a small Japanese resort near Kobe, named Takaradzuka, for a period of recuperation. Walter improved rapidly in the better clime, and after three weeks they moved from there to an appointment in Yokohama.

Chapter 2
BLIGHT O'ER EDEN

'Quel pays de verdure et d'ombre, ce Japon, quel Eden inattendu [5]'

Pierre Loti

Yokohama in 1890 could be a form of earthly paradise for a young married Englishwoman, if she could overcome homesickness (no problem for a brisk pragmatist such as Edith Carew), and if her husband proved to be a congenial partner. It was unusual, to be sure, for a mayor's daughter from Somerset to find herself in such an exotic location. The Orient was still profoundly mysterious. Although there is some documentation, the life of small settlements of Europeans and Americans in Japan is not nearly so well known as that in Victoria's actual dominions. These pockets of foreigners clung to the rim of the Japanese islands by virtue of mere paper treaties, not outright conquest, although not without remembered, antecedent violence.

The way of life in Japan was cosmopolitan, more sophisticated, less rigid, circumscribed and oppressive than under the Raj at the same period — freer, airy and light, more of a game than an ordeal. The climate was an important part of the difference. Although not British, with summer humidity and winter cold, it was bearable, and the daily timetable did not have to turn around extremes of weather. Floods and typhoons were not on the whole so threatening to the foreigners as they sound, but it was the rains which above all had the power to disrupt and spoil the quality of life. When it rained, it rained:

> *Et il pleurait, pleurait: il faisait presque nuit, tant cela tombait épais ... Il y avait du vent aussi; on l'entendait hurler dans les ravins avec une voix profonde.* [6] (Pierre Loti)

Earthquakes were the worst threat. A fearful quake, crowned with firestorms, was waiting, impendent, to kill nearly 150,000

people in Tokyo and Yokohama in 1923.

There was only one poisonous snake. The other nine species were harmless, if capable of causing a shudder.

Sport did not knock you up too badly, and cricket, tennis, baseball for the Americans, bathing, sailing, riding (usually a pony of sturdy, stubborn Mongolian type) and racing on the permanent racecourse were all pursued by the unquiet foreigners. Getting around the town was done by jinrikisha. The first railway line, from Yokohama to Tokyo, had opened in 1872, and the telegraph and telephone system had been installed. It was not yet general for houses to have private telephones, and jinrikisha men criss-crossed the streets, carrying chits and messages.

There was a Masonic Lodge in Yokohama. Tiffin and the Club, mail day and the P&O Line, *were* traditionally colonial, but the servants (often Chinese) were treated with less despisal than in India. It was wiser so.

The Western doctors, lawyers, bankers, merchants were by 1890 of good rank, by no means misfits. The community was small, and all members of the same caste were known to one another. Although the consular staff held to their eminence, the hierarchy was less fiercely enforced than in the Raj. Missionaries were more highly regarded: some were respected for their scholarliness. English-language newspapers were well presented.

While those (the great majority) who did not mix with the natives preferred the wide, occidental streets of the European quarters, some few men of literature, such as Pierre Loti and Lafcadio Hearn, were drawn to all that was Japanese, and sometimes to intermarriage — which *was* considered beyond the pale. Hearn's Yokohama, where he disembarked in 1890, is delightfully contemporaneous with the Carews' Yokohama. As Edith and Walter settled into their house on the Bluff — the best address, in its commanding, pine-wooded position, with mansions and luxurious bungalows — Hearn, below, explored the Japanese shrines and temples, gardens and shops, finding in Japan 'Forty million of the most loveable people in the universe'.

Staying at Carey's Hotel on the waterfront, run by an American mulatto, his fellow-guests sailors and sealers, he marvelled at the limpid air, the elfishness of objects and people, the prevailing touch of blueness, and the perfect snow cone of sacred Fuji-yama pendant at dawn above Yokohama. As he set off in a jinrikisha he saw the fleeting vistas of the narrow, blue-hung streets over the dancing white mushroom-shaped hat of his sandalled runner.

The Carews lived first at No.57 the Bluff, and later, from April 15th, 1895, at No.169. Both houses were rented. Walter's appointment in Yokohama was that of manager of the Yokohama United Club (Kipling's 'Overseas Club', originally the United Services Club) which had been organised by the departed much-missed military with their regimental bands. It was not so august a position as those which he had held in the hot lands, but it was congenial enough, and it suited him. He undertook his duties conscientiously, and bar and billiards were on tap.

Still an outdoor girl, Edith modelled her lifestyle on the Glastonbury pattern, with her own pony, tennis, shopping trips and outings. One feels that she found sightseeing rather a drag. 'At Homes', teas, dinners, dances, she tolerated. The ritual of social calls was her duty. She hated formal picnics, and was none too keen on sailing with Walter in his boat, the *Cocktail*. Books were popular novels. It was all trivial, extravert activity, seizing the moment.

Except for the latent and intermittent malaria, her health remained good. She was not a woman of strong maternal feelings, but it was expected of her that the marriage would be fruitful, and quite soon a daughter, Marjorie, was born, on March 3rd, 1891, followed by Benjamin, on August 4th, 1892. Edith did not go home to England for the births, but the Carews did spend much of 1892 at Zushi, a summer resort on the south-west shore of Tokyo Bay, just south of Yokohama.

In March 1893, however, leaving Walter at his job, Edith returned to Glastonbury on a long visit which began with a kind of absurd triumph. She was received like Cleopatra: 'The bells of the churches rang out merry peals of welcome; the town was illuminated and decorated; arches were erected; and the Town Band preceded a procession of great length, numbering hundreds of people, which accompanied her carriage from the railway station to her parents at Edgarley, enlivening the proceedings with fireworks and cheers en route'.

Back in Yokohama, Walter was having a bad time. He was

embarrassed. It was deuced awkward. The pain was excruciating, and he knew that he had to seek professional help. Otherwise, he was going to explode! Walter had a low opinion of doctors, and usually preferred to dose himself with home remedies such as Mother Seigel's syrup, but this predicament was different. Dr Edwin Wheeler was his family physician, but he and his wife and daughters were on visiting terms with the Carews, and Walter felt quite unable to reveal his complaint to him.

The only thing for it was to steel himself to consult another medico — Dr Neil Gordon Munro, who was also in practice in Yokohama. According to Dr Munro, who could not achieve precise definition, the consultation took place in the spring of 1893. It is possible, therefore, that all this was going on *before* Edith had left for home. Walter's encounter with Dr Munro was painful. He was suffering from a very severe stricture of the urethra, and at first the doctor could not pass even the smallest instrument.

As he was being tortured, Walter indicated to the doctor that he had, in the past, taken a remedy for the pain of his stricture. So this was not his first attack. 'Once a stricture, always a stricture', as Dr Munro later recited. Walter's stricture could have been variously caused. Plain trauma, such as falling astride a boom on the *Cocktail* is most unlikely, and in that case he could have expected sympathy from Dr Wheeler. An enlargement of the prostate gland would be somewhat unusual in a man of Walter's age. Inflammation of the prostate gland, resulting from infection by the common gonococcus, or the tubercle bacillus, was possible.

By far the most common type of urethral stricture met with in young and middle-aged men is caused by the inflammation of the genito-urinary tract that is set up by gonorrhoea. In such a case, if the original infection had been adequately treated the stricture would not have recurred. At the time when Dr Munro first saw Walter and treated his stricture he diagnosed 'no complications' and the patient was not suffering from 'anything else'.

Mere bashfulness at having metal bougies inserted into his penis by a friend often encountered at dinner parties is, to be fair, a possible explanation for Walter's aversion to seeking the help of his own doctor. Even the most bluff and confident men have their moments of social weakness. Common sense, however, indicates

1 Edith at Exmouth.

2 Walter Raymond Hallowell Carew.

3 Edith May Hallowell Carew.

4 Walter Bagehot, economist, related to Edith on the maternal side.

5 Abbey House, Glastonbury. Edith's early home.

6 Glastonbury Tor.

7 Glastonbury in 1860.

8 Admiral Sir Benjamin Hallowell Carew. Walter Carew's grandfather.

9 Edgarley House, Glastonbury, where Edith grew up.

10 St John's Church, the interior.

11 St John's Church, Glastonbury, where Edith was married.

12 Walter at the Yokohama United Club.

13 At the house on the Bluff, 1896. Edith (*seated on wall*), Walter (*standing at rear*), Mabel and Marian Schwann (*on steps, not able to differentiate*), Reginald (*with dog*), Mary Jacob (*left forefront*), Marjorie (*seated on lower step*), stableboy, Benjamin (*on pony*).

14 Yokohama United Club.

that a married man of 39 with a stricture that is not new, and who shuns his own doctor, is most likely to have a history of gonorrhoea. The more so since several months later, while Edith was still absent, an even more embarrassed Walter Carew was again driven to consult Dr Munro. This time the diagnosis was unequivocal: the doctor treated him for gonorrhoea, and, later again, for the catarrh of the bladder which followed the gonorrhoea.

Still in Edith's absence, Walter then felt it necessary, for such was his desperation, to consult a physician of some eminence, Dr Elwyn Otto Edward Baelz, Professor of Medicine of the Imperial University of Japan, in Tokyo. His chief complaint was of pain in the bladder, which troubled him more than all his malaria and liverishness, and of much irritation caused by his stricture. Dr Baelz did not use any instruments, but gave him a prescription which he found helpful for 'those cases'.

This palliative gave Walter some relief, and he had it made up several times. Indeed, he later encountered Dr Baelz at the holiday resort of Miyanoshita and told him that his remedy had made him feel better. It is obvious that Walter's enjoyment of life was impaired by his chronic stricture, because the fibrous tissue of that stricture had a constant tendency to contract down again after dilation. Alcohol and malaria will have been contributory factors.

Two years afterwards, in 1895, there is evidence of the continuing problem of the stricture. Max Kaufmann, a German friend of Walter's, and a fellow billiards player, happened to be using the urinal at the Yokohama Club, and could not avoid noticing Walter's pain. There must be a boundary in the etiquette of the shared situation beyond which a failure to express concern over a friend's groans and grimaces could be interpreted as a lack of civility! Gonorrhoea in the 1890s, long before antibiotics, was a frightening business. Only as recently as 1879, Albert Neisser had discovered the gonococcus, and in 1885, Ernst Bumm had succeeded in proving the relationship of the gonococcus to gonorrhoea.

Secrecy was all. In the houses of Glastonbury, Edith will never have heard the ugly syllables of the venereal diseases uttered aloud, nor probably will she have known how to pronounce them. The complications of gonorrhoea no longer spring easily to the mind, but they are severe, including nephritis, epididymitis, septicaemia, endocarditis, pleurisy, pneumonia and intractable rheumatism. The sufferings of women can include inflammation of the uterus, fallopian tubes and ovaries, often leading to sterility. The blindness of babies born from infected mothers is still well remembered in this country.

The legal position in the 1890s was that a wife could obtain a separation and maintenance order from a magistrate's court if her husband, while himself suffering from a venereal disease, and knowing that he was so suffering, had insisted on having sexual intercourse with her. Even if there were such an insistence, this is not the kind of relief that a woman of Edith's class would have sought.

In the divorce courts the transmission of a venereal disease was not of itself a ground for dissolution. The matter was subsumed under legal cruelty, but in a strictly defined limitation: wilfully and recklessly to communicate syphilis or gonorrhoea was cruelty, ie., such conduct as to have caused danger to life, limb, or bodily health, or as to give rise to a reasonable apprehension of such danger. Any such legal action was so scandalous as generally to be unthinkable. Matrimonial recriminations tended to be confused by the fact that the absence of any discharge clinically is no evidence of the absence of gonorrhoea even years after an infection, and as long as the gonococcus is latent the patient is capable of communicating the disease. Dr Munro's treatment of Walter will have been by antiseptic means: internally, by oils of sandalwood, cubebs,[7] and copaiba,[8] prescribed in capsule form, and externally, by irrigation with, typically, a weak solution of permanganate of potash.

Edith did not return to Yokohama until December 1893. Three-quarters of a year does seem to be an unconscionable length of time to abandon one's husband of only three to four years in a foreign land. It might well indicate disenchantment.

At some time after their reunion, Walter told her about his illness and the doctors whom he had consulted. There were to be no more children of the marriage. Neither party, however, at the time appears to have had any fixed desire to separate. There were very young children to be considered, and the weight of the disapprobation of the Porchs and the Carews. Sexual relations, or sexual relations of a sort, may have been resumed, but an entirely new mode of married life was now entered into, a compromise. This was the ancient device known as the *mari complaisant*. Edith, while preserving the status and outward form of a respectable married woman, was 'permitted' the latitude to enjoy flirtations of questionable intensity with a number of interested young men, even concurrently. At least one such experience approached a serious *affaire*.

Walter was supposed to bite his lip, turn a blind eye, and nurse his stricture! It was an explosive situation, and Walter simmered. In an unconscious attempt at lightening the stress of jealousy (Walter's) and guilt (Edith's) facetious nicknames were bestowed upon the rather muddled courtiers: the Ferret, the Ice Cream Vendor or the Organ-grinder, and the Youth. Walter brooded, and did a spot of spooning on his own account.

Edith knew her Tennyson, but she must have skimmed over the doomful words:

> *I hold that man the worst of public foes*
> *Who either for his own or children's sake,*
> *To save his blood from scandal, lets the wife*
> *Whom he knows false, abide and rule the house.* [9]

And so, with the trees in Eden blighted cruelly early in the marriage, the charade continued for a couple of years. The two children grew and flourished, and were set on ponies. Edith's letters home spoke of the sparkling social agenda of Yokohama. Walter, forever under the weather, fretted in his dead-end job and dreamed of an occupation that was more influential, and more remunerative. It is difficult to say who was the more discontented, but there were still daily enjoyments; life was not without hope, and it was comfortable.

The verandahed, two-storied house on the Bluff was peopled by a team of servants, and by 1896 they are identifiable. Edith did not, as a matter of fact, know all their names, but it didn't mean she was a bad person! Kee Chong was a Japanese steward, Yasuda Yasunobu a cook, Kitamura Kichiro a general coolie, Kuroyanagi Junya a *betto*, or groom, with his small stable-boy, and Ah Kwong, a 12-year-old Chinese boy, who waited at table and opened doors.

Edith tended to lose patience with female servants, and amahs came and went. On March 18th Rachel Greer — a Japanese subject, but actually a Eurasian girl — was to come down from Miss Crosby's Missionary School in Tokyo, and soon find her niche. She could read and speak some English, and exerted a degree of dominance over the native servants. Loyal and feudal in her attachment to her mistress, there was something scheming and tricky about her. On August 27th, Rachel's cousin, Asa, joined the household. Over this establishment of small kimonoed figures, this doll's-house, Edith exercised her administrative and social skills for the man whom she no longer loved.

Chapter 3
THE PLAINS OF HEAVEN

New Year's Day of 1896 was fine and bright, but Edith did not enjoy it. Walter went off in the morning for a picnic, leaving her in bed with a cold. It was a bad start to the year, and she wryly recorded it in her new saxe-blue Letts Colonial Office Diary. Edith kept the kind of diary which charts life's movements but rarely its emotions. It was guarded, with the careful entries which a marital partner makes on the off-chance that the other might be tempted, or driven, to take a peep.

Her diary bears witness to her wide circle of acquaintances: it is packed with their names, and the tiffins, teas, concerts and dances of heedless days lost beyond recall. The weather as it alternated was faithfully logged as a matter of priority, since it dictated the pattern of her entire day, which might encompass four or five separate activities while Walter was down at the Club on the Bund. Her stamina seems astonishing, with little rest and repeated changes of clothing.

By the following day Edith, typically, had quite recovered, and rode off at 9.30am for the Bank picnic. The day was not a success: the weather was showery and raw, and 'You never saw such a crowd of tailors' — a rare, snobbish comment. Walter took a half-holiday, it was Edith's afternoon to be 'At Home', and Benjamin fell off his pony. There were two ponies in the stable for the *betto* to look after, under the exacting eye of the mistress: a small one for the children, and Edith's special, keen mare, Babel or Babelle. Babel was Edith's baby, more prominent in the diary than Ben and Marjorie. Edith worried about her ailments — it was difficult to keep her sound — and treated her herself, in the absence of a European veterinary surgeon.

Babel was Edith's vital means of escape, and her alibi, from the

house on the Bluff to the Plains of Heaven above the town. Without Babel she could not canter up freely like a huntress in search of Ferrets and Youths. Gino Corti, who was the Ice Cream Vendor, aka the Organ-grinder, aka the Italian, frequented the Plains. In the house Edith was giving him English lessons. Walter made no objection when Signor Corti dined with the Carews.

January the 4th was a glorious day, but Edith felt 'seedy' — a euphemism for all manner of ills: malaria, influenza, headache, menstruation. She did manage to ride up to the racecourse, which was another meeting-place, but Babel was stiff and did not go well. Ben was in the wars again — the little pony in the public gardens on the Bluff gave him a nasty kick, or it could have been a bite.

The Sabbath was not observed in Yokohama as it had been in Glastonbury. Edith didn't think the minister was up to much, and Walter attended the Anglican church once in a blue moon. As long as the weather was right, every Sunday was regarded as a kind of Bank Holiday, or picnic, with excursions, sports and sightseeing. On January 5th Walter went with a friend by train and bicycle to Oiso, and had a 'jolly' time. It was one of the loveliest days they had had, and Edith took Babel out for two hours, but she was still not right. The Youth called. This was Harry Vansittart Dickinson, a bank clerk at the Hong Kong and Shanghai Bank and a friend of both the Carews for some five years, who was beginning to take a more affectionate interest in Edith. Later Edith went to church with Mrs Wheeler, who was the wife of the Carews' family doctor.

By Tuesday Babel was still stiff in the off-shoulder; it was such a nuisance. Edith made some calls in the afternoon, and Mrs Dunlop drove her home. The Dunlops lived at No.6 Bund, the main street on the waterfront — he was a merchant — and were good friends of the Carews. Ambrose Berry Walford, a youngish barrister practising in Yokohama, came to tea.

The next day Mr Easton sent her her photographs, and she thought that they were very good. He was the Ferret. His tenacity quotient was paradoxically low, but perhaps he was strikingly blond. On January 9th there was a long and severe shock of earthquake. Then it was another fine Sunday, and Walter cycled to Tokyo with a friend, while Edith rode out with the Ferret. That night Walter dined and slept in Tokyo, and a zigzag sign appears in

the diary, as it does on other occasions when Walter is away.

On Monday Walter was not well — not surprising after his 17-mile ride to Tokyo. Edith bought some lotion and powders for Babel from Schedel's, the German chemist. The following day Babel went beautifully, so that Edith thought the remedies had done her good. On the racecourse, she saw Mr Black's Australian horse fall, most mysteriously, and break his leg. Walter went home early, and retired to bed. On Wednesday he stayed in bed, but Edith was out and about — it was not her practice, when Walter was seedy, to stay at home and minister to him. He was better by Thursday and dined at the Club. Gino Corti called.

On Friday Edith went to an excellent concert with Harry Dickinson, and Walter went to bed. The Sunday was dull and very cold, and Walter stayed in bed, feeling ill. Edith rode out with the Ferret, but it was not a pleasant ride. The Ferret seems to have been causing trouble of some kind. On Monday she went skating with Gino Corti. Walter was still not well, and she wished that he could get away for a few days. Marjorie was always suffering from toothache, and Edith took her to the dentist, Dr Smith, two days running, and eventually he fixed her up. Corti's devotion was becoming silly but the skating was good fun, especially when the ice was perfect.

When Edith wished that Walter could get away, he quite often did so, and on January 21th he went off by train to Miyanoshita, taking Marjorie. Kamakura and Miyanoshita were resorts much favoured by westerners, and Walter's recurring fantasy was that a holiday in either place would make him a whole man again. An amah will have gone with the party, to look after Marjorie and her toothache. The Corti boy called on Edith, and on Saturday she saw him on the Plains of Heaven. She wrote one of her sparkling, chatty letters to Walter, and he wrote to her. That night Ambrose Walford dined with her alone, and they went on to a concert, which she enjoyed so much.

Sunday was warm and sunny, and at 9.30am, with a party of friends, she rode over for lunch at the hotel in Kamakura. Corti and Walford were of the company, and the Italian was asked back for tea. She was tired, and went early to bed; Ben slept with her. On Monday she heard from Walter that Marjorie was in pain with her teeth. A zigzag suggests that although it rained hard until 3pm, the day without Walter was not altogether dull.

The next morning Edith woke to a thick fog. The children's new saddle arrived, and she took Ben down to the station to meet Walter and Marjorie. The Eldridges called, (Dr Eldridge was to prove a loyal friend). On Wednesday Edith went to 'Tea and Tableaux' at Mrs Moss's, while Walter had his annual general meeting at the Club, and came home rather the worse for it. Then he caught a cold at the skating, and was very seedy by February 1st, on which day Edith met Corti on the hills.

Walter was still feeling very unwell on Sunday the 2nd, but he struggled out for a day's shooting with a friend; the result — 'sport nil'. The foreigners' guns had wiped out the pheasants, pigeons, woodcock and snipe which had once been plentiful. Discouraged, Walter did not go shooting again, just as he had given up long bicycle rides. His list of recreations seemed to be fast shrinking.

Thursday the 6th was a paradigm of the good life in Yokohama, and Edith knew it — 'What a lovely time we're having!' The weather was glorious, and she rode for two hours in the morning. Probably she met someone. She does not always say so. Fannie Eldridge tiffined with her, and they rehearsed for *A Fair Encounter*. She was 'At Home' to a stream of callers, and that merged into her dinner party of seven, with music and cards afterwards.

At 1am fire broke out further along the Bluff and seven houses were burnt to the ground; Edith rode past and saw what a bonfire it had been. There was a thunderstorm on Sunday the 9th, but Edith went alone to the Early Service: 'It is high time Mr Irwine resigned'. She felt very seedy and stayed in bed on Monday morning. Then she got up, went to a rehearsal, paid some calls, and went to a dinner party of 12. 'Good fun'.

On Tuesday she rode out for two and a half hours with the Ferret, and Gino Corti came for his lesson. It was Ben's turn to have a bad cold on the 12th, and there was an unpleasant incident, an ominous marker, which soured the flow of jolly days that compensated for rebellious thoughts. *Walter*, she wrote, *very angry with me over my extravagance, and inability to keep accounts.*

Walter's criticism was unfair. The short point is that he was after Edith's money. The flimsy marriage was also beset by those financial quarrels which often march with sexual differences. Her own private fortune was considerable — £400 per annum of her own money, and £100 per annum as an allowance from her father. Twice a year, in June and December, £250 was sent out to Yokohama, and until recently had been placed to *Walter's* account at the Hong Kong and Shanghai Bank.

From this he had doled out money at her request, until in June 1895, tiring of the arrangement, for what good reason, she had prevailed upon him to open a separate account for her at the Chartered Bank. Here when the half-yearly allowance arrived (and it was in Walter's name) he deposited a sum in Edith's name, varying from $500 to $800. The remainder was understood to be used by him at his discretion, and he also gave her a monthly allowance for household expenses. This pernicious set-up, more suited to a true and committed marriage, was, it may be noted, operative after the Married Woman's Property Act of 1882, so that the income of £500 per annum was not automatically Walter's money, and all parties concerned should have known so.

Aggrieved then by Walter's attack, Edith telegraphed home urgently, to Papa for £50, to keep the peace. It was snowing, and she felt very seedy and sick all day (probably as a result of the upset). She had to leave an afternoon dance after only two dances, and go home to bed. On Sunday she ordered some plants, rode with the Ferret and entertained the Corti boy in the afternoon. After dinner the Ferret came in to see the Magic Lantern.

Then she felt seedy, as if she had influenza, and went out to a deadly dinner party. On Pancake Day, £50 arrived from home, and she thanked goodness, but she had a horrible day, paying bills and arguing with Walter until her head ached. Walter went off to bed at 3pm and the next day he dined at the Club. On Saturday she bought a china dog, a good one, made in 1810, and rode out with Corti, upsetting Mr Auger from his bicycle. On the Sabbath she rode to the Plains of Heaven with the Ferret. Babel went very well. Ambrose Walford and the Ferret stayed to dinner on the 25th, and the barrister went with her to a rehearsal at the Public Hall.

Edith's engagements with her admirers came thick and fast. Corti came for his lesson, she walked with the Ferret, and she lost Snipe, one of her dogs; Harry Dickinson found him and brought him back. By March, Walter was looking far from well again, and how she wished he could get a change! Indeed, on March 3rd she sent for Dr Wheeler to have a look at him, and that same day he sailed off to Kobe on the *Bombay* in the hope that a sea trip would buck him up. Edith gave a big children's party for Marjorie's fifth birthday, with geishas, perhaps rather surprisingly. There is a zigzag for March 5th and 6th.

Sunday was so perfect that it should have been put in a glass case. Edith went down to the Early Service, and rode to the Plains of Heaven, the best ride she had ever had in Japan. Walter turned up at 6pm, the *Verona* having made a good passage, but he was still not so well as she would have liked to see him.

The Italian's English was getting on. Walter took Edith to the Masonic Ball, and she enjoyed it ever so much. On Friday the 13th there was much friction in the letter line between the Ferret and Edith. Walter came home early, not feeling well, and went to bed. She did likewise. Then she sat up late helping him with the copying work that John Lowder, their barrister friend, had given him. Certainly Lowder did not have a clerk, but was Walter really so hard up?

Sunday was the most perfect day that any being could desire. Walter (on a hired horse), Edith and Corti rode across the Downs to Kamakura, meeting a party of officers from the *Edgar* on the same excursion. While Walter slept during a rest on the way, they all talked scandal. Walter returned by train and Edith rode home with the Italian — a nice, quiet ride, taking just under three hours. Edith felt worried about Walter on March 20th; he was far from well. She herself had been occupied for days with shopping and arrangements, because three visitors were due to arrive from England on the 21st. Mabel and Marian Schwann, the two young girls steaming to Yokohama via Hong Kong, on their holiday of a lifetime, were Edith's two cousins, and Mabel had been one of her bridesmaids. Their visit, an exhausting round of sightseeing, took more out of them than out of Edith. She seemed to enjoy their company, except that dalliance was inhibited, and no doubt Walter was on his best behaviour. He felt too rotten to be troublesome, anyway.

Reginald Colmore Porch, aged 19, Edith's next-to-youngest

brother, (despatched abroad in the hope that he would make something of himself), was a convenient chaperon for the two sisters on the voyage out. His achievements at Malvern College had not been outstanding, and unlike his three brothers, he was set neither for university nor for a distinguished army career. In May, after quite a search, he was to take up an office post in Yokohama with Samuel Samuels & Company. The job was not to last.

Reggie was on excellent terms with his sister and brother-in-law, and participated with gusto in all the sporting and social activities that were open to him. He was a little too young, and unfunded, to be an eligible bachelor about town, but he was certainly a manly companion for Walter, who conceivably was sometimes lonely, and shared his liking for sailing. There is something rakish, dandiacal, charming, almost precociously dissipated about the young man who ruffles the dog in the family photograph (see plate 13).

It is impossible to guess how much he knew, saw, or gauged about the state of the Carews' marriage, but Edith was unable to hide from him the attentions of the Ferret and other encroaching, burrowing creatures. As an envoy from home (where his sister's behaviour would have been viewed as shocking beyond belief), he must at first have been totally disconcerted.

The day of their arrival dawned very cold with sleet and snow, but Edith got up at 5.30am and rode to the racecourse. She could not hold Babel. Then she was glad to get some breakfast on the *Ancona* where she found the girls and Reggie all well and eating their breakfast. On Sunday Dickinson dined with them, and they played whisky poker [10] (surely not Mabel and Marian; the Philharmonic Concert practice would have been more suitable). Gino Corti also came in to dinner and to be introduced.

After a few days of recovery from the voyage, Edith took Reggie and the girls by train to Tokyo, and settled them in at the Imperial Hotel. She herself, for some reason, caught the 4.50 back to Yokohama, and Walter, after work, caught the 7 o'clock to join them. A zigzag pops up in the diary. Edith rose early and caught the 7.30 to Tokyo. After breakfast she took the party to Nikko to see the famous painted buildings, the temples and mausoleums writhing with wood carving, lacquered in red and gilt. Home at 4.10. The Pollards came to dinner, and Mabel and Edith went on

with them to the Literary, where Edith sang.

Still, she was up early again the next morning, and in the afternoon went for a last ride with the Ferret, who gave her an affecting parting at the front gate. She does not seem to have been too moved. The next day, a lovely Sunday, a party of nine set out at 9.30am and rode to Kamakura via Kawasawa, where Mabel rode over a child, otherwise no damage. Six of them rode home over the Downs. Reggie managed very well on Wisdom, but Mabel had her work cut out to get Edgar back — sluggish was not the word for him.

On Monday, Edith went on board HMS *Pique* for tea, by invitation of Mr Grant. It poured steadily for the whole of Wednesday, and she got drenched trying out a new mare, Civility, on the racecourse. Consequently she developed an attack of malarial fever, and had to lie down most of the afternoon. After dinner they all went to the Philharmonic Concert, for which she had been rehearsing for ages, and it was decidedly *not* a success. The next day, after her 'At Home', she gave a dinner party for 12. Her dinners were always a success; she was efficient in everything that she undertook.

It was Easter in Yokohama, Good Friday, and Edith went down the town with the girls; Marian had her photo taken. Reggie and Dickinson went for a walk, and the latter came back to tiffin, after which he took Marian and Reggie for a sail on the *Maid*. Edith went for a short ride with her Organ-Grinder, and Walter dined at the Club.

Glorious weather on Saturday. There was a jolly sail on the *Maid*, and a ride, with Edith on Civility, who was going well. They all dined out at a Japanese Tea House, which made Edith feel sick, and she *was* sick at home. The geishas weren't up to much, either. Easter Day was perfect. A party of eight left at 10am and rode over to Plains to Kawasawa, where Reggie and Dickinson (who were becoming very friendly), were waiting for them on the *Maid*. Some of them strolled up to the Observatory before riding home, and Marian chose to sail home. Edith was feeling tired and seedy and went early to bed but was kept awake by Marjorie and her toothache. On Easter Monday Mr Boag dined with them, and they went to a most rotten entertainment at the Augers.

It poured without ceasing on Tuesday, but Edith and Mabel in jinrikishas managed to pay a fair number of calls, and Walter took Edith and Marian to a jolly dance at Mrs Mitchell's. Then there was a wedding to attend, and another English house was burnt to cinders. On April 9th Edith let Walter ride Babel for once, and she took Civility. Mabel was *not well*, but recovered enough to leave with the Carew party to Miyanoshita, where she went to bed. They played billiards at the hotel, did some shopping and walking, and caught the 2.04 train home.

On a warm sticky Saturday, Walter and Marian went off to Kamakura, and Edith went for a ride with the Organ-grinder; Civility was awfully fidgety. Dickinson called, and there is a zigzag in place here in the diary. On Sunday Edith went to church at 8am, Corti called and stayed to tiffin, and then they rode out together. The box from home arrived the next day; Edith unpacked it, and wore her new dress to the Bachelors' Ball, to which the returned Walter escorted her, with Marian.

They were up early in spite of the late night at the ball, and off by train on a long, tiring journey to Kioto. Mabel was ill on arrival. Edith, indefatigable, took the girls to a theatre, to a 'Cherry Dance', a ballet and the tempting shops, where Mabel bought a very good bronze for $20. Then on by train to Osaka, Nara, Kioto, where Marian took to her bed, while the other two did Lake Biwa, a temple and some potteries, and Edith, the daredevil, took the rapids, but the wetting give her a nasty sore throat and fever. On to Nagoya, but Edith was feeling awfully seedy, and they must have been glad to get home on April 23rd, to find all well, and that Reggie had started at Samuel Samuels & Company.

Next day Dickinson called, and told Walter that he was much taken with Marian. Edith's dry comment was that she thought Marian ought to tell him about Norman Walter, a frequent interested visitor to the house on the Bluff. No doubt Edith was jealous, because she soon called Dickinson an ass when he was becalmed in a boat with the girls. April 30th was a day that should have been blotted out of the almanac, with sleet and wind which drove everyone frantic. No one could possibly have pretended to enjoy the races. Marylands, Mr Slater's baby half-bred, was knocked against the rail by the wind, and fell, breaking her back.

May 1st was Edith's birthday. 'Twenty-eight. How old I'm getting'. May 4th was her seventh wedding anniversary. It rained all day and she did nothing much. The diary entries go through a phase of terseness and general dissatisfaction. Walter was very angry with her on May 9th, because she was again overdrawn at the Bank. *She told him that was not surprising, considering that he had never given her any of the allowances from home.*

On May 13th Mary Jacob arrived at nine in the evening by the *Hohenzollern*. Mary Esther Jacob was the Carews' new nursery governess. Marjorie and Ben had reached an age of unruliness, and a stronger figure than an amah was needed. Edith had never met her, although she knew of her, and her family; Edith's mother had chosen her locally, and on February 7th Mary had written to Mrs Porch an ingenuous letter confirming her willingness to travel.

'I will call on you soon after 3 o'clock on Monday afternoon. I shall be very glad to have the matter decided. My friends worry me a good deal, trying to frighten me with tales of malarial fever, earthquakes, and all other ills that flesh is heir to! Unfortunately I cannot prove to them from any book of reference I have, that Yokohama is a healthy climate — 'tho I am sure I have heard that it is — I have quite made up my mind from the first, that I would like to go — and I feel sure I can do all that Mrs Carew needs and the sooner (in reason) I can go, the better, I think, for I shall only be teased about it all the time. My friends say I must ask £30 per annum — and I will remain three years if needed.'

Mary was born at Edgarley on March 11th, 1866, so that at the age of 30 she could be expected to be more responsible than a young girl. Her parents, John Helliar Jacob, a farmer and Ondine (formerly Edwards) were dead, but she was not alone in the world. Before the frightening voyage to Yokohama, she had been living with her aunt and uncle and her sister Kate at Strathalbyn, a sizeable and most attractive house which still holds a lonely position in the small hamlet of Baltonsborough, some six and a half miles from Glastonbury.

Balanced in the privileged but awkward intermediate situation of governess, homesick up in her room, with only her banjo for company, struggling with the worrying presence of the established native servants, Mary was to find herself one close friend in July, a much-needed confidante. Elsa Christoffel, a Swiss national, had been in Yokohama since November 1894, as nurse to the Dunlops' children, and she could therefore initiate Mary into a number of mysteries. They giggled and gossiped and anatomized the limited circle of Europeans among whom they were trapped, their own future uncertain.

Edith was kind and dutiful to her useful new acquisition, taking her to church, giving her confidence around the shops, and teaching her how to travel by train with the children. Soon it was noticed that Marjorie was improving much in her behaviour.

Walter was sailing his boat, the *Cocktail*, whenever he could. He had taken a shine to Mrs Tocque, and liked her to be his passenger. Edith rode with her Organ-grinder, who fell into a ditch. Mary Jacob went to the theatre with Miss Winstanley.The fleet was in, and on Whit Monday Edith tiffined on the *Alacrity* with Captain de Lisle, and went on afterwards to a big 'At Home' given by the Admiral on the *Centurion*. In due course, Captain de Lisle came to tiffin.

May 29th was a sad day, spent in doing the girls' packing, and Edith saw them off at 10am on the 30th. She discovered her helpful new steward, Satar, to be a thief, and turned him out neck and crop, which upset her a good deal. She played and won the Ladies' Final Double Handicap at the tennis courts, but lost the Mixed Doubles Final; her partner played abominably. The Ferret called twice, and she said goodbye to him again. Ah Kwong, her Chinese boy, was badly bitten by the Baynes' Skye Terrier, and she had to take him to the doctor to be cauterized.

On June 13th she felt seedy. Then she had a row with the Italian, and an awful row with the *betto* for leading her cherished Babel badly. She had to send for Dr Kokkaku, who told her that Rachel was really ill, and gave her many directions about treatment. Walter sailed his race, and just lost the first prize by two seconds, which was hard lines. Rachel had to go to the hospital, and Edith saw Miss Crosby, the missionary, about her. Edith felt that she was getting an unfair amount of worry with servants and washerman. Walter was refusing to pay a washing bill, and Edith thought that she might have to go above him, but he did eventually settle up, and Edith thanked God.

The old money problem with Walter had recurred, in spite of the new procedure. The snag was that the cheque went out to Yokohama in Walter's name. Edith knew that the June remittance had been sent from England, but there was no sign of it in her account at the Chartered Bank. Either she was very tactful or she was afraid to ask Walter what had happened, because she did not tackle him about it until July. In what must have been a painful scene, he told her that the money had come through, but that he could not let her have any of it. He refused to explain. She appealed to Dickinson, and he wrote home for her. A better arrangement was made, at the cost of increased alienation within the marriage.

Chapter 4
A LIFE SO DREAR

Rachel came back from the Negishi Hospital after her undefined illness, and then Edith found that Babel was badly lame, with the off-hind fetlock much swollen, probably from a blow. It was several days before she was sound again, and Edith missed her daily ride. She saw Reggie fail to distinguish himself at a cricket match, and went to a big Musical Tea at the Litchfields'. Henry Charles Litchfield, a barrister of some eminence in Japan, was her lawyer. Dickinson's pony come down with him. Walter had neuralgia.

On American Independence Day everyone watched a game of football between Tokyo Upper School *v* US Men of War on the Cricket Ground, an excellent game, won by the home team, followed later by fireworks. Walter had one of his bad sick headaches (migraine?) and came home at noon. Edith rode up to the fortifications, for a reason which she did not care to specify.

July 23rd was a glorious day. 'Mais chaud comme tout', (Hot as anything). Babel very excitable, shied and reared. Mr Storer, of the *Prometheus*, called unexpectedly. Edith had her first cold bath of the year, and Ben played at riding competitions in her bed, all night long. Walter had gone away on his own to Nikko and Chuzenji, and on July 24th, a cloudless day, Edith wrote to him. Her tone is propitiatory, and there is no sign, or symbol, of financial warfare. The animated prattle of her conversation is well preserved in the living words:

My own darling,

Your first letter from Nikko arrived last evening, the second from Chuzenji early this am. I know your short cut and sympathise with you. The girls and I came down that way on our return. I am so glad Mr L. is up at the Lake; it will be nice for you. You do not

say how long you proposed remaining at Yumoto. I fancy Chuzenji will be more to your taste. Yumoto ought to be the coolest though. We are having real summer weather now, hot as anything. I send you the Gazette and Lloyds.

Reggie dined at the Club with Mr Dickinson and came home at 1 o'clock: I was having my solitary dinner when the front door-bell rang. Rachel answered it, and after much palavering came back saying a very big foreigner had come asking for Mr Carew. Rachel said Mr Carew had gone to Nikko, whereupon the unknown man vanished into the night — ten minutes afterwards, more ringing, more mysterious conversation between Rachel and somebody — so I went boldly out, and did not say `Your money or your life' but 'Hullo, Mr Storer, what are you doing here?'

You remember Mr Storer of the Palinurus *who came up and dined one night with us at 57. He is now on the* Prometheus. *He came up to see us, and on Rachel telling him you had gone to Nikko he went up to the [Japanese] police-station and asked which house Nikko was, and eventually came back here to say he couldn't find Nikko! I packed him off then and there as I was alone, but he is coming up to tiffin tomorrow (Saturday).*

At 10.10 I went up to bed, having deposited the key under the door-mat for Reggie. (First of all I must tell you that Ben and Marjorie were taking it in turn to sleep with me while Father is away.) I opened the door, when suddenly there was a squeal and the door stuck; there if you please was your son and heir lying just inside the door like a little dog. I picked him up and put him into bed — ten minutes after, bump, right through the [mosquito] curtain on to the floor and so on all thro' night. Once he crawled under the bed and there I found him when I woke up at 5am. No more Ben for me during the hot weather. Mary says he is so restless that she constantly expects him to throw himself out of the cot.

Rachel has gone into the country today to return tomorrow bringing her young sister with her. I went for such a long ride yesterday up to the old 'down' Race Course. Babel was angelic and I did enjoy it so. I never met a soul. Tonight Reggie and I are to dine at 7.15, meet Mr Dickinson outside the Club at 8.30 and go to some entertainment with him in Theatre Street — too hot I think.

Well good bye old Best.
Always with fond love from Pussy.
Your ever loving wife,
Edith

In fact, big, dark Mr Storer dined with Edith, and afterwards they went out together in the *Cocktail*; naturally, he was the helmsman. So much for Edith's assurances as to her solitary propriety. On Sunday she felt seedy all day, although she kept on her feet. Marjorie nearly killed herself by taking a header down the stable steps. Ah Kwong was giving her a lot of trouble. A strong typhoon wrecked a boat and eight men drowned off Hommoku.

It was much cooler on July the 27th, after heavy rains. Dr Wheeler called to advise on Edith's malaria, and she felt well enough to try out Sacha, a new mare from Morton's and a beauty to look at, but still very green. Walter returned, looking better. By Thursday the hot weather was back, and Dr Wheeler gave Edith a tonic. She was never a person to give in, and she played tennis the next day in the heat, which made her feel seedy again.

An ambitious expedition was planned for the weekend, and she had to be fit for anything. On the Saturday morning, as she was busy packing, there was a slight earthquake, and an ominous squally wind. Walter, Marjorie, Rachel and the provisions left at 2pm in the *Cocktail*, bound for Tomioka, and had many adventures. The boom broke as they were putting about to go home because it was too windy, and they all got very wet. Eventually they changed into jinrikishas and were taken across from Sujita in a sampan.

Reggie and Edith meanwhile had ridden down, and were much alarmed when they arrived at 6.45 to find that the rest of the party had not turned up. At last they were relieved to hear Walter's whistle. Poor Marjorie was awfully tired. They spent a feeble evening at the Halls', and had a wretched night, with fleas in myriads. At 2am Babel broke loose and explored the temple grounds.

They got up at 6 o'clock and had tea and cocoa. Marjorie, Walter and Reggie bathed early. Some European yachts came in, bringing a fair number of mosquitoes. They had a good tiffin in the temple gardens, and all left in the afternoon, except Edith, who rode home alone with Mr Tanner on his bicycle. It was not Edith's sort of trip, and she was dead beat.

August Bank Holiday was more enjoyable; she rode out with Gino Corti, he on Babel, she on Suzanne, a beautiful mare with good paces and very showy, but with a hard mouth. August 4th was Ben's fourth birthday. 'Fancy how time flies.' There was a birthday party for 12, and Rachel collapsed and had to have iced bandages. Edith herself got fever badly and had to go to bed early.

Walter had his anchor, ropes and small boat stolen on Saturday. Dr Wheeler's Kilaloo ran away and injured several people. Some coolies set upon and tried to murder the Konsul, Mr Baelin. The eclipse on August 9th was not up to much. The Carews sent a lovely basket of white flowers, costing seven and half dollars, for the Thomases' silver wedding. Dr Wheeler suggested that Edith should go away, since her fever was still troubling her, but she told him that she had decided not to go for six weeks.

On August 12th Mr de Flesch — with whom she often went riding — dined at the Carews', 'stays and all'! Walter was bitterly disappointed not to win a 'Box of Curios' raffle. Edith caught a monster moth. Then on a very hot Saturday, Walter contributed a farcical set-piece to Edith's commentary in the diary. He was taking his favourite, Mrs Tocque, off to a Yacht Club picnic, in the *Cocktail*, and just as they were starting he was so intent on spooning her that he ran into the *Wanderer*, tearing his sail and smashing his bowsprit. He was disgusted with himself.

As a result, perhaps, of the sailing disaster, Walter formed a resolve which was to disrupt Edith's precariously-balanced life pattern. He too, now that autumn was approaching, would have a horse of his own and join Pussy on those healthy rides which she enjoyed so much. It is also not at all unlikely that he felt a jealous wish to inhibit the secondary (or primary) purpose of her visits to the Plains of Heaven. Edith shows a decreasing enthusiasm for joint rides.

Towards the end of August Edith was still seedy, with a cold on the chest and a touch of influenza, she fancied. She saw the Morning Glories at the Gardeners' Association, but they weren't up to much, and went for a long hill walk with the 'dawgs', picking flowers. She and Walter were feeling worried about Reggie for some reason. She went down to see two geldings sold at auction for awful prices for such screws — $160 and $125.

Eventually she got in a hack called Merino, and tried him out herself, all round town, being completely without nerves. His trot was not up to much but Walter liked him, and either Edith or Walter (it is not clear which) bought him for only $50. He was probably a bit long in the tooth. Walter was thrilled with the horse, and took to going up to the racecourse in the early morning, even if Edith pleaded seediness and a touch of liver. He was dreadfully disappointed when Merino developed a swollen fetlock, and bought a new bicycle, but after a ride out with Gino Corti decided that he did not like the thing, and returned it.

Everyone felt seedy because of the humid weather, even the children, and Walter went to bed before dinner. Edith rode up on her own and saw an unpleasant sight — a man had hanged himself in the road leading to the racecourse. Marjorie was being very naughty. September 12th was Walter's 43rd birthday, and Merino was sound enough for a decent ride. Six friends came to dinner, including the Italian, whom Walter seems to have tolerated amazingly well — realizing, perhaps, that Edith found him callow.

Edith felt so tired and seedy on Sunday the 13th that she was thinking of seeing the Tokyo consultant, Dr Baelz, about her malaria. She felt no better when, after going to church with her, Walter showed her a plan of a house that he was proposing to have built, in the event that he failed to buy a property.

Dissatisfied Walter, thwarted of full access to Edith's allowance, was full of plots and plans, but it was always Edith's money that was at stake. Nice as it was, the house on the Bluff was only rented and Walter had conceived the desire to become a freeholder. Pushed by Walter, Edith obligingly wrote home and her father agreed to let her have £2,000 to invest in a house, on two conditions: Walter had to submit a satisfactory report on the house, and the title deeds had to be made out in Edith's name.

Clearly, the family were well alerted to Edith's predicament, but that does not mean that they will have been pressing for the dissolution of the marriage. Far from it: they were trying to prop it up, while at the same time protecting their only daughter from rascality and social demotion. A house belonging to a Mr Blad was

to be chosen, and a contract for $13,000 was soon to be under negotiation.

Walter's drive to better himself was also showing in a new dream — to give up his job and go into business in partnership in Yokohama, where there were contacts and regattas and life was good. Again, as ever, Edith wrote home, this time to Uncle Barnes, her trustee, and asked him if she could realize some of her money to enable Walter to buy into a firm, but her uncle (as was his absolute fiduciary duty) advised against any such action.

However, he did tell her that, if he approved of Walter's investment he would be willing to advance the legacy, of £8,000 to £10,000, which he had intended for Edith. Gladdened by tidings of this windfall, Walter asked around, and settled upon a silk farm. The principal was not resident in Yokohama and his consent was still pending.

Between September 14th and 22nd Edith felt very seedy or tired at least every other day. *(Walter Raymond Hallowell Carew now has only one month to live.)*

Harry Dickinson moved closer to Edith, to No. 160 the Bluff — the Jacksons' house. The mentions of frequent meetings with the bank clerk, so casually set down in the diary, lied by omission about the stage which their relationship had reached. When the coast was clear for a romantic encounter Edith hoisted a handkerchief on the verandah, which was a signal that Walter's complaisance extended only so far. One day in the last week of September, Dickinson wrote a tender, eloquent letter to Edith:

You ask me dearest to take time over answering your letter and in the same breath to give it to you at tiffin. An office on a mail day with all its interruptions is not an easy place and I do not know as I begin the how and where I shall end. What do you want me to say? It is impossible to go back to the old footing. He has altered all that and if you were a free woman I would ask you to come to me. You know this. Long ago when I first knew you something of a passion for you would now and then come over me and envy of the man who had you and now when you are thoroughly estranged and have come to me for help what I had easily checked before has risen again with a

strength that is multiplied a thousand fold by the knowledge that now you love me.

*Dearest, the scene of last night shall not take place again. We cannot help now I think loving. I know it is wrong but you are not to blame I think so much as I, but for others' sake than ours the grosser sin shall be avoided. Can we go on as we are? I do not see ** can help it. I went into all this ** beginning only with the honest intention of aiding you and cheering you up for ** and you enjoyed my coming. When I found your life so drear and empty of happiness that should have been yours my heart bled for you and I knew ** excuse anything you might do. It ** pity darling then akin to love and now I love you. I know that if you were free I would take you and keep you while ** lasted and therefore I now ....*[11]'

The letter from Edith which had drawn forth this really rather noble, courtly effusion had been destroyed by Dickinson. He made sure that none of her letters received by him survived. Edith intended to destroy his letters, but she was not thorough enough. How could she possibly have known that mischievous fingers would fish the torn-up fragments out of her wastepaper-basket in the dining-room, and *stitch them together?*

Mary Jacob was the original culprit. Her excuse for first going to the wastepaper-basket was that she was looking for letters from home which had been held back from her. If true this reveals a relationship with her employers which could not be guessed at from Edith's diary, in which Mary's social activities are charted as a member of the family. It does seem most unlikely that Edith, with all her worries, would have been bothered to act in such a way, with malice or curiosity.

The governess began her rifling activities on the 23rd or 24th September, and she sneaked off with the titillating fragments to her bosom friend, Elsa Christoffel. Although she had never done such a thing before, (perhaps), Elsa began a course of conduct of sewing the shredded letters into a coherent whole. No doubt she was nimble at patchwork. And *her* excuse for doing something that was so clearly anti-social was that she thought the letters might be useful to her friend if it should come out that various men, not friends of the family, were in the habit of visiting the house. She was afraid that Mary's character might suffer if the true state of affairs became known.

On Saturday, September 26th, the whole family left by train for Miyanoshita for the change of scene which Edith felt they much needed. At first, all went well; Sunday was glorious, and they walked to a spectacular pass, but Monday was gloomy, and Walter and Reggie had to leave for work by the very early train.

That evening Edith wrote to Walter from Fujiya's Hotel, Miyanoshita:

> *My dearest,*
>
> *Yamaguchi has just been to me about Ah Kwong not having a passport. He says it will be all right if I can give him one before we leave. Can you speak to Rachel or your clerk about it and send it me up. I hope you and Reggie got down all right. I gave Mrs **[12] your slippers and a pair of R.'s socks. I am sorry they were left behind. It has been an awfully dreary, dismal day here. Rain, rain, rain, thick fog, most depressing. I feel awfully seedy and wish I were back in Yokohama. I think the way we parted this morning had something to do with my depression. I hope you feel bright and cheerful, also that you have lost your indigestion. There's the dinner-bell, so I must go. I will write again tomorrow. Goodnight and goodbye, husband mine.*
>
> *From your loving wife,*
> *Edith*

On this same day, while it was raining in Miyanoshita, Harry Dickinson slipped into the library at Walter's Club, and took out a romantic novel, *The Playactress*, by S. R. Crockett. [13] This forgotten, pietistic tale is about the Lass in Black, which is the title of the second chapter. The actress with her pale gold hair was pale of face, with dark purple rims around her eyes, and she was 'dressed in a plain dark dress, with a small bonnet of brown and black.' Her air was mysterious, and she looked straightforward, with a set expression. Dickinson read the flimsy little melodrama and then passed it on to Edith on her return. He took it back to the library on October 9th.

Tuesday was a nice day, and they played pyramids after dinner at the hotel, but Wednesday was a day that Edith recorded in a most uncharacteristic way:

Rain

Did

nothing

but

grumble

at

the

weather

Thus emphatically in a kind of pyramid of discontent the stark words are arranged on the page of the diary, but Edith manages to write a controlled and conciliatory letter to Walter from Fujiya's Hotel:

> *Wed 10am*
> *Dearest Boy,*
> *Your letter of Tuesday arrived this morning during breakfast. I don't understand it very well. You are surprised that I did not send you a note with the slippers. I wrote to you on Monday, did you not receive the letter yesterday?*
> *You left here at 5.30am on Monday. I sent the slippers by the **s who left here at 9.30am, the same morning four hours after you. I do not see why I should be expected to write. Yesterday we all went to Hakone. I walked there and back, and as we didn't get in until late, I didn't write. Today is nasty, cold, raw, and intensely gloomy. I thank you very much for all the information about the house, it certainly does not sound a good investment, $15,000 is not exorbitant for No. 169. I quite concur in all you say on that score and will discuss it with you on Sat. I am to meet you am I not at Mr ** house at eleven? I am most sorry to hear you were not feeling well. I am not much better yet, but of course the change must be doing me good. M. and B. flourish. On second thoughts why don't you ask for a holiday on Sat? Come up here on Friday evening. I will walk down to Yumoto to meet you, and*

we can walk up together. Then you will get all Sat. and Sunday here and we can get a better chat. I can see the house alone if you think it necessary, but I certainly should not think of buying it after what you told me about the wall. I'll think this over. I want you. I think something is the matter with me I feel so awfully wretched and if it were not for the children you would see me in Yokohama tonight. Send a telegram in case letters miscarry and I will be down at Yumoto to meet the train that you came by before on Friday next. You will do this because I ask if you love me. We are going to walk to Kiga now if it doesn't rain.

Good bye husband mine,
Your loving little wife,
Edith

Back in England, Mary Jacob's aunt was writing a letter about Mary's sister Kate which indicates that Edith was actively forward planning:

Strathalbyn
Baltonsborough
October 1st, 1896
Dear Mrs Carew,

I thank you for your kind note, it is very good of you to take so much interest in Kate who will I think be quite ready and willing to leave England for Japan as soon as she hears definitely there is a situation ready for her which promises anything like the happiness Mary is now enjoying. We are pleased to hear she is so well and happy, and that she is giving you satisfaction and I must thank you for all your great kindness to her, and also for the photos which she has sent me. Mrs Porch and her nieces were here yesterday; they kindly brought us the little presents Mary sent. We shall indeed look forward to the great pleasure of making the acquaintance of Mary's little charges.

Believe me,
Yours truly,
E. Jacob

The diary continues:

October 1st, Thursday.
Rain
grumbled
still
more
at
the
weather.

October 2nd, Friday.

Rained and grumbled so much that at 2 o'clock I wired to W. to say I wanted to return. Ah Kwong and I with sweetest Tama [dog] caught the 9.30 train, arrived home at 11.55, all asleep and all well. Had a long talk with W. before I could get to sleep.

October 3rd, Saturday.

Lovely morning, but more rain in the pm. Walked round with Walter and had a look at Mr de Waepanert's house. It is a nice home but the grounds are poor, and being built at the edge of a severe bank is not in any way a desirable investment. W. left for Miyanoshita by the 1.26 train. I went down the Town with R.and took a walk in the rain. What awful weather we are having.

On this Saturday Dickinson wrote a letter to Edith which had been so finely shredded that even Elsa Christoffel's dexterous fingers were often frustrated:

*But come down to ** come about 2.3** goes up today we can have a ** I am still staying at the Jacksons but have told them not to expect me to tiffin as I wished to look out ** you down here. If you write me a ** it will be all right to send it ** the Bank as I shall leave ** instructions. Your letter reached me this morning. Should I alter my mind about tiffin I shall ** see you. Why do you ** this. You did not come ** I want so much to say stop down here ** and 2.6 train too ** the cricket field ** follow I must ** is there ** to meet you wet or* *fine ** thanks for Jude* [14] *. I send The Playactress.*

H.

I will give you The Playactress when I see you.

So, with his house plans dashed, Walter (also seeking a cure for seediness, and not at all deterred by Edith's bad experience in Miyanoshita) set off for his separate weekend.

Chapter 5
'LE MOMENT EST ARRIVÉ'

It was a Sunday without Walter, and naturally Edith turned to Harry Dickinson for company. Reggie, whether he knew so or not, was to have acted as chaperon, but for once the weather was on Edith's side. The diary carefully reduces the pleasures of the day, because Walter was becoming restive, even though he was conducting a flirtation of his own with a Miss Bolitho.

October 4th, Sunday

Dull morning which turned to heavy rain. Rode — along the Kawasawa Road. Reggie, Mr Dickinson and I had arranged to go and tiffin at Kawasawa. Mr D. and I rode out, and R. went in the *Cocktail* but as it came on very heavily to rain, he turned back. Mr D. had a feeble pony so as Reggie didn't turn up for Tiffin and it was raining hard we decided to walk to Kamakura and return by train, which we did. I cannot say the outing was a success. [15]

October 5th, Monday

Rained most of the day. Mary, M.and B. turned up at 11.45. W. seedy. We all feel most depressed at this weather. I don't ever remember such incessant rain. Of course I got malaria and went to bed before dinner.

In spite of the malaria, however, Edith had not been able to resist writing to Dickinson. The letter which follows is the only extant piece of writing by Edith addressed to Dickinson but in fact he never received it, because it was only a draft, consigned to the wastepaper-basket and the fascinated eyes of governesses: Dickinson *did* receive and duly destroy a letter couched in similar terms.

*Forgive me my dear, I always come to you in my trouble, there is not much the matter but I should like your advice on a matter which must ** early tomorrow ** is so far quite indifferent as to yesterday beyond calling you a few inelegant names. He is seedy, Miyanoshita did not suit him in more ways than one. Miss Bolitho wasn't ** owing to the rains. She was ** to leave us or get down ** Ikao. She however is ** Yokohama on Wed. and he asked ** and ** chaperon ** companion to dinner here Wed. ** the same evening. Can I refuse to meet them, or keep quiet by remaining passive? I rather think the latter will give him less of a handle to bully me. To add to the situation it would be nice to have you here on that evening. How would you like it? I haven't **'*

And there the fragment ends. There is something calculated about the need to draft what should be a plaintive cry for help and affection. Dickinson, ever more heavily involved, felt the same compulsion to write but in his case it was a flowing and explicit letter, gleefully recovered almost intact:

*I cannot go to bed my sweet without writing a line which I shall deliver if I can before I go down. Thanks for letter of today: I could not answer it as I stopped your coolie as he left the house and merely wrote acknowledgment. My poor darling — I knew you would suffer for yesterday but it revealed to me more than ever dearest how much I love you and how much you have become to me. I shall hope always that all this constant abuse of me will never cause you to look at me with other eyes than those you have now although I feel you think much too high of me. I feel so sure of your strength and steadfastness. And it is really after all abuse that is not deserved. I think he must think you care for me (without an idea that you [I?] know and return your affection) and though he probably does not know the extent that you have gone, he cannot but feel he has lost you and that you would if you could come to me. This must I think account a good deal for his horrible dislike for me. You know dearest in one way I care nothing for it. If I had you for my own I would laugh at his hatred. But I do feel it badly in another way that even he ** much as I despise and loath him ** should have this hatred of me. It's* *very childish but I cannot get over the feeling. But I would not give you up for all the hatred of the whole clan and family of Carews. I love you utterly my dear one, and the remembrance of yesterday will be ever with me. I have been thinking much about your probably having to meet this woman. I wish for your sake that you could refuse to but have come to think that you cannot well do so. Do you know anything against her; if not, you should meet her, I think. It would bring you endless bullying refusing and I want that to be avoided as far as possible. If you refuse on the grounds that he has insulted you before others and that you do not wish for a repetition, refuse first on these grounds and after that on account of his relation to her. That is to say — if you refuse at all. But I think you will have to stay and entertain her. If you cannot do it ask Mrs Jackson if you may come in here to dinner: it would make her think that there is no woman you could trust more than her.*

October 6th, Tuesday

Fine day at last but by no means settled. Rode to the Race Course in the early am. Babel very fit. Merino fairly well. Walked down the Town, saw Mr H. Jackson about drawing on Papa. Went to Dr Smith, played tennis, called on Mrs Wheeler, and walked home from the cemetery. Walter got a bad eye and went to bed before dinner. Busy until 11 pm over the tennis books etc.

October 7th, Wednesday

No news. Raining. Did not go to the course. W. went. Marjorie went to her first dancing lesson and I went to the Gardens.

And apparently no highly charged evening at No. 169, with Miss Bolitho and Harry Dickinson at the dinner table. Indeed, on (probably) Tuesday the 6th Dickinson had written:

Never mind my coming to dinner. I shan't feel hurt if I am left out of your parties. Nothing he can do will hurt my feelings now. It is worse for you than me to hear all his abuse. I am only afraid that he may say something rude to me before others and I shan't sit quietly under that. Only you would be treated worse than ever if we came to an open row again. I will leave the office early before twelve and come straight down. If you care to take a stroll along the road — if not wet well and good, I shall leave the office at a quarter to twelve. I tear the half sheet off and jot down points about your will. Are you coming to the Bank tomorrow? Goodnight sweet and take care of yourself.

Yours always dear.

H.

I will go and see Litchfield some time before he gets into a busy season. Tear all this up when you have taken a note of it — The notes re the will I mean. Of course you destroy letters.

Again, on Wednesday the 7th, Dickinson wrote:

*I think he was only bluffing this morning when he spoke about going in to ask ** your account. Can you send me line re your note to Litchfield to the Jacksons by a messenger. I want to know if you arranged an interview.*

H.

Tomorrow and Friday are both likely to be mail days, so do not miss today if possible.

By now, Edith had told Dickinson that she had written home to give her parents some indication of her marital predicament. She also told him that she did want to go home to Edgarley, and Dickinson nobly (or perhaps self-servingly, or ambivalently both) urged her to do so. He thought that if she went home for eight to twelve months she would find Yokohama a happier place on her return. Such a proposed leave of absence does tend to support the possibility that the previous long trip home in 1893 arose out of matrimonial fault. Referring to the letter home, Dickinson wrote:

Grown tired of you is good but not to my thinking strong enough. However you will know best what you can write. I call his treatment of you brutal. Not stand much in the way of your going home. I am not sure of this. When he finds his money supplies ceasing I think he will object. Ask Litchfield on Monday if in the event of your getting away with or without his consent if he can force you to return to him and if you find he has such a power then I should tell Mr L. the real state of of affairs — how it is impossible for you to really live with him as a wife, and your real wishes on the subject. That any wire they might send you, you would make arrangements about. Can you do this? When you next write say that if they wire they must address fully Mrs Carew, 169 Bluff, Yokohama. It would only cost ten or twelve shillings more and the expense is nothing compared with the importance of your receiving the message. Otherwise I can think of nothing that I wished you to write about.

I hope you said that the £100 which Carew had written for was done absolutely without your authority and that to say it was for you was simply a falsehood. It is obtaining money under false pretences, and I should like you to refer to this in your next letter, and say that any money he asks for of yours is deserving of only one name. I know you have said this less mildly, but there is no harm in impressing them with the importance of it. If you succeed in thoroughly impressing them with the fact that all the use he now has for you is your money — otherwise he is thoroughly tired of you and is treating you worse than any of his servants they will wake up to the fact of his being a scoundrel and a mercenary one.

October 8th, Thursday

Rode up to the Course. *Saw Mr L.* — Mr and Mrs Dunlop at the Course. Played tennis. N. Thomas and M. Rice played tennis singles and Nellie won. She has enormously strong joints. Walked home. Dr Hatton and the Simmonds dined here and we played Lap till very late.

October 9th, Friday

Dull and raining in the pm. W. went to the Course. I didn't — I went to Town. Tried to play tennis in the pm. Too wet. Walked home, found Walter in bed, tired out, and I was glad to join him. Arranged to go to Tokyo to see Baelz. Fever is no better and it is silly going on day after day. Heard from Father re the house, also from Harry. How odd about Mr Welch.

The entry for the 10th introduces a key figure — the 'Mysterious Visitor' — and is very legibly written, without errors:

October 10th, Saturday

Got up at 5. to find it pouring, so went to bed again. It rained hard until 3 o'c, most disappointing weather for the Regatta, which was held however in spite of wind and rain. As I never take any interest in it myself, it didn't upset me very much. Had a curious and mysterious visitor shortly after Tiffin, who called to see Walter. I went down to the Boat House about 3. and walked home about 5. as it cleared. Walter doesn't seem too well, and I wish he could get a thoro' change. I suppose it is the damp. I saw Dr Wheeler at the Boat House, and he gave me a prescription for my malaria.

Down at the Boat House, the exact sequence of events was that Dr Wheeler approached Edith and remarked that the trip to Miyanoshita had not done her much good. He might have said that she did not look so well. 'No,' she agreed, 'it was beastly weather, raining all the time.'

And then Edith said, 'I want you to give me those arsenic drops which you remember you gave me when I was opposite St John's at No. 57. Quinine does not affect me, you told me before, and you advised me to try arsenic.'

Dr Wheeler had previously prescribed arsenic for Edith's malaria, on three separate occasions, and he did not hesitate: 'Certainly: I will just write it out now,' and he tore off a piece of the Regatta programme and wrote out on it a prescription for half an ounce of Fowler's Solution — ie two grains of white arsenic in solution, also known as Liquor Arsenicalis. As is well known, two grains is the quoted smallest lethal dose of arsenic. The Fowler's was to be measured out in drops, and should have lasted about ten days.

October 11th, Sunday

Lovely day. Went to the Early Service. Walter stayed in all the am waiting for the 'woman in black' who however did not come. She appears to be shy. Reggie and I went for a walk to the Race Course and back and I got a short ride in the am. Walter not at all well and went to bed directly after Tiffin. I sent for Dr Wheeler about 5 o'clock, who ordered W. medicine. Not that it will do him much good I'm thinking.

On this Sunday domiciliary, Dr Wheeler found Walter Carew to be slightly weak and out of sorts, and a little nervous. He prescribed a mild stimulant to the liver in the form of Podophyllum (the May-apple, whose rhizome and roots contain a resin, podophyllin, and a constituent, podophyllotoxin) which was used as a cholagogue, to increase the flow of bile, and also as a cathartic. For good measure he added antipyrine to relieve any fever, and digitalis.

After his visit, even though it was a Sunday, a servant was sent out to the chemist's shop used by the household — Joseph Schedel, a German subject in business on his own account at No. 77, Yokohama — to have two prescriptions made up: the Fowler's Solution prescribed the day before for Edith, and the medicines for Walter. Meanwhile faithful Dickinson had been writing a Sunday letter:

I will come to church with Mrs Jackson and we will all walk up together if possible.

H.

and (a pencilled letter):

Say you do not know in the least about what steps he will take to get your money, but that it is your wish that none of yours be any more sent out to him on any account. Ask Litchfield to hurry up with the will, and do not over-hurry him and tell him you want a copy and that the original is to go home.

and:

*You have not said ** £150 you drew he is doing his very ** out of you by both threats and cajolery. Re your suggestion that* *the Bank would wire out the credit or permission for you to draw on your father. This can of course be done easily enough but it would be necessary to instruct the Bank (and in writing) that you had written to your father to this effect and that in the event of any such credit coming out of our London office either by wire or letter care is to be taken that the advice be sent to you and not to your husband. Such a letter would be best addressed privately. **Jackson you should ask him to treat the request in all confidence. I will draw up a letter for you before I go to Kobe.*

Against all this turmoil, the diary continued blandly:

October 12th, Monday

Fine, but doubtful. I rode to the Course. Walter didn't go. He wasn't feeling well enough, but he went down as usual to the office. Saw Mr Tennant and arranged with him about the report of the Races. Had a lot of trouble arranging about one handicap. Wrote home.

By Tuesday, Walter felt well enough to gallop.

October 13th, Tuesday

Rained a good deal in the am. Walter and I managed however to get up to the Course. Heavy galloping. Mr Pakenham has arrived. Kobe going well. Paid some calls and played tennis. Walter dined at the Club — and came home very late. He made me feel very much disgusted.

There is corroboration of Walter's late night, provided by Max Kauffman, that same good pal who had witnessed his difficulty in the urinal. They were playing billiards at the Club, after dinner, and Walter seemed to be in rather good spirits, just as a man would be after having a glass or two too many. In a kind of tipsy way, he kept repeating, 'Le moment est arrivé où il faut faire la chose'. [16]

During the day Schedel's had issued a repeat prescription of Dr Baelz's belladonna and morphine concoction for Walter's stricture, so it must have been playing him up again.

October 14th, Wednesday

Fine morning, in fact no rain all day, but dull in the pm. Played my Tennis Handicap and lost. Mons.Pernet was not up to much, but as I never expected to win, it didn't matter. I am sorry for him, tho'. Walter came home at 4 o'c, and went to bed. The result of last night's dissipation. Came home to find Reggie feverish and shivery, and sent for Dr Wheeler. Marjorie also has a bad croupy cold. Quite a Hospital!

Edith must have told Dickinson about Walter's 'dissipation' because his letter on Wednesday the 14th refers to the incident:

> *It will be necessary to be quite in accord with each other. On broad questions we must be able to answer alike. You first wrote to me about the money — writing to the man you could best entrust with some of your unhappiness. Money was a necessity and it was a very natural thing to come to me about it. This of course led to my advising you how to get it, and as the money proved a source of much anxiety to yourself on account of his attempts to get it, I often saw you at your house. If ever questioned re meeting on the hills we must admit it of course, as our meetings were for the purpose of talking generally over what was the best course to take as regards yourself. We met on no particular hills mind and never mention the fortifications, it is too near the cottage and if possible that should be kept out of it. We sometimes rode and sometimes walked. But our hill meetings have been so infrequent that it should be difficult to make any point against you.*
>
> *Our meeting place for the one or two occasions when we did meet must be the Tea-House near the steep hill or by the Race Course. We have rested of course it was easier to talk matters over thus but as often as not did not rest. The reason of our secret meeting was the double one of the (1) necessity of keeping the money matters from your husband (2) our mutual dislike of each other. We have met as friends and I am and have been always a good friend and nothing more and the sense that you had someone here whom (to some small extent) you could take into your confidence was a great comfort to you.*

I know nothing of the legal proceedings. You can say of course I recommended going to a lawyer in case your husband proved too difficult to manage about the money. Nothing more. As regards the not having taken proceedings before of course say you hoped things would improve. They have got worse however hence the compulsion. Your note with the cap [he had taken away someone else's cap by mistake] has disturbed me very much, it makes me dread to think of what you may be subjected to; please be so careful not to drive him into any violent act. He shall be punished but that would be but a small compensation for any harm done to you.

You must tell L. about last night and say that you really cannot say when you may be compelled to leave him from fear of personal violence. Ask his advice as to what you can do if you should ever get frightened. It will cause him to hurry up with the case anyway. It is quite clear to me now. At all risks, at all hazards, divorce. Your personal safety is of more importance to us all than any scandals and then you have your children.

If you succeed in proving the necessity for divorce you will have no trouble in convincing the Court of the unfitness of your husband to have the care of the children. You will then always have the comfortable feelings of having done rightly by the two little beings for whose lives you are responsible. Now and always I will help you in all things if you want me, as I know you do, and be with you while I may. Keep up your heart my dear one, and do not give in now under his cruelty and coarseness. If you are offered personal violence you must appeal to your brother and servants for immediate help and go to your lawyer for further guidance. Send for me whenever you may need me. Burn all this when you have read it and learnt the early part.

Harry Dickinson had compromised his own security, and he was now deeply worried for himself as well as for Edith. A certain weakness, and inadequacy of character, which will have been well perceived by Edith — whom he did not know at all — was beginning to show in the flurry of his fine words; frankly a buck-passing tendency.

A scandal would have wrecked his career at the bank, and he

was not anyway permitted under the terms of his appointment to enter into a marriage: Edith knew that. A cross-petition, with him as co-respondent, would have been ruinous for both. As a matter of fact, there is no adultery without actual penetration (be it ever so shallow, a mere nuzzling) but the cottage by the fortifications would have raised a strong suspicion, indeed, even if they had not gone so far as the 'grosser sin'.

However, Dickinson had no real need at that time to worry (although a horrendous scandal was lying in wait for him) because although Edith told him that she had twice seen Litchfield about divorce, such interviews by her own later admission *never took place.*

Chapter 6
'PLENTY DEADLY POISON'

Dr Edwin Wheeler, of No. 97, the Bluff, had been in practice in Yokohama for 23 years, and he was a decent colonial doctor of the old school, happy to mix with his patients socially, and willing to make home visits at any time of the day or night. In the afternoon of Thursday, October 15th, having received a note from Mrs Edith Carew that morning, which asked him to have a look at her husband — who did not seem to be in very good health — he examined Walter in his own office at the United Club. He did not feel greatly concerned by his patient's weakness and general state of being out of sorts.

'You are over-stimulating a little too much', he lectured Walter gently. 'You will have to go on a diet, and stay at home for at least two or three days and you must send a dozen Vichy Water up to the house, and drink only Vichy and milk.'

The doctor could hardly fail to notice that Walter's large eyes were muddy, with a yellowish tinge. It looked like a bilious attack, but to frighten him he issued the warning, 'If you don't watch out, you will get jaundice.'

After Dr Wheeler had gone, Walter wrote a dependent sort of letter to 'Dearest Edith':

Many thanks for your chit. I am feeling a little better but still very seedy; many thanks for sending me old Wheeler. He came to my office and talked a lot of rot about my being on the verge of jaundice and has knocked off all drinks except Vichy water, one dozen of which I have ordered to be sent to the house. I have been offered 13,000 dollars down for the house. Fearfully busy over the lotteries. W.

October 15th, Thursday

Fine day. I rode to the Course in spite of feeling very tired. Nothing very exciting. Reggie decidedly better, only a bad feverish cold. Wrote to the Dr and asked him to see W. at the Club. He doesn't seem at all himself. Went down the Town, played tennis, and on coming back at 4.30 found R. up and W. home in bed. He has been ordered a course of Vichy Water by the Dr. I wonder how long it will last.

In the quaint fashion of those long-ago days, Dr Wheeler called on Friday to check on his patient's progress, even though he considered that his condition was not at all serious. He found Walter in bed and much the same, except that he was also very drowsy — a classic symptom of sluggish liver. Edith did not think the domiciliary visit worth mentioning.

October 16th, Friday

Fairly fine. Reggie stayed in bed till 11 and remained in the house all day. Wrote to S.S. to say he was unable to go down to office. No news. W. stayed upstairs. I want him to keep quiet until Monday, if he will.

Walter's stricture must have been adding to his miseries, because Dr Baelz's secret prescription was filled again at Schedel's. Early the next morning, Dr Wheeler was back at No. 169. Walter was still drowsy, and he was nauseous. The doctor gave him some Podophyllum on sugar, whereupon he immediately vomited a small quantity of dark green, bilious-looking matter.

If only, Walter kept insisting, he could get to Kamakura, to the wonderful beach, he would feel better, but Dr Wheeler strongly advised him that he was in no fit state for such an expedition. The sickly patient was bitterly disappointed.

Although there was no cause for anxiety, the doctor returned that Saturday evening, and ordered a mustard sinapism — a plaster — because there had been continuing vomiting.

Edith, however, in spite of Walter's queasy condition, still managed to conduct a breezy day, packed with her customary activities:

October 17th, Saturday

Such a glorious day. Rode up to the Course. Lot of galloping. Mrs Dunlop, Pearson and Trixie were there. Dr came soon after breakfast, but did not care about W.'s going to Kamakura. R. and I walked round to Mr de Flesch to excuse W. from dining there. Got W. some books, and walked down the Town, taking Ben. Walter suddenly became very sick, I am glad he didn't go away. Dr W. says he is on the verge of jaundice. Dined at Mr de Flesch's and got home before 11 — Dunlops, Dodds, Festitices and de Waepanert there. Went to a cricket match in the pm. Reggie stayed with Walter. He is quite well again.

During that Saturday, Edith sent to Schedel's for more medicaments: 'Normal Dispensary. Please send one bottle quinine and refill the two accompanying bottle and tin. E.M.H. Carew, 169, Bluff, 17-10-96.' Joseph Schedel supplied a bottle of quinine, refilled the tin with salicylic dusting powder, and refilled the bottle with half an ounce of Fowler's Solution of Arsenic.

While she was down in town, getting books for the invalid, Edith ventured into a native chemist's — Maruya's, of Bentend-ori, which was also a bookstore. Perhaps she bought some books here, rather than getting them out of the Club library. What she did buy, presumably for her malaria, was a small tin box containing antipyrine.

Edith purchased it, she said from an employee named Hayashi Schichiro. Antipyrine is a white, crystalline febrifuge got from coal-tar products. She had bought a box before, on October 8th. Evidently the boathouse prescription for Fowler's had not thus, (assuming she had taken the full bottle of drops) been particularly successful.

Dickinson was about to depart to Kobe the next morning, to play cricket, but letters were still flowing in from him, destined to rise again from the wastepaper-basket:

> *Love you. I think of you always. I cannot give you up now. Time, separation, circumstances may in the future change us. Let us wait for the ** to develop and decide these things for ** It is 12 and ** I must go on ** the Hill and I cannot decide ** say we must*

*all as friends ** leave it for me to decide. It were ** to part altogether, but it can not ** sweet and I do not wish it. Let us talk it out again, not write, for I cannot write any more.*

On the Sunday, Edith ventured out only to church:

October 18th, Sunday

Fine day, colder. Did not ride. W. still quite seedy. Mr Stewart tiffined with us. Took the children to church. Mary went out with Elsa and a friend. Had dinner upstairs. Cricketers went to Kobe.

An emissary did go out, however, from No. 169. A jinrikisha man took a chit in the name of Carew to Maruya's, where Hayashi Schichiro supplied one bottle of chlorodyne and one bottle (one third of an ounce) of sugar of lead, both remedies for diarrhoea, the latter more drastic.

Lead acetate — sugar of lead — looks like loaf sugar, its crystals white or tinged with brown. Its taste is sweet, followed by an astringent or metallic flavour. It has the odour of vinegar. An abortifacient, it used to be given in doses of one to five grains for uncontrollable diarrhoea. Lead is a cumulative poison, seldom employed in homicide. One ounce of the acetate is not necessarily fatal.

Dr Wheeler did not hesitate to make a Sunday call, even though Edith failed to record it. The vomiting had improved, but there was still drowsiness, with a little epigastric pain. New symptoms were thirst and dryness of the mouth, and a feeling of constriction and pain in the throat on swallowing. The doctor thought that the dose of Podophyllum which he had previously administered had not had any effect (well, the patient vomited it up, didn't he?) and that possibly the tincture of Podophyllum which was in the house might be inert. He therefore prescribed a soluble Podophyllum mixture. He did *not* prescribe chlorodyne or sugar of lead. He was a Podophyllum man. There was no diarrhoea.

The following morning Dr Wheeler was back at Walter's bedside, still convinced that he was dealing with a very bad bilious attack. The patient was drowsy, slightly restless, with mild pain over the epigastric region, and pronounced pain when swallowing. He vomited some dark green matter, in the doctor's presence.

This time the prescription was for an effervescing saline draught — a purgative — and repeated mustard sinapisms. How inadequate these antiquated remedies seem now! And how surprised Dr Wheeler was when he returned in the evening to find no improvement at all!

Edith recorded neither visit:

October 19th, Monday

Fine day. Had such a restless night with W. Didn't go to the Course. Stayed in all day — W. no better. He talked about going to the office after tiffin, but he is not at all fit for it. Wrote to Mr Stewart at his dictation. Reggie went back to his office. Marjorie's cold still bad.

It is important to notice Edith's words — 'Stayed in all day' — as would indeed be expected of a wife whose husband was as incommoded as Dr Wheeler described. The importance lies in the fact that on Monday, *probably,* Hayashi Schichiro of Maruya's sold one bottle of sugar of lead and one full ounce bottle of Fowler's Solution of arsenic to a 'foreign woman'. He had never met her before. When he warned her that the arsenic was a dangerous poison she said that it was for external application. There was no doctor's prescription; she merely wrote the names of the two medicines on a chit, and added 'Mrs Carew'. The same foreign woman returned the next day and paid for the drugs.

On the Tuesday morning Dr Wheeler was seriously puzzled: his patient was much worse. The vomiting had increased, and there was now slight diarrhoea, accompanied by tenesmus.

To try to stem the vomiting, Dr Wheeler administered bismuth and hydrocyanic acid, but by now he was getting rattled, and he asked Edith if she would have any objection to a second opinion. He wanted to call in Dr Howard Todd, who was attached to the Royal Naval Hospital. 'Certainly not, bring him round,' was the expected reply.

At about three o'clock, after a consultation with Dr Todd at the hospital, Dr Wheeler drove him to the house on the Bluff, where the two doctors bent over Walter and prodded and probed, while Edith watched.

Dr Todd asked to see some of the vomit, but the basin had been washed out. Dr Wheeler ventured into the bathroom, and examined the motions. There was very little faecal matter, and a great deal of lavatory paper covered with a motion of dark greenish-black.

Dr Todd's opinion was that Walter Carew was suffering from some irritant of the stomach, aggravated by liver disease: on palpation, the liver was contracted. He recommended that the motions and vomit should be kept for examination and suggested some bromide, and pieces of ice for the throat.

At about 7pm Dr Wheeler made his third visit of the day. Edith told him that it was impossible to get Walter to take anything by mouth. The doctor had a go, but the patient turned away: 'It is no use. I am not going to take a thing that will burn the throat out of me.'

As an alternative Dr Wheeler administered by hypodermic injection a tabloid of one-quarter of a grain of hydrochlorate of morphine and one-hundredth part of a grain of atropine. This was to sedate a patient who was restless, vomiting, purging, and growing weaker by the minute. A modern view would be that he was becoming seriously dehydrated.

Dr Wheeler left the house that evening, well satisfied that he could do nothing more at that time, and covered and comforted by the second opinion. He happened to be dining out that night, just down the road at No 118 the Bluff, and was halfway through dinner when he was told by a servant that a lady wanted to see him.

Edith's diary records this incident:

October 20th, Tuesday

Dull but no rain. Walter no better. No news. Dr Todd came in the afternoon to see W. Ordered him ice. Went down Town in the am. Remained in in the aft. Walter rather alarmed me after dinner, and I went in search of Dr Wheeler who was at Mrs Mollison's. Mr Parsons came in in the aft. Had a very bad night.

Dr Wheeler left the table, and found Edith waiting outside in a jinrikisha. 'I am sorry to disturb you, Doctor,' she said. 'Walter does not seem so well. He is muttering and talking and saying things, and seeing insects and animals crawling over his bed.' Dr Wheeler stayed calm. 'That may possibly be due to the hypodermic, but it will pass off. You go back, and as soon as the ladies rise, I will come around.'

At about 11 o'clock, the doctor made his fourth visit of the day, and found his patient half sleeping, and muttering, complaining of stomach-ache, backache, and tenesmus. He was intensely thirsty, and asked with a certain pathos for a brandy and soda. What Dr Wheeler certainly did not know, as he left his bilious, muttering patient to live through another nightmarish night, was that on that Tuesday evening at about 6.15 Edith had sent a jinrikisha man, Ando Musaburo, to Maruya's with a note:

> *Mr Maruya,*
> *Please give bearer*
> *1 Bed Pan*
> *1 Bottle of Fowler's Solution of Arsenic.*
> *E.M.H. Carew.*
> *169, Bluff*
> *20.10.*

An apprentice, Yamada Masakichi, supplied the ounce-bottle and the bedpan.

Promptly the next morning, Wednesday, October 21st, Dr Wheeler was again in attendance, and found a change for the worse, with his patient becoming prostrated. Diarrhoea, acute now, of a dark greenish, greyish or black-greenish colour and very liquid was the most prominent, and unaccountable symptom. The Podophyllum and the effervescing saline draught might have induced a few loose motions, but the excessive purging now present was an inappropriate response. The vomiting had not stopped, and the pain in the throat was still deeply upsetting to the patient, with 'everything burning'.

Rather hopelessly, Dr Wheeler prescribed again: belladonna and opium to be sprinkled over a sponge and applied externally for the continuing pain in the back, and beef peptone, to make light beef tea. Walter was supposed to be drinking milk and soda all the time — but swallowing still hurt him.

That Wednesday morning Edith despatched Mary Jacob on some errands: she was to go to Moss's the furniture dealer's, to take a book to Curnow's, to take a chit to Joseph Schedel's, and another, in Edith Carew's handwriting, to Maruya's, which read:

Will Mr Maruya give bearer one bottle of Fowler's Solution, and one bottle of sugar of lead.

Edith gave her five dollars and said that she wanted change. The governess went to Maruya's last, leaving the two children outside in a jinrikisha. The man — who was Hayashi Schichiro — had a dreadful question for her. 'Why,' he asked, 'you bought so plenty deadly poison?'

Mary Jacob hurried homewards with the two little bottles in her little bag. As she passed Schedel's the youngest assistant, who was standing on the steps, beckoned to her, and asked her to take another bottle. The chit from Edith which Mary had previously put in, and which brought forth this bottle, read: 'Normal Dispensary. Please send a small bottle of Fowler's Solution of Arsenic the same as before. I cannot send the empty bottle as it has been broken. E.M.H. Carew. 169, Bluff. 21.10.' (The 'same as before' refers to the boathouse prescription).

The youngest assistant marked the bottle 'W. R. Carew Esq., 4 to 5 drops in water after meals. 21.10.96.'

At 11.30 to 11.45 Edith was waiting for the governess on the steps of the house on the Bluff, and Mary saw her put the two Maruya's bottles on the small writing-table by the window. She did not see what she did with the Schedel's bottle. At about mid-day on that Wednesday, Dr Wheeler received a note from Edith Carew, saying that her husband was not well, and asking him to call again. She also wrote: 'Shall I telegraph, or will you, for Dr Baelz?'

Dr Wheeler replied, 'I will', and sent a telegram immediately after tiffin. In the late afternoon, between five and six o'clock, the reply came:

Dr Wheeler, Yokohama. Tokyo 21.10. 4.7 p.m. Impossible today would tomorrow evening do. Baelz.

Before dinner Dr Wheeler took the telegram up to No. 169 to show it to Edith. 'You had better go upstairs and see how the patient is before you decide anything,' she said, rather formally.

And there was Walter in his bed, quite cheery, and inclined to talk, begging the doctor for goodness sake to give him a little brandy and soda as his throat was so dry and burning. Dr Wheeler gave him a nip of what he asked for, with a quarter of a grain of cocaine in it, to try to check the vomiting. He left three cocaine tabloids for the night. Before he went home he saw a zinc bedpan, and Edith told him, 'Oh, I have got a bedpan, Doctor. That will save him getting up.' As for Dr Baelz's visit, it was decided, since Walter had had rather a better afternoon, to wait until morning.

Meanwhile, at 2 o'clock that afternoon there had been a meeting at a dancing lesson which had far-reaching consequences. Mary Jacob and Elsa Christoffel took their respective charges for their lesson, and Mary blurted out the dreadful words of Hayashi Schichiro. For the moment neither young woman knew how to act, and that is very understandable. Mary did tell Reginald Porch, 'in a casual sort of way', but he thought nothing of it. 'The cheek of the man!' was his attitude.

Knowing none of these developments, Edith wrote in her diary that night an uncompleted entry:

October 21st, Wednesday

Cold but no rain. Agreed with Mr Parsons that Dr W. didn't appear to understand W.'s case, and wired thro' the Dr for Baelz. He couldn't come however. Had several callers. I am sure W. is really ill and I am going

Those are the last words of the diary of Edith Carew.

Chapter 7
MR BOAG'S FUNERAL

Thursday, October 22nd. A very worried man, Dr Wheeler stood over the diminished figure of Walter Carew. He was obviously much worse, hovering in a half-dream state, and extremely prostrated. Edith said that she had been up most of the night with him. She had sent for the doctor at 6.30am and it was now 7 o'clock. Dr Wheeler saw that the patient was exhausted, and so he administered a dose of 15 grains of hydrate of chloral, to induce proper sleep. He told Edith not to talk to her husband, and, if he spoke, not to answer him.

As he left to attend the funeral of a mutual acquaintance, Mr Boag, who appears in the diary, Dr Wheeler said that he would return, but in fact he had already made up his mind to get Walter admitted to the Naval Hospital. He had to confess to himself that he could not account for the grossly severe symptoms, the irritation of unknown origin which had occurred over and above the original bilious attack. The anxious words in his head were that he could not make head or tail of it all.

Mr Boag's funeral at nine in the morning was as much a milestone in the case as the dancing lesson. It was a moment of some trepidation for Charles Buchanan Dunlop as he approached Dr Wheeler. The matter that he was about to raise was beyond all bounds of Victorian family life and class.

Early that morning his nursery governess, Elsa Christoffel had come to him in great agitation to tell him about Hayashi Schichiro and his 'so plenty deadly poison'. Dramatically, as was her nature, she insisted that, 'If we do not speak now it will be on our consciences all our lives, should Mr Carew die.'

Elsa was especially importunate because she was bursting with her special knowledge of the Dickinson love-letters, but did not

dare at that stage to mention her discreditable little hobby. She so worked upon her employer that he agreed to issue a guarded warning to Dr Wheeler, and to ask him to go to see Mary Jacob himself.

Dunlop's whispered warning opened the doctor's eyes, and he hastened round to John Lowder's house, where the children happened to be spending the day, to confront Mary Jacob. She told him all that she knew about her shopping trip for poison, and, with a frightening burden of responsibility that was his alone, Dr Wheeler began a course of activity that kept him on his feet for hours. His priority was to get Walter safely into the hospital, but Dr Todd was away for the day, and his junior, Dr Percival May, was reluctant to take the responsibility of admitting such an unusual case. Temporarily thwarted, he went on next to see the British Consul, John Hall, to ask him to use his influence at the hospital.

His manner back at No. 169 had changed, as he told Edith shortly that Walter was only going from bad to worse, and that he had made up his mind to remove him to the hospital at once. Just after he had left the house, he met Reginald Porch. 'You go up,' he told him, 'as I fear your brother-in-law is getting arsenic in some form.' Reggie was told to stay in the room with Walter, and to see that he was given nothing but milk and soda, by Reggie's own hands. Meanwhile the Consul had gone to the hospital by jinrikisha, leaned heavily upon young Dr May, and secured admission.

An anonymous note came to Dr Wheeler: *'Three bottles solution of arsenic in one week, Maruya.'* His office boy, who knew such things, told him that it had been brought from No. 6, Bund, which was the home of the Dunlops, and Elsa Christoffel.

At 2.30 Dr Wheeler found that Walter had deteriorated alarmingly. On being spoken to, he struggled up on his elbow, in an automatic gesture of courtesy, but he was so weak that he fell back in a sort of tetanic spasm, and broke out in a cold sweat. As gently as he could, the doctor administered a stimulant, and he rallied.

They placed him on the stretcher and took him down to the hospital where he was put to bed, but they could not make him comfortable. He said that he had a terrible pain in his chest, going through to the back, and he tossed from side to side, sitting up and lying down in his struggle to breathe.

Confronted with this harrowing scene, Dr May was still able to make a clinical assessment: the pulse was feeble, rapid, slightly irregular, and 'running'. The patient felt that he was choking, his extremities were cold, his tongue furred and his mouth dry. The purging and vomiting seem to have been absent. There was no merciful loss of consciousness, although at times he lapsed into a low, muttering delirium, and pointed to the pattern on the quilt.

They put hot-water bottles and hot flannels to the patient's feet and stomach and gave him brandy and milk and soda water, all of which he retained. Dr May administered stimulants and ether hypodermically, but at about 4.15, Walter Hallowell Carew became quite pulseless, and at about 4.40 in the afternoon, his heart stopped beating.

Late that night, after he had been out to dinner, Dr Wheeler went up to No. 169, in response to an urgent note from Edith.

'Doctor,' she said, 'there is one thing I would like to tell you which I suppose I ought to have told you before. Mr Carew had a stricture and he had been in the habit of taking arsenic for it. Just a few days ago he asked me to send down and get a small bottle of Fowler's Solution of arsenic, and he also wanted some sugar of lead.'

Dr Wheeler's manner to Edith no longer reflected tennis parties and regattas: 'It is a pity: it would have simplified matters if you had told me so.'

Edith went on, 'But I cannot find the bottles. I thought they were in that drawer at the bedside.'

And so the terrible day ended. Perhaps Edith sat and looked at the blank page of her diary, because there is a single weak cross over the space for October 22nd. Reggie left his job. Dickinson returned from Kobe on October 23rd.

There had to be a post-mortem examination on October 23rd, performed by Dr Todd and Dr May, with Dr Wheeler looking on. The report was as follows:

Eighteen hours after death the body was first examined externally for any marks of injury and the orifices to see if they contained poison. The chest was then opened and the contents examined in situ. The organs were then removed and the trachea, bronchi, lungs, and larynx examined. Then the heart, its orifices, valves, and structure. Then the upper part of the oesophagus was examined. The abdomen was then opened and its contents examined in situ. The lower part of the oesophagus and the pyloric end of the stomach were then ligatured, removed, and placed in a glass jar. The small and large intestine were separated from their muscularies, ligatures applied, and the whole intestines placed in a glass jar. The liver was then removed, incisions being made in its substance, and the organ placed in a glass jar. The liver was of very firm consistence and a good deal smaller than normal, about 40 ounces. The spleen was then removed and incised, both kidneys and ureters examined and removed, left slightly larger than right kidney. One kidney placed in a glass jar with liver. The empty abdominal and thoracic cavities were carefully examined. The skull-cap was removed and the brain and membrane examined in situ. The brain was then removed and many sections made in various directions. The arteries were not atheromatous. The base of the skull was examined and the upper part of the spinal cord. The bladder was found to be small, very contracted and empty, some blood clots on the mucous membrane, which latter was much thickened. Negative symptoms not recorded.

There was, the doctors decided, no lesion of the body sufficiently grave to justify the issue of a certificate of death from natural causes. It was a suspicious death.

Mary Jacob was beginning to feel unsafe. By her own account, there was a fraught conversation on the night of the death; in Reggie's presence, Edith denied to Mary that she herself had written the note for arsenic and sugar of lead which Mary had taken to Maruya's on October 21st. Edith told her that the note was in Walter's handwriting, and that he had taken his own life; she had a letter in her possession, saying that he was going to do it.

On Friday evening, the 23rd, therefore, with Elsa Christoffel to support her, Mary did something that was enterprising and independent: she went back to Maruya's and demanded the return of Edith's note. Because she had paid cash for the two bottles, however, Hayashi Schichiro had torn the note up, and thrown it away, but he did find the chit of October 20th, brought by the jinrikisha man (for the bedpan and Fowler's) signed 'E.M.H. Carew', which he handed over to Mary in return for its payment.

On October 24th Mary Jacob moved to a refuge at No.2 the Bluff, to stay with Miss Harriet Gertrude Britain, a kind of American Good Samaritan who protected her from Edith's attempts to get at her. A strained correspondence ensued:

Dear Mary,
[October 25th]

Before you finally decide on what you intend doing, it is Mr Porch's wish as well as my own that you come round and see us. I have no wish and no intention to ask you to remain here against your will, but there are certain questions which it is my intention as well as my duty to ask you. I must therefore ask you to be good enough to come around here sometime this evening. I shall not detain you for any time.

Yours truly,
E.M.H. Carew.

No. 2, *Bluff,*
Sunday October 25th.

Dear Mrs Carew,

In reply to the note I received through Mr Lowder this evening I regard my engagement in your employ to be at an end. If you have any questions to ask me, please do so through Mr Lowder, your lawyer.

In respect to the message you sent me by Mr Lowder this afternoon asking me to take your children to Kamakura for a week, I do not intend to leave Yokohama at present, but if you will send them to me here it would make me very happy to have them with me.

Yours truly,

Mary E. Jacob.

Monday, October 26th.

Dear Mrs Carew,

Will you tell one of your servants to let the jinrikisha men have my two boxes, and also to take my banjo and the photo of my home from the wall and send them to me at the same time.

(Unsigned)

October 28th.

Dear Mrs Carew,

On examining the package you sent me this morning I find four articles which do not belong to me. I therefore return them by bearer.

Yours truly,
M.E. Jacob.

On Saturday, October 24th, the consul, in his occasional rôle as coroner — and it was he indeed who had ordered the post-mortem — convened an inquest at the place of death, the Royal Naval Hospital. In a most unusual manner, the coroner had been involved *before* the death, after Dr Wheeler had roped him in, and therefore he was already a party to the suspicion against Edith Carew.

John Carey Hall, born in Coleraine, County Londonderry, on January 22nd, 1844, had had a distinguished consular career, and also considerable legal experience. He entered the consular service for Japan in 1868, and was called to the Bar (Middle Temple) in 1881. His services were lent to the Japanese Commission for Prison Reforms in 1871, and he was Acting Assistant Judge of the Supreme Court for China and Japan at Shanghai, 1888-9. He was versatile, but his true function was that of consul: he acted or officiated at all the open ports of Japan.

A small jury of five men was the due form in the restricted community in Yokohama, and Messrs. T. Rose, J. K. Trafford, E. T. Nicholas, E. Powys and G. Blundell were sworn. A Mr Nicholas is mentioned in the diary. It is very likely that all the jurymen belonged to the Masonic Lodge. Walter Carew will certainly have been a Mason; Edith went to the Masonic Ball on March 12th, and

membership would have been expected of the Secretary of the United Club.

After hearing the primary medical evidence, and at the suggestion of the coroner, the jury made a submission in writing: 'We require that Dr Edwin Divers, of Tokyo, be summoned as a witness, and that a post-mortem be made by him with a chemical analysis of the contents of the stomach and intestines.'

It was now past noon, and the funeral of Walter Carew was fixed for 2.30 pm. There was no let or hindrance on the burial, because the viscera of the deceased had been held back.

Edith, who had been sitting quietly in court, arrayed in her new widow's weeds, spoke with the composure and hauteur which were to characterise her demeanour throughout; she wished to give evidence, but not until she had attended her husband's funeral.

When the inquest resumed at 2pm, in the new and more formal setting of the Court Room at the Consulate, John Lowder appeared to watch the proceedings on Edith's behalf. She needed him. Enquiries at Schedel's and Maruya's had revealed that there was too much arsenic and sugar of lead associated with the Carew household.

Mary Esther Jacob, tremulous first witness of the resumed hearing, was not going to be of any help to Edith. '*Why you bought so plenty deadly poison?*' did its own damage. She had not known that any had been bought before. Hayashi Schichiro told her that 'Some had been bought the day before and the day before that, and that I must warn Mrs Carew to be careful how she used it.'

'Do you know who went to make the previous purchases?' the coroner asked.

'Maruya told me Mrs Carew on the 19th and the boy on the 20th.'

Mr Trafford, of the jury, 'Did he ask you where you had come from?'

' "Yes," he said, "Are you Mrs Carew?" I had never been to the shop before. I did not know Mrs Carew had been there until he told me.'

John Lowder, invited to examine the witness, said, 'I am not sufficiently instructed to ask questions. I might ask whether the witness knows the writing in which the paper was.'

Mary Jacob: 'Yes, Mrs Carew's.'

'You are quite certain?'

'I am positive.'

Oh, dear!

Reginald Colmore Porch, a most uncomfortable witness, could not tell why the arsenic was purchased. He had no idea. He thought it very extraordinary when he heard the quantity that had been purchased. Mary Jacob did not tell him how much. He did not know it was against Dr Wheeler's orders, because he understood that arsenic was sometimes used as a medicine. He was about to leave the room when the governess told him about the chemist's observation; he understood what she said to be a comment on his impudence.

Lowder elicited that the Carews' marriage was a picture of harmony and affectionate concern.

Edith, returned from the funeral, and not at all prostrated by that occasion, had just entered the courtroom, so that Mary Jacob had been spared her aquiline gaze. On being sworn, under examination by Lowder she presented her own spirited version of events, every word of which must be recorded here, because this was in effect her defence, and also the net in which — so early — she confined herself. Only *two days* had passed since the death. There had been precious little time for her to test her version of events in conference with Mr Lowder. There was no solicitor to advise her.

Meanwhile, was she going to try to persuade the court that Walter had committed suicide?

My husband had been ailing for some weeks past, but was not taken really ill until the Thursday, when he said Dr Wheeler had ordered him to take Vichy water, and to keep as quiet as possible. He had had several attacks of liver complaint during the last eight years, and I thought this was another. He did not get better on Saturday or Sunday.

On Saturday he expressed a wish to go to Kamakura on the Monday, and I wrote to Dr Wheeler, asking if he could do so. Dr Wheeler, after examining him, said he was afraid he might catch a chill and advised him not to go. He gradually became worse, and on Monday I had twice to send for the doctor, and also on

Tuesday. At tiffin time on Tuesday Dr Wheeler asked if I had any objection to his calling in Dr Todd, as he would like to consult him.

I entirely agree with the evidence Dr Todd gave this morning as to what he told me. I was present at the consultation. Dr Wheeler told me that afternoon that my husband was to have nothing but milk and soda, and no stimulant. I cannot recollect whether it was before Dr Todd's visit or after that my husband expressed a wish that he should be given his usual dose of arsenic.

He has been in the habit of taking arsenic in small quantities for some time. I cannot state exactly what kind because I do not know. I told him that as Dr Wheeler was treating him, I thought it would be better if he would not take medicine on his own account. He insisted and begged me to give him some. I went to the cupboard where he kept his medicine, but only found an empty bottle, or perhaps a drop inside. I remonstrated with him a good deal on taking arsenic, especially as he was in his present state.

He then told me that when I was in England in 1893 he was obliged to consult Dr Munro, and later Dr Baelz, on a disease which he did not wish to mention to Dr Wheeler. I do not know whether Dr Munro prescribed for him at that time, but later Dr Baelz did. I have had his prescription made up from time to time. He told me that when he was suffering in such a way, arsenic was the only thing that gave him relief.

On Tuesday evening he gave me a slip of paper, which I have in my possession, on which was written, 'One bottle of Fowler's solution of arsenic. One bottle of sugar of lead.' I told him at the time I should not send for the things, but if I did eventually I should tell Dr Wheeler.

On Wednesday he spoke about the great pain he was in, and told me if I did not get the medicine he would get it himself through other means. I wrote out on another piece of paper what he had given me, and asked my governess to get them for me. When she brought them I gave them to my husband sealed in the paper in which they were received, and told him I would not allow him to take the mixture at the time, as he was taking medicine from Dr Wheeler.

I wrote to Dr Wheeler, telling him I should like to see Dr Baelz. Dr Wheeler came to see my husband again about half-past six or seven, and then told me he thought he was slightly better as he had retained his food, but that as he had had such a restless night, he thought it advisable to give him a hypodermic, and left with me two or three cocaine tabloids, one of which he told me to give him in a little milk, soda, and brandy, about eight o'clock.

During Mr Carew's illness, we experienced great difficulty in getting him to take medicine. I mixed it in barley-water, milk and lime-squash. Since Thursday morning, I gave him no medicine. The hypodermic Dr Wheeler gave did not have the desired effect. Towards nine o'clock, he became delirious, and very excitable.

Dr Wheeler told me he was dining out that night, so I went to the house where he was dining, and told him my husband was very excited and unable to sleep. I was absent about half an hour. When I returned, my husband was asleep, and apparently quite well. Dr Wheeler came about eleven o'clock, and seemed to think he was better.

He slept only a short time; was very restless and complained of great thirst. Dr Todd had advised me to give him at short intervals small pieces of ice. He complained of great pain in his back and side. I called up the servants, had the fire lighted, and applied hot-water bottles to his feet and sides, as I saw his temperature was very low.

At five o'clock on Thursday morning I did not like certain symptoms and sent for Dr Wheeler. He came at seven o'clock and gave my husband a cocaine tabloid, with a little brandy and soda, and a draught of hydrate of chloral to send him to sleep, but it had no effect.

At eight o'clock I felt so anxious that I wrote for Mr Parsons, who came shortly after. I told him I did not share Dr Wheeler's opinion as to the satisfactory progress of the case, and that I insisted on having some other opinion. Mr Parsons promised to see Dr Wheeler at once, and did so, and returned in a quarter of an hour. He told me not to alarm myself unnecessarily as Dr Wheeler was quite confident of the case.

At nine o'clock on Wednesday night my husband was never

conscious for more than a few moments at a time, and I saw he was getting weaker. Dr Wheeler came at twelve o'clock and said, "I have arranged to have him taken to the hospital; he is only going from bad to worse".

During Thursday I gave him some beef tea and some milk and soda, with a little brandy in it, according to Dr Wheeler's instructions. After tiffin, he complained of great pain in his chest and of feeling very sick, but being unable to be so. Thinking it might be indigestion, I gave him a little hot water, but it had very little effect in making him sick.

Dr Wheeler arrived about this time, and he was taken to the hospital. He was perfectly conscious when he left the house, and although I knew at the time he was admitted to the hospital that he was seriously ill, I had no idea of there being any danger. I told several people whom I saw I thought he was going on all right, and it was a great shock to me to learn at five o'clock that he had passed away.

Earlier in the day, my brother told me that Dr Wheeler thought, or knew, that he [Walter] was taking arsenic. I attached little importance to his remark at the time, as knowing from past experience that my husband had been in the habit of taking arsenic, it never occurred to me to be of any importance. After I had heard of his death, and had been told that a post-mortem would be held, I remembered the fact that he had ordered, and I had given him, a bottle of sugar of lead. I went upstairs and opened the drawer where he had put the bottles when I gave them to him, and found they were missing. I at once sent for Dr Wheeler, but he did not come down till eleven o'clock. I told him the facts, but he did not at the time say anything except, "It's a pity".

I have since ascertained that on or about the 20th, Mr Carew gave my amah a written order and she sent it to Maruya. Last night I thought it necessary to make a thorough search for the missing bottles, and after a good deal of trouble I found them at the back of the table on the floor, which stood at the corner of his bed. Without measuring, I should say there are six or eight drops of arsenic left in the bottle, and about half a bottle of sugar of lead.

At the time he ordered the arsenic through me, when he also ordered the sugar of lead, I told him there was a small quantity in a bottle in the stable which had been used as an emulsion for my pony, and I asked him what he wished to do with it.

He told me some years ago it had great effect as an external application for congestion of the liver, and I never thought of either of the two bottles till yesterday.

I should like to contradict a statement made by Dr Wheeler this morning that Mr Carew was invalided from the Straits on account of malarial fever. To my knowledge, he has never suffered from malarial fever. He was obliged to leave the Straits on account of nervous depression, due to the climate and overwork.

Edith Carew's first presentation was finished.

Chapter 8
'BAMBOOZLED'

By her given, early evidence, Edith had committed herself to the well-used Victorian defence that her husband was an habitual arsenic-eater. She would have to do better than Florence Maybrick, who had failed, in 1889, the year of Edith's marriage, and now languished in Aylesbury Prison. If Edith had indeed put up suicide to Mary Jacob, she had abandoned that line. During the course of her apologia, with its overt points, such as the 'usual dose' of arsenic, she had inserted a kind of hidden agenda. A clever touch was the implication that the calling of Dr Baelz *at her insistence*, however thwarted, was intended to treat the secret stricture *and to discuss the use of arsenic.*

The rigmarole about the hidden bottles had a covert meaning. They could not be found in some drawer or cabinet, because Walter with his thoughtfully provided bedpan was, as the week passed, too ill to get to them. They had to be within his grasp from his sick-bed, and they had to be concealed, as he swigged down arsenic against her wishes, and privately rubbed in sugar of lead!

It is very possible, incidentally, that half of the bottle of lead was left, because, as Walter took in less and less fluid, let alone solids, the distinctive taste became even more difficult to disguise. Surely she did not slip a last dose of Fowler's into the hot-water emetic, to speed Walter on his way to hospital, a *coup de grâce*, as he left her control?

Of course, she could not state exactly what kind of arsenic Walter was in the habit of taking, because she did not wish to pinpoint a source. Vagueness was essential. She realized that local chemists would not confirm that they were suppliers to Walter. Conceivably he could have bought some arsenic in Tokyo, or could have relied upon a large stock bottle from the past. Equally, he could

have bought solid arsenic surreptitiously from any Eastern bazaar, but since he had 'pleaded' for Fowler's, Edith had really limited his 'habit' to Fowler's, which could be got only from an orthodox chemist's shop, of whatever nationality.

Was Edith going to be able to produce the slip of paper in Walter's handwriting which explained away the governess' errand to Maruya's on the day before the death? She had also accounted, in her fashion, for the acquisition of sugar of lead on October 18th. Airily 'on or about' October 20th, *Walter*, she said, gave the amah a written order to Maruya's, but she must have feared the coming evidence of Hayashi Schichiro. That left unacknowledged the Fowler's and sugar of lead sold by Maruya's to a foreign woman on October 19th. Perhaps Edith hoped that by a miracle this occasion would be missed, or more likely, and crudely, she had not yet got her story straight!

Mr Rose, of the jury, took over the questioning: knowing that her husband had been in the habit of taking arsenic, she did not think it unwise to give in to him, but she now saw that it would have been much wiser to mention it to Dr Wheeler. She did it to please Walter; she did not think he would take it. Lowder re-examined: generally the marriage was affectionate but lately there had been unpleasant discussions on a certain point. She did indeed have the written order, in pencil, at home. It was not true that she herself had purchased medicine at Maruya's.

Mr Rose, persistent, thought that it would be necessary to call Maruya. That would be indispensable, said the coroner. It was now past four o'clock, and it was nearly dark. The inquest was adjourned until Monday, November 2nd, when Dr Divers would report on his chemical analysis.

Edith had a week in which to think and plan. On October 29th a plague of anonymous letters began to trouble Yokohama, as weird and dubious as those which were to rain upon Great Wyrley, back home in Staffordshire, in the Edalji case of 1903.[17] The first one read:

> *'beware dare to speak one word of the truth and you shall never leave japan alive'*

A servant found this feeble little message on the 29th, like an apport on the doorstep of No.169. On Sunday, November 1st, John Lowder, of Counsel, verily received a purple letter, dated October 29th:

Mr Lowder,

I do not know you, probably have never seen you, but I gather from Saturday's papers that you will be acting on behalf of the wife of the man who was to me the world and more than the world. Dead men tell no tales; no, nor dead women either, for I am going to join him. Do you know what waiting means for eight long weary years. I have watched and waited, watched till I knew he would grow tired of her, that silly little fool, and then I came to him. What is the result? We, between us, electrify Japan. I have never professed to be a good woman, but, for the sake of a few lines, I do not see why I should let a silly innocent be condemned for what she knows nothing about, and for what she never will know anything about, and for which, when you get this, no one on this earth could enlighten her. She is a silly fool, otherwise she would not have treated the last two weeks as she has done. By the time you get this I shall be well on my way to join him, my twin soul. You may call this what you like, but I think deep down in my heart I write this for the sake of the boy who is so like his father. Let his mother take heed that he enter not into temptation. I shall write to the coroner.

A.L.

On November 1st, that most flinty recipient, the coroner, also received a letter of similar hue:

Mr Hall,

I have finished a letter to Mr Lowder so cannot begin this to you in quite the same way. Shall I begin it with the truest and wisest saying on this earth 'woman is at the bottom of everything' in this case it is so, for between us we have bamboozled the lot of you. 1. The chemist, 2. The doctor, and last but not least that fool his wife. I stop here because my last act on earth shall be a merciful one, and as I am going to join him, my twin soul, I will exonerate that little fool from any share in helping us to meet each other. I have done my work well, [sounds like Jack the Ripper, 1888!] and am taking good care to escape the lot of you and the law. My two letters will not be posted till Sunday morning when I shall be — ?

The world will call me mad. I am, however, sane enough in what I have done and what I am going to do and sane enough to accomplish my end — that as we were divided in life we were not in death. I wonder whether out of all this community there is one who can sympathise with me who goes out to meet her maker.

29th October.

A.L.

By way of a neat coda, 'A.L.' sent another letter to Edith, the envelope postmarked November 1st:

I have done what I can for you. True, I have made you suffer, but I have written to Mr Hall and to Mr Lowder. Yokohama will be troubled no more by

A.L.

Although it was a good try, it was hardly likely that the absurd, artificial letters would dispel the weight of suspicion and gossip against Edith Carew, the 'silly little fool', and, when the inquest was resumed on Monday, November 2nd, Henry Charles Litchfield (he who was the divorce expert) appearing here, more alarmingly, as the Crown Prosecutor in Japan, represented Her Majesty's Government.

John Lowder, for Edith, was now fully instructed, and for good measure had a junior in court with him. This was Ambrose Berry Walford, who figured regularly in the diary as a friend more than an acquaintance, although not a close friend. Walford, born in 1857, was the only son of John Berry Walford, of Abergavenny. He was called to the Bar (Lincoln's Inn) in 1883, and practised in Yokohama from 1889 to 1900. John Frederic Lowder, it might be timely to state, was also a member of Lincoln's Inn. Born in 1843, the second son of the Revd John Lowder, of Derry Hill, Wiltshire, he had had an unconventional and adventurous career, having first in 1860 entered the consular service in Japan. He narrowly escaped being killed during the notorious attack on the legation at Tokyo by some 15 assassins who had signed a declaration that they would not stand by and see the Sacred Empire defiled by the foreigners.

He was promoted to consul in 1869, but was then called to the Bar in 1872, in which year he resigned from the consular service to take important legal offices in the service of the Emperor, from whom he later received the Order of the Rising Sun. As the Japanese Government felt able to dispense with the services of foreigners, in another reversal he decided to stay on in Japan and practise in Yokohama. John Carey Hall must have found him an uncomfortable presence in his court.

The coroner stated now that the case, so far as it had gone, tended to throw suspicion upon Mrs Carew, and therefore it would be better for her to hear the whole of the evidence before giving such further evidence as, he had heard, she wished to put before the Court. Here he thwarted the express desire of her Counsel for her to be heard first, in case the jury should think that she had 'set up a story' after hearing all the evidence.

Dr Neil Gordon Munro, graduate of Edinburgh University, the physician who had treated Walter painfully for gonorrhoea, in 1893, and devoutly hoped not to have to tell the Court so, must have displaced his anxiety to any suggestion of his having prescribed arsenic to the dead man! 'I have made enquiries at all the chemists' shops, and have a written statement from all to that effect,' he insisted, quaintly.

He was, however, more importantly, the first witness to attest to a history of arsenic-eating, which was obviously after Edith's evidence to be a central argument of the proceedings:

I have a dim recollection, although it is not a thing I could swear to, but I have a strong impression that Mr Carew told me at the time that he had occasionally taken arsenic; and I think it is right that I should state so.

I think he said he took it because it gave him relief from pain. I cannot say whether he said he used it for malaria. It is frequently used to keep off malaria. Arsenic has nothing to do with stricture. I certainly would not prescribe it. Stricture is frequently aggravated by malarial attacks, and in that case it might have connection with stricture but not direct connection.

Mr Rose, of the jury, thinking of Walter's 'plea' to Edith, 'He never asked you for arsenic or sugar of lead?'

'No.'

Hayashi Schichiro, of Maruya's, was bad news, and good news, for Edith. Alfred Ernest Wileman, who was acting registrar of the court, served as interpreter, and fielded the exchanges. Edith listened intently as he approached the occasion of the 19th, and something like a miracle *did* occur.

To whom, the coroner asked, did he sell the arsenic and sugar of lead on that day?

'I do not recollect very well, but probably it was Mrs Carew, I think.'

'When did she pay?'

'On the 20th, I think, but I don't know very well.'

'Then,' the coroner pressed, 'you met the buyer of the poison on the 19th, and a day or two afterwards?'

'I cannot recollect her face very well. I am not quite sure.'

The coroner addressed the interpreter: 'Ask the witness to look at the lady in black sitting beside Mr Lowder. Let him go round and look at Mrs Carew.'

None now could doubt that this was trial by inquest, as Hayashi Schichiro stared inscrutably at Edith's equally inscrutable countenance.

'I do not remember well,' he said. 'The person there has come to buy things before, but I do not recognize her very well now as the person who came on the 19th.'

Coroner, hot for certainty: 'Is it quite certain that that lady is not the person who came on the 19th?'

And, the dusty answer: 'I cannot say. I think it must have been someone from Mr Carew's house. I am sure that the words 'Mrs Carew' were written on that paper.'

When the foreign woman returned on (probably) the 20th, and paid for the two drugs, he tore up the paper, which could thus obviously never be produced in court. Apparently the woman at the same time paid for some previous purchases of medicine. The

question was asked: 'Did you receive payment yourself for the medicine sold on the 19th?' and his reply was, 'I had sold some before, and I received the money together with that.'

This detail, if accurate, rather knocked on the head the notion — not very seriously canvassed — that an impostor pretending to be Edith Carew bought the poison, unless (and this would be merely fanciful) the chemist asked for payment for past purchases and the impostor paid up, for greater verisimilitude.

Coming to the arsenic and the bedpan of the 20th, there were no miracles here for Edith because her actual note, retrieved by the two governesses on 23rd, was now put in as an exhibit by Litchfield. Edith's previous words that Walter had sent the amah on 20th with a written order rang hollowly in the memory of those present who understood the discrepancy.

The purchase of 21st, through the agency of Mary Jacob, was not of itself denied by Edith, and the chemist confirmed that the note for this occasion, not signed, had been in the same handwriting as the bedpan note. It could not be produced, because he had torn it up at the time of payment by cash.

The chemist admitted that selling these poisons to foreigners was contrary to Japanese regulations, which admission may in part explain his slipperiness as a witness.

Lowder: 'Do you enter the sale of poisons in a book?'

'No, we have the doctor's prescription.'

'Could the sugar of lead have been bought previously, on the 17th or 18th?' Lowder asked.

'No. I am sure because it is in the register that it was sold on the 19th.'

'But you just told us you do not keep books.'

'I do register in a book. I mistook the interpreter's meaning.'

On the 17th Edith had indeed bought some antipyrine from Maruya's, for her own use, but Counsel had small chance of showing that sugar of lead had been bought with it, because as he now discovered Hayashi Schichiro had not been in the shop at that time.

What did the foreign woman on the 19th look like, then?

'I don't recollect very well; but I think black clothes or grey clothes.'

Edith, at her age, would not normally have worn black. Grey sometimes, perhaps. Her riding habit could have been black. According to the diary, she did not stir forth all day. The 'Mysterious Caller' wore black. Had Hayashi Schichiro been got at?

Dr Elwyn Otto Edward Baelz, Professor of Medicine at the Imperial University of Japan, was a woolly witness — perhaps even deliberately so:

Mr Carew has been once to consult me, but unfortunately I cannot find any notes. I do not remember what I prescribed, but I got a prescription from Mr Lowder and when I saw it I remembered that Mr Carew came up to complain of pain in the bladder; at least I believe he came to complain of that but I am not sure. It is a prescription I use for those cases. There was no arsenic; at least there was no arsenic in the copy of the prescription I got from Mr Lowder. That is all I have got to say.

The g-word has still not been uttered in the court. Some people will still have had only the vaguest notion that Walter had suffered from some kind of bladder trouble. Dr Baelz withdrew, and was replaced by Dr Edwin Divers, Professor of Chemistry at the Imperial University, who had not yet finished his chemical examination of the viscera of Walter Carew, but could say that he had found arsenic, more particularly in the liver, sufficient to cause death.

He found it difficult to speak about lead, for fear that what he said might affect the minds of the jury. He would say that he had met with a substance which promised to be lead. Arsenic was certainly used in the alleviation of malaria and the stomach troubles of so-called 'liver'. A full medicinal dose of Fowler's Solution was eight drops, and a fatal dose would be half an ounce.[18]

Arsenic had a recognized use in the treatment of spasmodic diseases, and it was quite possible that it would be helpful in cases of stricture of the urinary passages. (Lowder will have been very pleased with this unexpected and creative suggestion, which fitted nicely with Dr Munro's recollection that Walter had told him that he took arsenic for the relief of pain. Incidentally, the diary refers to Walter's sick headaches, for which arsenic used to be taken.)

However, Dr Divers knew of no record of such use for stricture, and so, he admitted, it was only a supposition. It would have been written up in a medical journal. (This is the sort of qualification that a jury forgets!)

The Styrian peasants,[19] with their rubicund complexions and well-expanded lungs, came now, clomping over their Alpine meadows, as they always did sooner or later, in these contests over arsenic. With their exception, Dr Divers was not aware of any examples of arsenic-eating for pleasure and recreation.

Walter Carew's illness lasted seven or eight days. The symptoms varied in acuteness. Arsenic was a non-cumulative drug, rapidly eliminated from the system, principally in urine. The deceased must have received the poison in several dangerous doses, and not in one dose at the beginning of the illness. Fowler's Solution was coloured and flavoured, so that it might not be mistaken for water. The doctor's next point was surprising, and had the effect of making the hot-water emetic a perfectly innocent act of mercy: 'Here I may say that the stomach when examined by me was quite fresh. It was opened by me and there was not the slightest odour of volatile poison or of lavender, which serves to give an odour to Fowler's Solution.'

As for self-administration by misadventure, that was most unlikely, because of the great difference between the medicinal and poisonous doses. In ordinary cases, too, the rapid power of becoming accustomed to the drug, which necessitated higher and higher doses, was not a clinical reality. As for suicide, although arsenic had often been used, 'there is such a result produced by an *attempt* to poison with arsenic that it must be very rare indeed that anyone with suicidal intent would administer to himself a second or third dose, because the effects of arsenic are very depressing upon the mental and bodily faculties, taking away all determination to do anything.'

Therefore, Dr Divers concluded, 'the deceased died from the effects of arsenic, administered by another person, unknown to himself.' Now it had been said, and all who had suspected, and had acted upon their suspicion, were publicly vindicated.

After tiffin the jury would not let Dr Divers get away with his cryptic comments about lead, and, blustering a bit, he did allow that the contents of the intestines yielded a black sulphide:

'After suitable chemical treatment, I have a black compound, and sugar of lead would produce such a compound: arsenic produces a bright yellow.' There probably was lead in the stomach. 'It is probable that half an ounce of sugar of lead would cause death, and the symptoms would be somewhat similar to those of arsenic, but it is not probable in my opinion that sugar of lead caused death. *Lead might have been administered to check haemorrhage, and haemorrhage is a known result of arsenical poisoning.*' (Certainly bleeding was no part of Walter's symptomatology.)

John Lowder went straight to the weak point: 'What quantity of arsenic did you find in the viscera?'

Dr Divers was a man of *personalitas sensitiva,* and he was becoming self-justificatory.

> *That is just a question I cannot answer. I can give you an opinion, but I have not yet been able to prepare it fit for weighing. In any case, it would be very small, perhaps one-tenth of a grain, perhaps only one-twentieth, and one-tenth in the liver. There was much less in the contents of the bowels, some traces — certainly unweighable quantities — in the stomach.*
>
> *I intended to devote myself to that matter afterwards, but it is too late for this inquest, unless it is adjourned.* It is not my fault. *I have lost no time, but have devoted myself to the case day by day, and I cannot possibly be to blame for not being ready. The only thing that I can be blamed for is in answering hurriedly, by telegraph, and saying that I could be ready by Friday. I have worked alone and I am responsible for the examination, so that I can swear to my own evidence.*

Lowder was unmoved by this outburst. Indeed, the professional man who found himself out in Japan in the 1890s had to be prepared to function without back-up, to go it alone.

Lowder: 'Should you consider it a startling proposition that a person accustomed to take arsenic in the shape of Fowler's Solution could take an ounce bottle in from four to five doses without harm to himself? I ask you because the evidence I wish to adduce in this case is that the deceased was in the habit of taking this solution, and that he divided a one-ounce bottle into only four or five doses.'

Dr Divers floundered. He could not deny the academic possibility: 'That would be very startling. It would be in accordance with some medical cases, but not with persons that one usually mixes with. I wish that Dr Baelz had been asked some questions on that point. So far as my knowledge of practical work and of reading and studying medical works and medical jurisprudence goes — and I was lecturer for some years on the subject — such cases are not recognized as occuring amongst Western Europeans.'

Lowder: 'Then I take it your answer to me is not derived from the very latest authorities on the subject?'

Wrong!

Divers: 'Yes, from the very latest' — and he referred to the up-to-date work of Dr Lauder Brunton, of St Bartholomew's Hospital. It was just slightly unfortunate that he could not remember the title of the relevant tome on therapeutics.

In case anyone should imagine that Fowler's is somehow less lethal than solid white arsenic, Dr Divers gave it as his personal opinion that arsenic was at least as active in solution, or rather it ought to be more active, *because* in solution: 'Solid arsenic sticks in the stomach, but when it is in solution, the passing into the body should be more rapid.'

Joseph Schedel, the German chemist, was examined by Litchfield. In the same way as Maruya's, he could not offer up any old prescriptions for arsenic for Walter Carew. In some triumph, Lowder produced a Schedel's bottle which pleased him, because it bore the label:

W.H.R. Carew, October 21st, 3rd time. [The order of the initials is wrong.]

The explanation only slightly vitiated Lowder's advantage: 'Because there is no address on the prescription. It might have been Mr or Mrs Carew. My assistant [he who stood on the doorstep and beckoned to Mary Jacob] wrote on it because he said Mrs Carew bought it.'

Rachel Greer, under examination by Litchfield and members of the jury, said that *she* had sent the messenger to Maruya's on October 18th for medicine (i.e. the first purchase of sugar of lead): 'I received a memorandum *at the hands of my master.* It was not a large bottle.'

John Lowder, who had sat by quietly, delighted with this evidence, carefully underlined the point in favour of his client.

'Was not Mrs Carew at church?'

'She was out.'

'Was it not on a Sunday?'

'It may have been.'

'What time of day was it?'

'I do not remember well the hour. It was perhaps about 4 o'clock.'

Lowder was well enough pleased with the first footings of Edith's arsenic-eating defence, but he was also intent on another line, which he now revealed, or rather adumbrated, in an application to the Court:

'It is very important for Mrs Carew to obtain the evidence of a person named Annie Luke. She was in Yokohama on the 29th of last month [he was referring to the start of the anonymous letters] and probably is now. I myself have made every attempt to ascertain the whereabouts of this woman and have failed to do so, and I apply to you now to take such measures as it is in your power to take to ascertain the whereabouts of Annie Luke, to secure her attendance.'

Coroner: 'Very well then, gentlemen of the jury, tomorrow being the birthday of the Monarch [the Emperor Mutsuhito] in whose territory we are residing, I propose, as a mark of respect, that we adjourn the case until Wednesday morning at 9am.'

Chapter 9
THE WOMAN IN BLACK

The entity know as 'Annie Luke' has made her first appearance in court. The series of 'A.L.' letters has not yet been made public. Edith has told her Counsel that she knows the identity of 'A.L.' — she is a woman from Walter's past, named Annie Luke. Lowder is determined to play upon what we may now call the Annie Luke letters. It is not that he has abandoned the classic, arsenic-eating defence, in regard to which he is already scouring medico-legal textbooks, but that he has taken up the position that he is also, in parallel, duty-bound to investigate Annie Luke as one of the possibilities of the mystery. He takes the 'confession' and the 'exoneration' very, very seriously. Annie Luke actually serves nicely to obfuscate anxious matters such as the trail of messengers scurrying to the house on the Bluff with their small bottles of deadly poison.

Edith has told Lowder that the 'Woman in Black', the 'Mysterious Visitor' of October 10th, must have been Annie Luke, and on Wednesday, November 4th, she offers herself for re-examination at the inquest, with the full intention of fleshing forth the Annie Luke apparition.

First of all, there was some rebuilding to do. One false impression which she particularly wanted to correct shows the power in a courtroom of a single word, in this case "then". Lowder asked her about her evidence that Walter '...*then* told me that when I was in England in 1893, he was obliged to consult Dr Munro.'

'I should have left out the word "then",' she said now. 'I should have said he told me *again* that he had been obliged to consult the doctors; and the reason he mentioned it on that occasion was because he was afraid that during his last illness I should mention the fact to Dr Wheeler.'

It will not have been a mere slip of the tongue. The first variation was to colour the urgency, the secrecy of Walter's condition. However, on reflection she will have wished to be seen as long privy to the secret, in order to have gone along with his self-dosings.

A much more serious volte-face, which dented her credibility at this early stage, was to do with her denial of sending a jinrikisha man for Fowler's and a bedpan on October 20th. The production of the actual 'bedpan chit', with her signature, had forced her to a lame recantation: 'In the evening I recollect writing to Maruya's for the bedpan. I cannot say that I have any recollection whatever of writing for arsenic, but I know that I must have done so, as my writing is conclusive evidence.

> *The amah brought me on Tuesday night the parcel which she received from Maruya's. She gave it to me as Dr Wheeler and I were leaving the bedroom, and I told her to put it on a chair in the passage upstairs. The bedpan was not taken out of its wrapping until the following morning. I am positive that I had no idea that arsenic had come into the house that night, because I have no recollection whatever of ever seeing the bottle which is said to have contained arsenic.*

Shuddering inwardly, John Lowder passed on to the surer ground of the Carews' finances, and then to Annie Luke. Walter had mentioned this woman to Edith soon after their marriage. She lived in Devonshire, Edith believed.

'At that time he told me very little except that he had seen a great deal of her. The conversation at the time made so little impression upon me, but as far as I can remember, he gave me to understand that he had been amusing himself with her, prior to his meeting me, or marrying me.'

Lowder: 'Did this arouse any feeling of jealousy in your mind?'

'None whatever.'

'And you never mentioned her name particularly between you, until quite recently?'

'Last month.'

As if to buttress the idea of Walter Carew as a man of dubious

morality, the better to give Annie Luke a real presence, Lowder invited his client to betray a family secret:

'He also told you that prior to his marriage he had begotten children who were still alive?'

'Yes.'

'For one of these children you provided support?'

'Yes.'

'That did not create any dissension between you or any jealousy in your mind?'

'No. I should like to add that the circumstance of which Mr Lowder is speaking was in the Native States of Singapore, and I never knew of this until some four months after my marriage.'

It was not Annie Luke who had the children; they were a Singapore woman's and the implication is that there had been a ménage out in the jungle. The impression of Edith's broadmindedness and generosity went to showing her good character. No independent evidence ever turned up, however, by way of chits, dockets, receipts or thank-you letters to prove Edith's charitable disbursements.

Counsel had to get Edith to repudiate all sentiments of jealousy in case jealousy should somehow be thought to be a motive for murder. He would come back to Annie Luke, but he wanted to get in some new evidence of Walter's arsenic habit.

In Sungei Ujong, about nine months after they were married, Edith learnt that he took arsenic. She had no idea why. The chief medical officer at Singapore Hospital had prescribed arsenic. She had no recollection of the prescribed dose, but on Walter's return from Singapore she would suppose that he was taking four or five drops three times a day. (Drops would indicate Fowler's.)

Lowder: 'Did he continue to take arsenic from that time periodically — I do not say consecutively [he covered himself] — till the day of his death?'

'Yes, indeed', she said, 'and without its being prescribed for him'.

'To go back to the earlier portion of your married life, were you frequently in the habit of administering arsenic to your husband?'

'Frequently, every day.'

'And you measured it out in drops?'

'Yes, always.'

'Latterly he has always helped himself — dosed himself?'

'Yes, it was only during his illness in the Straits that I was accustomed to give him the arsenic myself.'

'And latterly he would use this arsenic without measuring it, would he not?'

'Yes, he has been in the habit of doing so for some time because it was such a habit with him to take arsenic as a 'pick-me-up' that he would pour a small quantity out and mix it with water.'

Lowder produced another small bottle which, Edith said, Walter had kept on the sideboard. After breakfast — generally just an egg — he used to pour out a dose from this bottle.

'You have made an experiment,' Lowder addressed Edith solemnly, 'with an ounce bottle by filling it with water, and pouring out the amount which he was in the habit of taking?'

'Yes, and I have found an ounce bottle would contain for him five doses.'

Another, broken bottle was put in. Edith said that it was the broken Fowler's bottle which she had mentioned in her note to Schedel's on October 21st. She had knocked it off the mantelshelf and it had fallen on to the fender directly underneath. The fender itself had been carted into court, and Lowder asked for it to be analysed, to show spilt Fowler's Solution. As for the bottle itself, Edith said that Asa, the amah, had found it, on the previous morning:

'I told her it was necessary that the bottle should be found. She said she could not find it, as it had been thrown away some days previously. As I knew she had been the one to sweep up the broken glass, I knew she must know where she had thrown it. The bottle was found, so she tells me, in an ash heap at the back of the servants' quarters.'

After tiffin Edith handed her Counsel yet another bottle, containing Dr Baelz's stricture medicine, which was supposed to be innocent of arsenic. However, having smelt it, Edith said, she believed it to contain arsenic. Her implication was not that contamination had occurred, but that Walter himself had added arsenic for better effect or easier taking. Lowder, putting it in, invited the coroner to have the contents analysed.

Then he opened the entire matter of Annie Luke. The anonymous letters were read out in court, and he suggested that they were all in the same handwriting. He recreated the occasion when, as so clearly recorded in the diary (which had not yet been produced) the 'Woman in Black' had called on the wet afternoon of October 10th, Regatta day. Edith described her as slight, tall, fair rather than dark, and very heavily veiled. After the visitor's departure, Edith now testified, she had written a letter to Walter, which, she said, she had found after his death among his papers. Marked 'Urgent', it read:

Dearest Walter,

A most mysterious [mis-spelt as 'misterious'] lady came here just now and asked to see Mr Walter Carew. I told her you were not in, when she said she would call again early this evening, about 4.30, as she must see you. She would give me no name nor any reason for her visit. She came about ten minutes ago (2 o'clock) and seemed much distressed at not finding you in. I promised to let you know, and said you would be back [tear in paper] then. She said this afternoon or tomorrow morning I must see him. I shall go round to Mrs Walter's about the tennis cakes at any event. I think it is too wet to go down to the boathouse, but may come if it clears. Will you be back to see your 'Woman in Black'? If not, what message shall I tell Rachel to give her? Enclosed is her card.

Yours,

Edith.

The card was produced with the letter. Lowder found it necessary to explore the possibility of corroboration of the mysterious visit. Edith told the Court: 'I mentioned before half-a-dozen people at the boathouse of the visit of this mysterious lady, and he [Walter] was subjected to very much chaff on that occasion.'

Lowder: 'Did you ask him if he was going up to keep his appointment at half-past four?'

'Yes; he told me he received my note and that he had replied to it. I must have missed the messenger on the way. He said he would go up at half-past four. I remained at the boathouse myself for a couple of hours. I was subsequently given to understand that the lady did not keep her appointment.'

Counsel: 'The following day was Sunday, I believe, and it was customary for the nursery governess and the children to lunch or dine with you at the middle of the day. Did they do so?'

'They did, as well as Mr Porch and my husband. The conversation turned upon the lady who had called the previous day.'

'Was it a serious conversation?'

'Quite the reverse.'

'In fact, you were joking with your husband about the mysterious woman in black?'

'I was under the impression that the lady was more or less a hoax or a myth, and that she had no business with my husband, as she did not keep her appointment.'

Also amongst Walter's papers after his death Edith had found, so she said, a plangent letter marked 'Private':

> *'I must see you.* [Lowder read aloud.] *Why have you done nothing since you got my two* [sic] *cards? Or perhaps she never let you get them. I cannot meet her again; she makes me mad when I think of what I might have done for you. I cannot give you any address. I am living wherever I can find shelter, but you can find and help me if you will, as I know you will, for the sake of old times. Annie.'*

This undated letter, or at least its envelope, had definitely been posted. There is a stamp on the envelope which bears the date October 13th. Two tags affixed to the letter itself bore the same date. On the night of October 13th, Edith went on, Walter came home late, at about 1.45am., and he was not quite sober.

Lowder: 'Was he in the habit of coming home in such a state?'

'No.'

'Not quite sober' would appear to be some kind of ladylike litotes, when put against the diary of that date, and Max Kauffman's evening when *'Le moment est arrivé'*. Anyway, thus Walter's drunken evening and his receipt of a stimulating letter were neatly linked. On the 16th or 17th, Edith further testified, she received anonymously, in an envelope which she destroyed, a letter in Walter's handwriting, addressed to Miss Annie Luke, Post Office, Yokohama:

'I feel greatly distressed about you, [Lowder read aloud]and ever since I got your card last Saturday have been endeavouring to find you. I wish to, and will help you if I can only find you. Meet me this evening at 5.30 pm on the Bund, opposite the Club Hotel.

Wednesday, October 14th.

W.'

During the middle of the night of Monday, October 19th, Edith testified, Walter was very restless, and spoke to her about Annie Luke.

'He expressed to me a very great wish to see her, and, without telling me very much, made me believe he had treated her very badly, and told me that he meant in some way to make amends to her.I purposely refrained from telling him that I had in my possession an anonymous letter. All Monday he seemed to me not so well, and I did not wish to worry him in any way, but I told him we would discuss the matter more thoroughly when he was better.'

Lowder, confronting a possible motive for malice: 'Did you raise any objection to his making any amends to her?'

'No, the whole of the conversation about her did not last more than ten minutes, and I did not see that a conversation on such a subject could be discussed in a short time.' (She has missed the point.)

'Did he say anything about having led her to believe that he would marry her?'

'He did not say so to me. [The instructions seem to have gone awry here.] He only gave me to understand that in some way he had behaved very badly, all of which had occurred previous to our marriage. He did not tell me whether he had met her on the 14th, and I did not ask him.'

'Didn't you tell him that you knew he had been in correspondence with her?'

'I told him that, but I didn't tell him I had any letters in my possession.'

In the evening of October 20th, said Edith, 'When my brother had come back from the office, I was called downstairs to see a visitor, and Mr Carew, who was then more or less wandering, seemed to believe that the lady who had been to see me was Annie

Luke. Seeing this, I said to him, "I have had a visitor — guess who it is?" — and he immediately replied "Annie". I said, "Yes she has been here, and I have had a long talk with her. I am going to look after her and take care of her". This was of course, absolutely untrue, as I said it merely to pacify him, and he never mentioned the matter again in my hearing.'

Lowder: 'You say your brother was present at that conversation?'

Edith: 'Yes.'

Lowder returned, but soon wished that he had not done so, to the slip of paper in Walter Carew's handwriting from which, Edith had said, she had reluctantly copied the order for Fowler's and sugar of lead, to give to Mary Jacob to take to Maruya's on October 21st.

'I have forgotten to put it in,' said Lowder brightly, 'Is this the piece of paper?'

Edith: 'Yes.'

Lowder scanned it, and realized his mistake. The names of the drugs were *not* in Walter's handwriting, although some unconnected writing on the back, about a letter which had miscarried, *was* in his hand. Desperately, he tried unsuccessfully to convince the coroner that it was he, Lowder, not Edith, who had made the assertion, the promise which could not be fulfilled: 'As a matter of fact, I am responsible for that. I had not seen the paper, nor had her attention been as carefully drawn to it as it should have been. Now, however, the witness wishes to correct that impression. Is that not so, Mrs Carew?'

Edith: 'Yes.'

Counsel: 'You do not know in whose handwriting the order for the medicines is?'

Edith: 'I have never seen it before.'

A better point, well supported by other evidence, was that Edith would under no circumstances have signed a chit 'Mrs Carew', as the foreign woman was stated by Hayashi Schichiro to have written on the disputed date of October 19th. Her usual, more socially acceptable signature was 'E.M.H. Carew'. (Someone impersonating Edith Carew might have got the signature wrong! Or Edith herself, pretending to be an impostor, might have signed wrongly!)

Finally, John Lowder put it before the Court that he had been unable to find the woman going under the name of Annie Luke, as his client had instructed him.

Dr Divers was back in court to report on his completed examination of the viscera. He had found arsenic 'in more or less quantity' to be universally present in the organs sent to him. There was one-sixth of a grain in the liver. These findings were expected, but next he was to produce a bombshell which was to cause confusion where there should have been scientific precision. Two poisons at issue were bad enough, but now he had found a *third*.

Let him speak, in his bumbling, anxious way:

> *In the stomach when opened and the contents poured out, there were on the surface near the entrance — near the gullet entrance — very minute specks adhering to the stomach, of a white, pasty substance, which was just in the gullet before it passed into the stomach — two or three little white particles.*
>
> *The whole of this matter, very minute, altogether consisted essentially of white arsenic; that is to say, consisted of a substance which is not a solution of arsenic, but a white solid.*
>
> *It is practically impossible to think that the white arsenic could have been regenerated from the solution taken, by the action of the stomach. The only conclusion I can draw is that solid white arsenic was one of the substances exhibited to the deceased. When this white arsenic is swallowed, causing death, it is usual to find patches of white pasty matter sticking to the walls of the stomach. Finding these white specks was, however, to me a surprise.*

As for sugar of lead, Dr Divers was prepared to commit himself at last:

> *The intestines, which were sent to me unopened, contained nearly a quart of liquid matter, entirely devoid of the usual odour of such matter — odourless, in fact, practically, but of a slate-black colour. These contents of the intestines I have found to contain lead in very small quantities — small but distinct positive qualities — enough to have coloured the intestinal organs from the well-known blackness of sulphide of lead.*

A silence which was perhaps as ominous as it was stunned greeted

Dr Divers' revelations. No one wanted to question him.

Lowder: 'My client is rather exhausted by the long examination, and although she makes no application which will be inconvenient to the coroner or the jury, she would prefer to undergo her cross-examination tomorrow.'

Mr Blundell, of the jury, 'Tomorrow is mail-day.'

Coroner, (cruel): 'Mail-day or no mail-day, this case must be heard. The inquest will stand adjourned till ten o'clock tomorrow morning.'

Chapter 10
THE EPSILON LETTER

The Crown showed a sinister disinclination to cross-examine Edith on Thursday, November 5th, and only the coroner had a question for her. It was a good one:

'Have you any knowledge from what source your late husband obtained the supplies of arsenic which you say he was in the habit of taking? Was it from a foreign or Japanese chemist or druggist?'

Edith: 'I am afraid I cannot give you any definite information. Mr Lowder may possibly be able later on to give you information.'

Then Harry Vansittart Dickinson was called by Lowder, in his persona as loyal friend of the family, not yet as epistolary lover. He lied: Mr and Mrs Carew lived together on affectionate terms. After the money difficulties had been settled towards the end of August they had continued to live on the same affectionate terms. Yes, indeed.

Additionally, he could help with the fast-building defence in preparation: 'I recollect, years ago, when he was living at Zushi, that he told me that on one occasion when living in the Straits he had nearly killed himself by an accidental overdose of arsenic.'

To strengthen the second prong of the defence, he produced a touching story: on the day of Walter's funeral he saw a woman standing loitering near the Water Street entrance of the United Club. She had been crying, and seemed to be trying to repress an outburst of distress. He had never seen her before (so it was not Mrs Tocque) nor since, and it was possible that he could recognise her again. He had not taken sufficient notice of her dress to be able to describe it. She was five feet four to five feet five, and slim. She was '*more fair than dark*.' Just so; had not Edith said that the 'Mysterious Visitor' was '*Fair rather than dark*'?

Young Reggie Porch came forward in his consistent position as

loyal brother. His most important purpose at this time was to corroborate the Annie Luke apparition. He remembered perfectly well the jokes over Sunday lunch, the next day. He corroborated too Edith's merciful white lie in the sickroom on October 20th; her saying that Annie Luke had called, and that she would do her best to help her.

Mr Nicholas of the jury, suspicious, asked if Reginald had seen the Annie Luke letters. He replied that he had seen them on the evening of the 22nd, not before Walter's death, but, prompted by Lowder, he did see the card with M.J. and A.L. on Saturday, October 10th.

Kobayashi Beika, who was described as a naturalised Japanese subject, was examined by Edith's Junior Counsel, Ambrose Walford. He had come forward to bear witness, as he did now, to Walter's arsenic habit. About one year ago he had been tiffining at the Club, and shared a table with Mr Carew. He happened to mention to Walter that he had taken a medicine which contained strychnine, to buck him up.

'Oh! that's nothing,' Walter had boasted. 'I take enough poison to kill six men. I am obliged to do so.' Mr Rose asked Beika if he knew where Walter purchased arsenic, but he did not know.

The amah, Asa, was called by Lowder to testify to the broken bottle incident. Unfortunately she could not remember the date of the actual breakage, although she was clear about being told to find it two days previously, as she did, beside a broken lampshade by a small bush.

John Lowder had himself sworn, in order to testify, and disclosed his special relationship with his client. He had known the Carews well, he might say intimately since 1890, and had always known them to be on the most affectionate terms. In particular — and how contrary to the codes of the Bar all this personal involvement sounds — he wished to put on record a certain conversation with the deceased which had taken place a long time ago.

'On seeing me about to enter Brett and Co's shop, he said, "Why do you go to a European drugstore; unless for some particular prescription, I always send to the native drugstores." '

This must have been Lowder's 'explanation', as heralded by

Edith, but the snag here was that all native chemists *competent to make up Fowler's Solution* could easily be checked. Lowder must have been milling over the significance, the advantage, of the solid white arsenic detected by Dr Divers.

As if reading his mind, the coroner announced that in view of the new aspect given to the case by Dr Divers' latest evidence he had considered it his duty to request the Japanese authorities to order an inspection of the Japanese stores with the view of ascertaining the supplies of white arsenic to customers during the month of October.

The following day, Friday, November 6th, the coroner had to report that the Japanese police could find no address at which white arsenic had been sold to foreigners recently. (These findings were not, however, definitive, because, as has been explained, white arsenic was easily obtainable under the counter.)

Edward Owen, an employee of the Peninsular and Oriental Steam Navigation Company in Yokohama, called by Lowder, was an interesting witness whose testimony was, curiously, never greatly regarded, referred to, or relied upon. He corroborated the reality of the 'Mysterious Visitor' *in Walter's mind,* although not her notional name. There is no evidence that he was a particular friend of Edith's, and he had a decent job, in a career structure, which he would scarcely have wished to jeopardise for an inducement. On October 15th (later corrected to 13th) he remembered that Walter Carew came into his office. He was well acquainted with him. It was about 2.30pm. He asked Owen if a lady had been in. She was fair, tall, and wore a dark dress and a veil: *Mrs Carew had seen her outside the P&O gates.*

Owen assured him that no such person had been to see him. Walter said that he was mystified as to who the lady was who had called, asking for him. He thought that she was possibly the girl to whom he had been engaged in England. He had received two cards from her. The first one bore some initials. Owen could not remember what those initials were. The second one also had initials on it, with 1888, and gave him a further clue to the identity of the caller. He searched in his pockets but could not find a card to show Owen.

The coroner called a witness of his own, George Kircher, court usher, whom he had instructed to make all possible diligent enquiries for a person by the name of Annie Luke. He had found no trace of her in Yokohama.

Mr Rose asked if it might be necessary to require a handwriting expert to make an assessment of the Annie Luke letters.

Coroner: 'If you gentlemen of the jury consider it actually necessary, we will get an expert, but I would suggest that the point be reserved for further consideration.' (A clear message of the way his mind was inclined.) Mr Trafford, of the jury, abrogating some legal knowledge: 'The question is one for the jury to decide whether it is necessary to have an expert.'

Coroner: 'The inquest has already extended to a great length. I think the jury will be able to form from the handwriting some sort of an idea as to whether the letters are all in the same handwriting. You are all practical businessmen accustomed to read different handwritings.'

Mr Rose: 'To my mind it would be important to have independent testimony.'

The coroner had the letters passed to the jury, and continued:

'I will ask you, Mr Rose, to compare the first letter and the last of the series, to form a tolerably sound judgement as to whether these two were written by the same hand. *I would also remind you that there is not necessarily any further relation between an envelope and the message it contains than there is between a bottle and the cork with which it is stopped.*'

John Lowder liked none of this; he felt that the jury should compare all the letters, and he particularly took exception to the comparison with a bottle. He so pressed the coroner that he was obliged to tell the jury that 'It will be your bounden duty to give full weight to the consideration that Mrs Carew has sworn that particular letters were inside particular envelopes.'

Only Mr Rose (and John Lowder) persisted in wanting a handwriting expert, but he was overruled. 'The point in my opinion has so very remote a bearing upon the issue before you', and thus the coroner began his summing up of what he called a very difficult and complicated case.

His address went strongly against Edith Carew. The testimony of Mary Jacob as to her procuring arsenic by Mrs Carew's orders was 'clear and explicit and unshaken by such slight cross-examination as she was exposed to. Her testimony was that of an unwilling but truthful witness, and upon every material point her evidence remains unshaken.'

The jury had the cause of death; the duty of the jury was reduced to the one point of who administered the arsenic. There was hardly a tittle or jot of evidence for suicide. Dr Divers' evidence had gone against an accidental overdose, in spite of Mrs Carew's evidence which was calculated to suggest that explanation. The coroner did not doubt that Mr Carew *had* taken arsenic medicinally. If not Mrs Carew's, whose hand administered the arsenic?

> *The case which the able Counsel for Mrs Carew has been endeavouring to make out, I take to be this, that on or about the tenth of October last a woman named Annie Luke with whom Mr Carew had previous relations in England or elsewhere, came to Yokohama, and during the course of Mr Carew's illness, in an interval in which Mrs Carew was not at the bedside of her husband, found entrance to the deceased and administered the poison. If that is not the implication, I fail to see what the object of all this evidence as to Annie Luke can be.*
>
> *Gentlemen, I take upon myself the responsibility of saying that in considering your verdict you need not complicate your minds much as to the share which such a person as Annie Luke may have taken in the tragedy. If you reject the story of Annie Luke as largely imaginary, suppositional, impalpable, intangible and unverifiable, you are necessarily driven to the conclusion that arsenic must in some way have been administered by Mrs Carew.*

The jury retired for one hour and twenty five minutes, during which time they asked for refreshments, which the coroner did not allow: this just might have turned them away from the verdict which he had solicited.

The foreman — not in fact pushy Mr Rose but quiet Mr Blundell — read the verdict, an open one, that Walter Carew had died from the effects of arsenic, but by whom the poison was administered there was no direct evidence to show.

The following day, John Frederic Lowder, in all tongue-and-cheek seriousness, as an alternative to the search for Annie Luke, caused to be published a notice which offered five hundred dollars as a reward for the identification, by specimens of handwriting or otherwise, of the writer or writers of the Annie Luke letters and envelopes. The open verdict had offered him little comfort, because he knew that the Establishment was moving against Edith Carew and that he had to prepare for a long fight. In England there was much comment in the press, and it was felt that his client's conduct demanded a most searching investigation. In fact the evidence at the inquest had been of such a nature that Sir Ernest Satow, Her Majesty's Minister and Consul General at Tokyo, had instructed the Crown Prosecutor in Japan to take steps to bring about a magisterial enquiry.

A date was set for November 11th, and on November 10th Edith wrote to Mary Jacob:

> *Dear Mary,*
>
> *I hope for the sake of Edgarley and the old people at home that you will see Mr Porch who will take this letter to you. If this will not appeal to you perhaps you will see him for the sake of Marjorie and Ben. I hope Mr Porch (my father) will soon be here and trust that if you won't see my brother you will see him.* [Her father did not go out to Yokohama.]
>
> *Yours sincerely,*
>
> *E.M.H. Carew.*

So soon after the inquest, on November 11th, appearing on a summons, Edith found herself back in the same courtroom, charged with murder, with the tribunal constituted as magisterial proceedings, the equivalent of English full committal proceedings. The general rule was that the law of England followed a British person when he or she entered upon foreign soil. The legal situation in Japan in 1896 was governed generally by the Foreign Jurisdiction Act of 1890, supplemented by such Orders in Council as might be necessary for giving due effect to the jurisdiction.

In 1865, by an important Order in Council, a Supreme Court for China and Japan had been created at Shanghai, presided over by a judge and an assistant judge. China and Japan were divided up into districts, in which the wants of the English subjects were to be supplied by provincial courts, as at Yokohama. In 1878 the Court for Japan was created separately, but it still held a subservient position to the Supreme Court for China and Japan. The Court for Japan had the power to try capital offences. Appeal in all cases lay to Shanghai, exactly as if the Court for Japan were still only a provincial court.

The foreign community in Japan was remarkably litigious. Some of the lawyers combined their work with running a newspaper, which explains why the law-reporting was often so good. The Consular Court in Yokohama, sitting as Her Britannic Majesty's Court for Japan, thus, with certain local procedural differences, operated as if it were situated in England. In particular, the law of evidence was not changed. Judges and Counsel were of formidable competence, charged with a pride — perhaps an anxious pride — in keeping up standards.

Counsel now for the Crown and for Edith Carew were the same, but the consul had been replaced by an assistant judge, James Troup. John Lowder left the court to make application to the available judge in chambers (ie not sitting in open court) — who happened to be the senior judge, Mowat, who will appear later in all his importance — for bail for his client during the hearing. This was granted upon Edith's own surety and that of J.D. Hutchison and R.B. Robinson, 'Substantial British merchants resident in Yokohama', whom she had brought to court with her. The amount of bail was kept private. After some formalities, the Court rose until the following morning.

During that first day Lowder received another 'A.L.' letter at his accommodation at Wright's Hotel:

Mr Lowder,

It never occurred to you did it that 'my way' to join him might be by the French mail, it never occurred to you did it that I can disguise myself as well as my name, it never occurred to you did it that you never could and never would find me. Who am I and what is my name eh? Is it A.L. or M.J. or was I during my stay in Yokohama passing under some other name eh?

A.L.!!

The small courtroom was crowded on November 12th. The trio of doctors, Wheeler, Todd and May, repeated their inquest evidence. Dr Wheeler was already finding himself in difficulties as to discrepancy: 'When a man gets over fifty, especially after living for a number of years in the East, his memory is not sufficiently good to go back half a month with any degree of accuracy.'

Early in the morning of October 13th Edith wrote an extremely unwise letter to Mary Jacob, which was later produced against her as evidence of intent to tamper with a witness:

> *Dear Mary,*
>
> *I went round to see you this morning early, I suppose it was Miss Britain I saw, who said you would not see me. I am very sorry you wouldn't. However, I suppose you know your own mind best. I have a fair idea of what you will be asked and what you will reply in court today, and I want to tell you that it depends entirely upon you today as to the result in everything. You yourself must see that, and I hope you will remember and bear this in mind for the sake of Marjorie and Ben, if for none else.*
>
> *Yours,*
> *E.M.H.C.*

In court, however, uninfluenced, Mary Jacob examined by Litchfield gave some damaging new evidence relating to October 19th, the day of the sale of Fowler's to an unidentified foreign woman, the day on which Edith noted in her diary that she did not go out. The governess had detailed memories of meeting Edith in town; with Marjorie she went 'by appointment to the Post Office to meet Mrs Carew, who had taken her little boy, Ben, down town. I remember Ben running across the road this side of the Post Office to meet me. Marjorie was not feeling very well and we changed. Mrs Carew said she had left her jinrikisha at the chemist's to follow her, but she did not know where he had gone.'

John Lowder chose to cross-examine hardly at all on this occasion. He did not suggest that Mary Jacob had mistaken the day. No one asked her if Edith Carew had been wearing dark clothes, as described by Hayashi Schichiro. If she had been, Lowder (who will have known) would not, of course, have wanted it brought out. If she had been wearing bright clothing one would think that at some stage he would want that to be known. Perhaps he feared malice; these were early, tentative days. As for why Litchfield did not ask (unless it was an oversight) he probably ought ethically to have asked, even if he knew that Edith's dress was bright.

By this time the two governesses had handed over to Litchfield their treasure trove of the stitched Dickinson love-letters, and against fierce opposition from Defence Counsel, they were produced in court and identified. They brought a whole new dimension to the proceedings; Edith had lost her dignity, and soon choice phrases would be on the lips of those who had previously bowed to her in the social round.

Elsa Christoffel, who had not been called at the inquest — when the letters were a secret — although she had attended to support her friend, now found herself aggressively cross-examined by John Lowder. He made her write to his dictation extracts from the Annie Luke letters, with the clear implication that he suspected *her* of being their author.

The following day, Saturday, November 14th, Edith committed a frightful indiscretion, a sudden reckless act, which damaged her credibility and made people think that she was capable of anything. The exhibit marked *Epsilon* was found to be missing from the envelope of Dickinson letters which, upon request, the Clerk of the Court, Mr Moss, had handed to Ambrose Walford. The letters had been spread out on counsels' table, where Edith was sitting, and when they were returned to Moss and checked, *Epsilon* was no longer with them. *Epsilon* was the particularly compromising letter — 'I love you utterly my dear one, and the remembrance of yesterday will be ever with me.'

The court was cleared, and Mrs Moss, wife of the Clerk of the Court, was deputed to search Edith Carew. *Epsilon* was found hidden in the sleeve of her black dress — a Japanese expedient — between the cloth sleeve and the crêpe cuff. The governesses had, in fact, handed the Dickinson letters to Litchfield on Sunday, November 8th, just after the inquest, and their existence will have been disclosed to the defence in good time, but the shock of seeing them spread before her in public must have caused a panic in Edith.

She was now in disgrace, and, on Monday, November 16th, she

was no longer allowed the privilege of sitting with Counsel, but was conducted to a seat at the side of the dock. Her Junior Counsel, Walford, felt that he, together with the Clerk of the Court, might have been very seriously compromised. 'I therefore find it impossible to act any longer for the accused in this case,' he announced. 'Had I been engaged alone, I should naturally have hesitated before retiring, but I am glad to think that the defence remains in the hands of my able and learned friend, and that the interests of the accused will in no way suffer.'

He then left the court! His dramatic withdrawal — which was not at all necessary, and was not the action of a tough criminal lawyer — *must* have caused serious damage to his already disgraced client. The suspicion must be that he had no stomach for the fight; his previous friendship was an embarrassment, he was worried about his own reputation, and *Epsilon* was a weak excuse for extricating himself. Lowder, sophisticated and robust, was not rocked in the slightest, and carried on alone.

By unfortunate juxtaposition, Harry Vansittart Dickinson was called on next, *by the Crown,* exposed as lover, not family friend. Subpoenas had been issued, and he must have been there against his will. They made him read out his love-letters, and established the incident of the novel, *The Playactress.* Then they let him shuffle off with as much dignity as he could muster.

On Wednesday, November 18th, Dr Divers made a nervous witness: 'I have no wish to testify, nor do I wish to keep anything back.' He told the Court something of his professional background: before his 23 years in Japan, he had been Professor of Materia Medica and Therapeutics in the Medical School of the Queen's Hospital, Birmingham, and then Lecturer in Medical Jurisprudence in the Medical School of the Middlesex Hospital.

He had not examined the kidney — an omission which Lowder quietly noted for future use. The liver was small but not noticeably unhealthy. The absence of inflammation of the stomach and duodenum pointed to the ingestion of arsenic largely in solution, not as solid white arsenic. The specks of solid white arsenic were now quantified as eight on the wall of the stomach, and two just inside the gullet. He did not quantify the lead found, which though minute in quantity was most marked in the contents of the bowel and in the bloody fluid outside the bowels, which probably contained pancreatic fluid. Again, Lowder bided his time.

Rachel Greer was tested once more, and held to her previous evidence that her master had given her the writing on October 18th to send out by jinkrikisha for medicine. She could not remember well whether it was one or two bottles. She was still in Mrs Carew's employment. They let her sit, because she was in rather bad health.

John Lowder called no evidence, and Henry Litchfield asked the judge, forthwith, upon the evidence laid before him, to commit the accused for trial before a jury.

The medical evidence points to the fact of death by arsenic or some other poison. The evidence I have laid before you shows that arsenic in considerable quantities was introduced into the house shortly before his death. Part of that arsenic was traced directly to the hands of Mrs Carew. It was shown that Mrs Carew had the chief duty of nursing the deceased during the time of his illness. It was also shown, I submit, in spite of all appearances to the contrary, that the accused led one person to believe that there were serious and almost irreconcilable differences between them.

Judge: 'I am of opinion that the evidence is such as ought to be placed before a jury.'

Edith Carew had no statement to make. Harry Dickinson was sworn in his own recognisance of $100 to appear to give evidence at the trial. Mary Jacob would have received similar treatment, but she had disappeared.

Edith was allowed to go home in the custody of the Constable of the Court to collect some personal articles. A later application for bail was refused.

She was from now on barred from the Plains of Heaven.

Chapter 11
DIVERS OPINIONS

Back home in Glastonbury the belief that it was all a dreadful mistake prevailed. The trial was set for January 5th, 1897, which happened to be one of John Albert Porch's mayoral years, and he did not stand down. A set-piece in the *Japan Gazette* conveys the atmosphere of the opening day:

Those wending their way past the Post Office end of Main Street on Tuesday morning, January 5th, at five minutes to ten, might have noticed a closed 'rikisha, proceeding at a walking pace and followed by two men. The 'rikisha was occupied by a lady in deep mourning, and that lady is accused of a crime of which the penalty, should she be found guilty, is death. Yet her manner was composed, and when later she saw her Counsel, she smiled. Outside the British Consulate stood a large number of men engaged in serious conversation. There was none of the hilarity which is usual with men. All comported themselves with becoming gravity as conscious of the grave duty which they had been called upon to fulfil. By ten o'clock the little courtroom was filled to overflowing, and those summoned, unable to find seats, or even standing room, blocked the entrance hall.

Mrs Carew, accompanied by her brother and the warder, entered within two minutes of the hour, and as she took her seat at the back of the place reserved for her Counsel it was noticed that her face wore an expression of cheerful composure. Mr Wilkinson next entered in wig and gown, but passed through to the Consular Offices, returning a minute later with Mr Litchfield, also in wig and gown. Hardly were they seated when Mr Lowder, in a morning-coat and with his overcoat over his arm came in and had a brief talk with the woman whose cause he is championing.

The chat was evidently pleasant, for both Counsel and client smiled. Mr Lowder then left the room but soon returned, this time in his barrister's robe, and took his accustomed seat.

Soon after Judge Mowat entered garbed in a white wig and a crimson robe, having a lining of ermine, and collar and cuffs of the same material. He was accompanied by Mr Troup [the assistant judge] *who also sat on the bench. When the Judge was seated Mr Moss, Clerk of the Court, impressively read the charge, to which Mrs Carew replied in clear and distinct tones, without betraying the slightest quiver in her voice, 'I am not guilty.' Mr Lowder then said, 'I have to apply under advice of her medical attendant that the prisoner be allowed a seat.' 'Certainly,' replied the Judge. Mrs Carew then moved into the dock, Mr Kircher bringing a chair.*

Judge Mowat was a scrupulous judge, anxious, obsessional, but not inflexible; strong counsel could bring about an alteration in his decisions on evidence. Born in 1843, called to the Bar in 1871, he had been Acting Chief Justice in England in 1879, 1881,1888 and 1889. He had been appointed Judge of H.B.M.'s Court for Japan in 1891. Whether or not the matter at issue was to affect him, the fact is that 1897 was to be the year in which he retired on pension to 10 Grand Avenue Mansions, Hove. He did not die until June 7th, 1925.

For the Crown, Henry Litchfield had now been joined — at the special instigation of Sir Ernest Satow — by Hiram Shaw Wilkinson, H.M.B.'s Crown Advocate in China. Born in Belfast in 1840, called to the Bar in 1872, he succeeded Judge Mowat as Judge of H.M.B.'s Court for Japan from 1897 to 1900. He was then appointed Chief Justice of the Supreme Court for China from 1900 to 1905 and was knighted in 1903. He retired to Moneyshanere, Tobermore, County Londonderry, and died on September 27th, 1926.

Edith rested all her hopes, and Porch family money, on one counsel in the person of John Lowder, who was to prove ever intrepid and ingenious on her behalf. She herself had no right to speak — it was not quite 1898 — and was bound by the hasty statement that she had made before the coroner.

Those summoned to serve as jurors showed a marked reluctance

to appear, and the judge handed out swingeing fines of $50. Names such as Henry Moss, who had put in a medical certificate, and H.I. Chope, are familiar from the diary. The final list of five male[20] jurors — five as the jury was constituted in the Court for Japan — consisted of Joseph Davieson, Robert Courtney Johnstone, Duncan MacLaren, Andrew Patterson (foreman) and Arthur Henry Cole Watson.

In his opening address for the Crown, Hiram Wilkinson formulated a limitation; the jury was to decide as to the administration of arsenic only. There was no evidence to show that sugar of lead caused death. It might have delayed the purging (and haemorrhage) of arsenical poisoning. The Crown was clearly discomposed by Dr Divers' finding of white arsenic. Wilkinson allowed that the prosecution could not trace the source of the substance, except that the *betto* would say that on two occasions Mrs Carew gave him some white powder to sprinkle on the pony's food.

Counsel challenged the prisoner's statement that her husband always kept a small bottle of arsenic on the dining-room sideboard. It was not even a consistent statement, because she had previously said that she went to the cupboard in the dressing-room, where he kept his medicine.

Was it credible, anyway, that arsenic would be put next to a bottle of cod-liver oil for the children which, the governess would say, was kept on the sideboard? If the deceased had been in the habit of taking large doses of arsenic, 'there ought to be some place from which he obtained it.'

The Dickinson letters were such as 'no modest woman who still retained her fealty to her husband could accept from any man whatever.' Although, of course, it was not necessary to prove motive for the murder, the letters *might* be taken to show one. Edith Carew either lived in peace and comfort with her husband, and wrote a concoction of lies to Dickinson — when, perhaps, the question of motive became more obscure — or she was truly in fear of her life, which *would* be a motive.

The Crown was not, however, leaning towards the explanation of Walter seen as a homicidal brute, meet for extermination. Wilkinson was beginning a course of argumentation that all Edith's

complaints to Dickinson about Walter were outright lies. This view had already been aired in Litchfield's closing words at the magisterial proceedings, but it is against the evidence of the diary, the medical history, the other men, Walter's flirtations, and the money problems, which indicate that there *were* 'serious and almost irreconcilable differences'.

The force of the Crown's ongoing contention was that in telling a tissue of lies to an outsider about her marriage, Edith had demonstrated such a moral turpitude, such a disposition for falsehood, that her evidence in general was worthless, and that she was thereby shewn forth as a person capable of murder.

Although a belief that this was a crime of passion stayed with the Carew case, *it never was the submission of the Crown that love for Dickinson was the motive for murder,* and this was a most creditable restraint. It would have been easy to use the letters as evidence of an eternal triangle *tout court,* and certainly they were placed before the jury as an important part of the case against Edith Carew.

The Crown, quite frankly and expressly, was unable to suggest a sufficient motive. By denying the failure of the marriage, the prosecution had as it were neutered itself in that respect. The defence too, for obvious reasons, was bound to represent the marriage as cordial and affectionate, so that, curiously, both sides argued here in harmony.

And now the Crown made the preposterous suggestion that the defence had asked the coroner's jury to conclude that poison was supplied to Walter Carew for the purpose of suicide, by the hands of one Annie Luke. John Lowder had to make a fully justified interruption at this point, to disclaim any such intention. Wilkinson accepted his denial, remarking merely that the implication was one that the jury might have thought was intended to be drawn, taking into account too that his learned friend had had no opportunity of addressing the coroner's court.

Another suggestion, Counsel went on, might be that the existence of Annie Luke would account for uneasiness on the part of the deceased which might, with other things, have led him to suicide. He would, however, wish to put it strongly to the jury that Annie Luke was the mere creation of the prisoner, whatever reality

she might have had in Walter Carew's earlier life.

Mary Jacob would swear that the card which she saw was inscribed with only 'M.J. 1880', not, additionally, 'A.L'. The fact was impressed on her mind by the similarity to her own initials. She would also say that there was a good deal of chaff about the 'Mysterious Visitor', but that the name 'Annie Luke' was never mentioned at that time.

If Edith had been tinkering, there were two possibilities here, although Counsel did not articulate them. Supposing that there had been no 'Mysterious Visitor' at all, and Edith had manufactured the card, it looked as if, first casting about (perhaps in haste) for random initials, she had lighted upon those of her governess, but had later improved on her artefact.

Suppose that a genuine 'Mysterious Visitor' had turned up at No. 169, then she was M.J. indeed, and nothing to do with Annie Luke, but no one produced the merest shadow of such a person. Finally, Wilkinson read aloud the three ill-judged letters from Edith to Mary Jacob in her place of safety with Miss Britain, and the jury marked them well.

Crown Counsel had finished his opening remarks, and after tiffin he began to call his witnesses. Dr Wheeler had prepared his evidence carefully, and achieved an admirable degree of clarity and recall. On the second day of the trial, January 6th, only about 20 members of the public attended, because medical evidence was expected. The Crown had a doctor — Dr Tripler — present, to act as adviser, and the defence had brought Dr Eldridge, Edith's friend; he had a formidable array of scientific tomes in front of him.

Dr Wheeler was recalled, to state that he had never heard of arsenic and sugar of lead being used as direct remedies for stricture. The only possible way in which sugar of lead could be used would be as an injection, to check the urethritis of stricture. Sugar of lead was often given to check diarrhoea, because of its astringent properties. Up to a certain time in Walter Carew's illness — the Tuesday — his bowels were not active, so much so that purgatives were given.

Arsenic was often used as an anti-periodic in malaria. Although the doctor had the impression that Walter had suffered from malaria, he had never complained of it to him. There is ample

independent evidence that Walter had had malaria in the past. The first prong of the defence — that of self-administration of arsenic — would be greatly aided by a history of malaria. So Edith's denial at the inquest of such a history was self-defeating, plainly malicious, or a double-bluff.

Once, Dr Wheeler said, he had wondered if copper poisoning might be causing the puzzling symptoms, and he had asked the Carews if they used any copper pots and pans. 'No,' Walter had told him. 'We have splendid pots and pans, all porcelain-lined.'

John Lowder then entered into his first cross-examination of the trial. His favourable points elicited from Dr Wheeler were as follows:

There was no haemorrhage from the bowels of the deceased during his illness.

The implication was that sugar of lead *had* been ingested, and that Walter had taken it himself to control arsenical bleeding.

Sugar of lead could not have been administered to the deceased in any quantity by another person without his tasting it.

It was possible but not probable that the deceased was *already* suffering from arsenical poisoning (from self-administration) on October 15th, when Dr Wheeler warned him that he was on the verge of jaundice.

Edith Carew was anxious that Walter should get a change in Kamakura, and the plan probably was that she would not accompany him there.

During the week at issue Edith was busy with repeated sinapisms and other nursing duties, and was always present in the morning. Because of the exigencies of the doctor's profession, she could never predict the exact time of his arrival. '*She was always there*'. In particular she was there on the morning of October 19th, when Mary Jacob had said that she met her employer in town.

She had seemed rather pleased to have Dr Todd brought in. Here the judge meanly extracted the qualification that the doctor had not noticed Edith's expression!

Both Edith and the doctor had difficulty in persuading Walter to take any medicine. *Ergo* — he was not easy to poison. It was Edith Carew herself — on the Wednesday, after the doctor had said to her, 'You must be tired', — who had suggested getting in a nurse,

a coloured man named Hunter.

The request for the boathouse prescription occurred in the natural course of conversation.

If Walter Carew had previously suffered the effects of an accidental overdose of arsenic he might have recognised the symptoms if someone else were administering it to him.

If the kidneys had been diseased — and here Counsel was entering on a new line of argumentation — the burden of eliminating (self-administered) arsenic would have been thrown upon the bowels and skin, and that might have accounted for arsenic being found in the bowels.

Dr Wheeler, during the course of the illness, had found a trace of albumen in the urine. If present there in large quantities it might well indicate kidney disease. Long-standing stricture and catarrh of the bladder were usually followed by affection of the kidney.

Crown Counsel re-examined on this point: 'Did the quantity of albumen found in the urine lead you to think that he was suffering from kidney disease?'

Dr Wheeler: 'I inferred kidney disease; but albumen is found in the urine in cases of arsenical poisoning.'

And there Dr Wheeler was released, to be replaced by Dr Todd, who read the post-mortem report, and, examined by Litchfield, stated that he had found the kidneys to be 'quite healthy by all indications'.

Lowder could not leave it at that: 'The kidney, though apparently healthy to the naked eye, might be found to be seriously diseased if examined under the microscope?'

'Not seriously, but commencing to be diseased.'

Lowder: 'Had you any particular object in sending the kidney for chemical analysis?'

'It is the organ which excretes irritant poison from the body. It was not on account of any disease that I detected.'

Not discouraged, Lowder pressed on hopefully, and gained the notional point that, unusually, one kidney might be diseased without the other.

On the following day, January 7th, even fewer members of the public were present. Dr May was the first witness, and his most useful contribution to the proceedings was that there had been none

of the blue line of lead poisoning on the gums. Although generally associated with chronic plumbism, a blue line might occur acutely if large doses of lead were taken over a short period.

Dr Edwin Divers was sensitive and vulnerable. All too soon during his examination-in-chief, he heard the judge himself interpose with the one question which he dreaded — 'And the lead?'

Divers: 'The lead was in such small quantities, I did not attempt to weigh it. The lead was everywhere, but it was small. The most lead I got was in the contents of the intestines.

'In connection with this not attempting to weigh, I have to mention that the work of examination was carried out by me single-handed. After the inquest was finished, I had other engagements and was utterly exhausted and undesirous of touching the matters again.

'I mention this because I might, if I had gone on, have collected all the lead and weighed it, and all the arsenic and weighed it, but it was in consequence of exhaustion and the conviction of the non-necessity of going on any further in the interests of justice that I stopped.'

He had scraped the Carews' bedroom fender, and tested the matter for arsenic, but the stain consisted only of human urine, *not*, as Edith had proposed, spilt Fowler's from her broken bottle.

Edith had, however, been right about the bottle of Dr Baelz's secret stricture medicine which she had produced. Although it should have contained only belladonna, morphia and distilled water, some hand had added European Fowler's Solution (as from Schedel's rather than Maruya's.)

Dr Divers had conducted some recent research especially for the proceedings, and had found that Japanese Fowler's generally lacked the odour of lavender and the red colouring of sandalwood, as ordered in European Fowler's, although indeed those additives were similarly ordered in the Japanese pharmacopoeia. Nor did strong sunlight bleach the European solution into a simulacrum of the Japanese version.

Hiram Wilkinson moved from questions of fact to questions of opinion. Dr Divers thought that the case was clearly one in which soluble arsenic was given repeatedly and in increasing doses. He knew of only one anomalous patient who had developed tolerance

to Fowler's Solution: tolerance was normally to solid white arsenic.

To kill by sugar of lead, one and a half to two ounces would be required, and there would be a strong effect on the mouth and throat, as ingested. He saw nothing of lead poisoning in Walter Carew's symptoms, except for the slight constipation. Acute fatal lead poisoning was extremely rare.

The sixth of a grain of arsenic found in the liver was a full and sufficient quantity to establish death.

John Lowder rose to cross-examine: 'Finding two poisons present, ought you not to have ascertained the quantity of lead?'

Divers: 'What do you mean by "ought"? Do you mean morally, or my responsibility to this Court?'

Lowder: 'Yes.'

Divers: 'No, I should not, nor the arsenic either, judging by all precedent known to me.'

'You were unassisted, I think?'

'Entirely; by a servant, even.'

'If you had not been so utterly exhausted and tired of your work, as you told us this morning you were, do you not think you would have proceeded to determine the amount of lead?'

Divers, confessing: 'I think I should have collected the lead and determined it, and the arsenic and estimated it, and I think I should have tested it afterwards.'

Lowder : 'If not weary of work?'

'Yes. I would have carried the case further if I had the curiosity, but I had the unpleasant matters about my laboratory, and my colleagues had to be considered.'

Under relentless pressure from Counsel, Dr Divers admitted that he could not assert positively that the lead did not contribute to the death.

Satisfied, Lowder moved on to the tempting subject of the absence of smell when the stomach was opened. Surely if Fowler's were therein there should have been a scent of lavender? He avoided the inconvenient point already made that Japanese Fowler's lacked lavender. It might also be pointed out that the larger one-ounce acquisitions of Fowler's all came from Maruya's towards the end of the week, with the exception of the last half-ounce from Schedel's.

Dr Divers' reply was somewhat vague: 'You see, deceased died on the 22nd October, and his stomach was opened by me on the 26th, and the stomach remained in the body of the deceased for a day, I think, before it was removed. We don't give much for smells in those cases.'

Under further pressure, Dr Divers weakened his previous opinion by the admission that he could not positively assert as a deduction from what came under his own observation that arsenic had been taken or administered *in solution*. Lowder was playing with the existence of the ten little solid particles of arsenic and substantially eroding the integrity of the prosecution case.

Then the kidney.

'I examined it and looked at it and thought of analysing it.'

Should he not have analysed it?

'I should not have done more than I did. I could not do everything. It was open to me to choose as a chemist what parts I examined. I could give you motives if you want them or reasons why I selected certain parts to examine.'

He could not be brought to say that the kidney appeared to be diseased as a result of stricture. 'I did not examine it microscopically, but I could see that it was not a kidney that would not excrete urine. It was to all appearances a healthy kidney.'

Judge Mowat asked an important question, which if resolved would have hardened the case for the Crown. It is possible that he had taken advice. Could the specks of white arsenic have arisen from decomposition of Fowler's Solution?

The very last thing that Lowder wanted was a simplification, a reduction, and Dr Divers' uncompromising opinion — and he may well have been wrong — ran straight into the hands of the defence: 'That is a matter that has engaged my close attention, and my conclusion is that it could not, both from my knowledge and my experience through this trial. I cannot connect one with the other.'

At last, on the following, fourth, day of the trial, Dr Divers was released and allowed to surface, dented and scarred by the experience.

Chapter 12
TWIN SOULS

Edith's studied poise occasionally deserted her, when she flushed a deep, dark red, and on January 8th, she was about to suffer the worst kind of embarrassment. John Lowder had decided to bring in the subject of the gonorrhoea himself. He will have warned Edith.

Dr Neil Gordon Munro had just been brought by Wilkinson, in all fairness and quest for the truth, to attest to his treatment of Walter's stricture in 1893, and to repeat his recollection of the conversation in which Walter had said, to the doctor's expressed surprise, that arsenic relieved the pain of stricture.

Apparently — and Dr Munro's memory improved under the stress of the trial — Walter had asked him to explain why arsenic gave him relief, and he had been able to give the patient no explanation except that it might be so. Already delighted with this history — for surely a man suffering such agony would continue to seek the medicine that eased it, if only a continuing source of supply could be found — Lowder began to cross-examine. Circuitously, he approached the unsaid area, arriving at the crux: 'Did you treat him for anything else?'

Dr Munro: 'Am I obliged to answer, my Lord ?'

Judge: 'Yes, I think so.'

Dr Munro: 'I treated him after his recovery from stricture. He consulted me about an attack of gonorrhoea, and the bladder catarrh followed the gonorrhoea.'

The extent of the shock caused by the sounding of the word in the courtroom can be gauged by the fact that the word was never uttered there again. Lowder will have hoped that some sympathy might have attached to his client, so that she could be seen as less of a wanton. Otherwise he needed all available medical evidence of chronic and distressing illness for which the remedy of arsenic was

taken in increasing dosage. This was a stronger imperative than James Maybrick's hypochondriasis.

Dr Munro continued to perform the service that Lowder was intent on extracting: 'I knew arsenic was *par excellence* the specific for neuralgia and malaria, and I thought that stricture complicated with malaria might cause pains which arsenic might relieve.' He did not think that Walter's stricture would ever have been wholly cured. It was a very bad case anyway.

Lowder: 'Would the presence of the stricture cause pain in micturition?'

'Undoubtedly.'

'And so, I presume, would inflammation of the bladder?'

'Very much so.'

'Now, this pain in micturition is also a symptom of arsenical poisoning, is it not?'

'Yes.'

'With strangury?'

'Yes.'

'Might the pain, if actually proceeding from arsenical poisoning, be easily mistaken for that produced by stricture or inflammation of the bladder?'

'Yes, undoubtedly.'

Lowder: 'So that if the deceased took arsenic habitually to alleviate, to relieve, the pain of suffering strangury, he might be unwittingly inducing the very pain he was taking arsenic in the hope of stopping. And finding no alleviation, he would be apt to take larger doses perhaps in the hope of stopping it?'

Munro: 'It is certainly possible he would do so.'

Lowder sat down, well pleased with his and Dr Eldridge's research, and the neat if dialectical model which he had constructed. He will not have been so happy with the Crown's immediately consecutive evidence drawn from the three European chemists in business in Yokohama that, going back to around 1892, there was no record of the sale of arsenic to Walter Carew.

By way perhaps of taking the sting out of this mass of theoretical evidence Lowder, cross-examining Frederick William Thomas, manager of Brett & Co, revealed that, somewhat irregularly, he had been allowed to encourage this prosecution witness to make some rather tenuous experiments which were calculated to show that sugar of lead could not have been administered to Walter without his knowledge.

The judge enjoyed this part of the proceedings, and took the keenest, interposing interest as the chemist related that one grain of sugar of lead mixed with a full tumbler of soda water gave a slightly milky appearance. Two grains gave a slight taste. Three grains gave a marked change in both appearance and taste.

Lowder was eager to cross-examine Joseph Schedel, the German chemist, in order to dispel the lingering suspicion in the courtroom that Dr Divers' ten specks of white arsenic might have had their provenance in the Carews' stable.

Edith herself, in her first statement before the coroner, had appeared to say that there was a small quantity of arsenic in a *bottle* in the stable, which had been used as an emulsion for a pony. Later it was thought that she had been referring to sugar of lead. Kuroyanagi Junya, her *betto,* had been called at the inquest to clarify what drugs had been in use. In the spring of 1896, he said, Mrs Carew had given him a *white powder* to sprinkle on the fodder of a pony that had taken cold. In the autumn, Mrs Carew had put two or three drops of a *fluid* in a bucket of water for him to apply to a pony which had fever in the leg. He did not know the name of either medicine.

Asked for more specificity at the inquest, Edith had testified that sugar of lead had been purchased for the pony in the June or July for external application, to be dissolved in water, but had not been used afterwards as far as she knew. The fluid was Elliman's Embrocation. She was not asked about the powder.

Called at the trial, the *betto* said that the white powder had been wrapped in a small paper packet. In June or July, by Mrs Carew's orders, he had given the remainder to a pony. In the summer he had bought ten cents' worth of sugar of lead for a horse with white legs, which was lame. Half of it was left, and he used it up after his master's death. It was in the *betto's* possession throughout.

There was then almost certainly sugar of lead kept on some shelf in the stable. Remembering that there was never any evidence of purchase of white arsenic, could the white powder for the pony that had taken cold have been white arsenic? Schedel's evidence was the opportunity for some if not total refutation.

In 1895 and 1896 he had supplied powders of salicylic of soda to Mrs Carew for a dog and a small pony, both suffering from 'rheumatism'. He had also dispensed nitre and bicarbonate of potash for a pony, an ointment for a running sore at the side of a horse's mouth, and a bottle of Elliman's. There was no arsenic in any of these remedies.

Saturday, January 9th, was devoted to the coroner's formal proving of Edith Carew's statement at the inquest. The depositions on oath of a witness at an inquest are evidence against him should he be subsequently tried on a criminal charge, and the coroner's duty was to show forth that the prisoner had not been improperly compelled to answer questions. John Carey Hall chose to affirm, because taking an oath was contrary to his religious belief. He must have been a Quaker. Since the inquest, he had been transferred, and was now H.M. Consul at Hyogo and Osaka.

John Lowder must have been far from happy when printed copies of his client's first statement were distributed to the jury. The second, amending statement of November 4th was merely read aloud, and then the Court rose at noon.

Although Lowder was doing well with what might be termed the Maybrick defence of arsenic habituation, he must really have been despondent, even desperate, about Edith's prospects, because over the weekend he set in motion a singular course of events which damaged his reputation, affected the health of an innocent person, and curtailed the liberty of his own client. It cannot ever be wise to defend a good friend upon a capital charge.

That Sunday, January 10th, on John Frederic Lowder's private prosecution, Mary Jacob was arrested on the charge of murdering Walter Carew.

Shortly after 2pm, equipped with a warrant issued by the Consulate, George Hodges, the British constable and gaoler, proceeded to No. 2 the Bluff and removed the governess — who was nursing someone's baby when they arrived — to the gaol at the Consulate, where Edith was accommodated in a separate cell.

Miss Britain, Mary's protector, was an American citizen, and therefore Hodges was accompanied by Mr. R. Chance, Deputy Marshal of the U.S. Court, who held a document from the

American Consul-General, empowering the British official to make the arrest on the premises.

There was general consternation at this development. It is worth remarking that no barrister in the entire affair had the benefit of instructing solicitor. All on his own John Lowder had prepared his case, interviewed witnesses, and had conferences with his client. Another professional mind might have acted as a buffer, a restraining influence.

On Monday, January 11th, very early — at 8.45, with a large crowd in court — Lowder brought about the spectacle of the governess far from home and afraid, like a Brontë character, being charged before James Troup, Assistant Judge, with the murder of her employer.

Lowder appeared in person — not professionally, he said — at these magisterial proceedings, 'But simply as a member of this community who considers it to be his duty to prefer this charge.' Henry Charles Litchfield appeared to watch the case on behalf of the Crown. Mary Jacob was represented by Counsel, George Scidmore.

'May it please your honour...' Lowder began. It soon became apparent that he sought to show that the Annie Luke letters were the fabrication of Mary Jacob, in which case she stood self-accused of the murder — another of his dialectical conclusions.

It is an academic point that, by appearing in the case against Mary Jacob as a private person, Lowder was not instructed by Edith Carew to take this line. However, the two concurrent hearings merged as to their matter, and Edith must share the responsibility.

To establish his contention Lowder produced a couple of letters (see plates 18-21) in the undoubted handwriting of Mary Jacob and invited the Assistant Judge to compare them with the 'A.L.' letters.

In particular, he pointed to similarities between 'Lowder', 'Yokohama', 'ght', 'f', and 'er'. He is surely right when he says that 'A.L.' has difficulty in disguising her 'f's.

Continuing, Lowder stated that Rachel Greer was going to testify that on several occasions between August and October, 1896, she had seen Mary Jacob in the act of copying and practising Edith Carew's handwriting. 'Rachel, come here,' the governess had said to her. 'I want to show you something. See what

Mrs Carew does in mischief!'

Then the governess had pieced together two halves of an envelope, on which the spying Rachel Greer had seen her writing the previous evening, and the amah read the words:

Edith Dickinson. Edith Eason. Edith Carew.

She could not remember the proper order, and there might have been another name as well.

Then, Lowder continued, Rachel would state that the governess had said, 'She has written this to see which she loves the best. It is just like Mrs Carew's handwriting — it must be her writing — you must think it her writing. What fun it would be to show it to Mr Carew!'

Additionally, Lowder stated, 'I have a telegram in my possession relating to the character of the accused, which will probably render necessary the attendance of witnesses from home.' Of this information more later; suffice it to say that it may have sparked off the hounding of Mary Jacob.

'It might be argued,' he went on, 'that the accused was not acquainted with Annie Luke. On that, I would point out that there is nothing in the 'A.L.' letters alone to show that the writer was aware of Annie Luke. Annie Luke was the name attached by the deceased to the letters. 'A.L.' appeared on the card in his wife's letter to him.

'On the other hand it will be shown that the relations between the accused and the deceased were apparently of so intimate a nature that it is quite possible she may have heard the name of Annie Luke from him, or as she came from the same part of the country, it may be that she was acquainted with the name of Annie Luke or that she knew Annie herself before she left home. That is shortly the nature of the case I shall present to you.'

What is this, this poisonous imputation? How can he establish such a scandal? Conceivably, perhaps, the governess might have had a crush on Walter Carew, a dark, dominant, very masculine presence; might have been sexually disturbed by the erotic atmosphere generated by Edith Carew, but proof of an intimate relationship would seem to be a fanciful hope.

The committal proceedings were not the tribunal for a discussion of motive for murder, but what would be available for canvassing? Mental imbalance? Sexual jealousy?

Reginald Porch, fighting for his sister, identified Mary Jacob's birthday-book, which he had found on the children's toy box in the nursery on January 1st or 2nd. He said that he had taken it down to the dining-room, and upon opening it on January 8th, he had found inside a loose piece of paper:

M.J. M.J? 1888
a.L. A.L.
Dearest Walter
My own
D.D.D.D.
Jacob

John Lowder's proposition was that the birthday-book paper showed characters identical to those of the 'A.L.' letters, and that 'Dearest Walter' and 'My own' were an imitation of Edith Carew's handwriting.

Counsel for Mary Jacob objected strongly at this stage, when Lowder applied for a week's remand: 'I am busily occupied, as your Honour is aware, in the defence of Mrs Carew, whose case goes on from day to day.' The Assistant Judge supported him; the hearing was to resume the following morning, and Lowder hurried off to the other court, where Judge Mowat had taken his seat (rather late) on the sixth day of the trial. Because of the sensation caused by the arrest of the governess, there was a large attendance.

John Carey Hall was still proving the inquest evidence. Lowder indicated his desire to ask a question or two but discomposed perhaps, by the pressure of his double rôle he accidentally led the coroner into a new and embarrassing passage of independent evidence:

Lowder: 'Your suspicions on October 22nd were not aroused towards any particular individual?'

Coroner: 'I can answer that quite in the affirmative: I suspected Mrs Carew.'

Lowder: 'You suspected Mrs Carew?'

Coroner: 'Yes, for a reason that has not been stated.'

Lowder: 'For a reason stated to you by Dr Wheeler.'

Coroner: 'Not entirely by that.'

Lowder: 'Not entirely by that?'

Coroner: 'No.'

Lowder: 'Will you tell me how your suspicion had otherwise been aroused?'

Coroner: 'On the 17th, I had met Mrs Carew walking up apparently from the native town. [On that day, she had sent for half an ounce of Fowler's from Schedel's, and she had gone down town — the diary says 'taking Ben' — and bought some antipyrine from Maruya's]. When we met, myself and my wife were walking down towards the native town, and Mrs Carew was walking up towards the Settlement.

'I stopped Mrs Carew and spoke a few words to her about an entirely different matter, something about the lawn-tennis ground. I was very much impressed by Mrs Carew's manner. She seemed labouring under very strong mental excitement and was at that time very much preoccupied. At that time I put it down to anxiety about her husband's illness. I had just heard of it that morning

'But when Dr Wheeler made his communication to me it at once suggested an entirely different explanation to account for the singularity of Mrs Carew's behaviour at that time.'

Powerless during this vivid recital, Lowder's only recourse was to criticise the coroner for not taking Walter's dying depositions.

'I did not think he was then dying. I thought I should have been in time to save his life by hurrying him into the hospital.'

Hayashi Schichiro was Wilkinson's next witness, and something seemed to have happened to him since his two previous appearances in the witness-box. He was more awkward than before to question, through a Japanese interpreter, Mr Uchiyama, and this resistance to direct questioning, and use of ambiguity in reply, went beyond the restraints of his own culture.

The most vexing part of his testimony was an insistence that he had previously been mistaken, and that in fact there had been no purchase of poison at all on October 19th. On October *20th,* he now said, there had been *two* separate acquisitions of poison.

First of all, before noon, the unidentified foreign woman had bought Fowler's Solution and chloral, not sugar of lead — that had been another of his mistakes, he now said. She had paid $2.65 for

these two items on that day, which sum also covered the sugar of lead and chlorodyne taken on October 18th by a jinrikisha man bearing a chit with the name of Carew, together with antipyrine delivered to No. 169 the Bluff on October 8th. On the second occasion on the 20th, a jinrikisha man had taken the well-established Fowler's and bedpan paid for by Mary Jacob on the 24th.

Edith was thus, in a way, well-served. The chemist still failed to identify her as the foreign woman, and his evidence contradicted Mary Jacob's. Certainly her diary for the 20th states 'Went down town in the am.'

The prosecution naturally did not like the new version, and it made their previously strong witness appear unreliable. Lowder was not altogether pleased either, because the foreign woman of the 20th seemed to draw purchases of drugs more closely than before around the name of Carew.

At the request of the Crown there was no trial hearing on January 12th, when the Jacob committal occupied a full day. The courtroom was crowded. Edith had not been present at the first day's hearing, but this time, 'Shortly after nine o'clock, Mrs Carew was brought into court and later was called as a witness. She gave her evidence coolly and clearly and appeared to be in good spirits, although, as Mr Lowder afterwards stated, she had not then partaken of breakfast. Miss Jacob also appeared quite cheerful and evinced the keenest interest in the proceedings.'

George Scidmore asked if his client might be allowed to sit during the examination — 'It is quite trying for her to remain standing' — an important indication of the state of her health, which was to have certain consequences.

The constable and gaoler, George Hodges, gave details of the arrest and search of Mary Jacob's room, from where he had taken a box made of Miyanoshita woodwork, which was filled with letters and papers. John Lowder — who got into a lot of trouble with the Assistant Judge for having, with the permission of George Hodges, taken this box overnight to his room at Wright's Hotel and there perused the contents — tried not very successfully to show that the governess had papers in her possession which should not have been there.

In particular, Hodges swore that he had taken from Mary Jacob's room the letter from Strathalbyn dated October 1st, 1896, written by Mary's aunt to Edith about the possibility of Kate's coming to Japan. Edith was to say that it had never reached her hands, but it is the sort of letter which Edith might have given to Mary to keep, and it is also the sort of letter which Edith read and then tossed into her wastepaper-basket.

Lowder, not making any striking progress, moved on to the matter of the romantic novels, attempting to associate them with Mary Jacob rather than Edith Carew. Giving evidence, Edith said smoothly that the governess was fond of reading novels, and books were kept in the dining-room, easily accessible. Certainly she remembered Dickinson's lending her *The Playactress,* but she had merely glanced over it, and found that she had read it before. As for the chapter headed *The Lady in Black* (Lowder should have said *Lass*), 'The first time that chapter was recalled to my memory was when Mr Litchfield mentioned it in court at the Preliminary Examination.'

Did the governess read it? It would have been so easy to say that she had seen her glued to the book, but all she said was, 'I have no idea.'

Referring now to the 'A.L.' letters and their allusion to 'Twin Souls', Lowder handed Edith a book entitled *A Romance of Two Worlds,* by Marie Corelli, and established that it came from the shelf in the dining-room. He did not ask her if she had ever read it. It was risky to produce it at all and positively reckless of him to intone, as he did, some ornate passages which only too clearly recalled the oleaginous prose of the 'A.L.' letters.

'Azul looked tenderly upon me and said: "When thou hast slept the brief sleep of death, when thou art permitted to throw off for ever thy garb of clay, and when by thine own ceaseless love and longing thou hast won the right to pass the Great Circle, thou shalt find thyself in a land where the glories of the natural scenery alone shall overpower thee with joy — scenery that for ever changes into new wonders and greater beauty.

' "Thou shalt hear music such as thou canst not dream of. Thou shalt find friends, beyond all imagination fair and faithful.

Thou shalt read and see the history of all the planets, produced for thee in an ever-moving panorama. Thou shalt love and be loved for ever by thine own Twin Soul; wherever that spirit may be now, it must join thee hereafter. The joys of learning, memory, consciousness, sleep, waking and exercise shall all be thine. Sin, sorrow, pain, disease and death thou shalt know no more".

'I was full of a strange unhesitating courage, therefore I said fearlessly, "He is My Beloved one, Azul — My Twin Soul; and wilt thou let him fall away from thee when a word or sign might save him?"'

To be fair, in 1896 Marie Corelli was at the height of her fame, and her books sprouted everywhere — even in Yokohama. Both Oscar Wilde and Wilkie Collins liked *A Romance of Two Worlds* (1886), which is not so much a Gothic fantasy as an early specimen of science fiction. It is a nice conceit to imagine Edith's mind receiving its seductive images:

'There are your murderous women with large almond eyes, fair white hands, and voluptuous red lips....I took an antique silver goblet from the mantelpiece, filled it with the cool fluid, and was about to drink, when the cup was suddenly snatched from my hand ... "Do not drink that" he said, "you must not!"'

Finally, having himself raised the aspersion, Lowder dissociated Edith from it: 'Had you any reason from anything that came under your own observation to suspect any impropriety between the accused and your husband?'

Edith: 'Absolutely nothing.'

Chapter 13
THE CHRISTOFFEL LETTER

Edith braced herself for George Scidmore's cross-examination, which proved to be positively biographical, going into the details of her married life, the constitution of her household, and the acquiring of Mary Jacob's services. Really, it was a kind of extended fishing expedition. He did have a stab at showing Edith as a skilled forger of signatures, but she easily stonewalled him. When Walter was Acting Resident at Sungei Ujong, did she assist him in discharging his duties?

'I! Never!'

'Did you not do some writing for him?'

'Never.'

'His duties included particularly the issuance of orders in writing to subordinates under him?'

'All his orders were printed. He had to sign his name, certainly, but his orders were government orders, principally leases.'

'Did you ever, at any time, during his illness at his request or at his direction sign any order or orders in his name?'

'Which illness are you referring to?'

'During any illness.'

'No, not at all.'

Moving on, Scidmore probed the lineaments of the 'Mysterious Visitor', and Edith added a few more, perfectly consistent details. She was taller than Edith (who was 5ft 3¼ inches in height) and slight of build. It was impossible to estimate her age except that she was not very old. She was thickly veiled. Edith went up close to her when she handed over her card. It was an extremely wet afternoon, and at the best of times the hall was dim.

The woman gave the impression of a person in disguise. She probably wore a long cloak. She definitely wore gloves. Her clothing

was probably that of someone in easy circumstances.

Counsel: 'Did her general air and manner indicate to you her station in life? That is —'

Edith, interrupting: 'I quite understand. I should say she was a lady.'

'Did she seem easy and collected?'

'Perfectly … What struck me more than anything else was her great anxiety.'

Counsel: 'When she left the house, did you notice which direction she took?'

'The right leads to nowhere, only to the back. She must have turned to the left.'

Counsel: 'When she reached the main road, I mean.'

'I didn't see her leave the premises. I only saw her leave the front door.'

'Did you hear the noise of a jinrikisha or other vehicle previous to her arrival or after her departure?'

'No, it is not probable that I should have done on such a wet afternoon as that, and I was not thinking anything about it.'

Counsel: 'Was there anything in her manner, dress, or the tones of her voice that sounded or appeared familiar to you in any way?'

'No, nothing whatever. Absolutely nothing.'

'Did she appear to speak in her natural voice, or did it appear disguised?'

'As I didn't know her natural voice, I could not say if she was feigning or attempting to disguise her voice.'

'Her voice didn't strike you as being disguised?'

Edith: 'No, not at all.'

Scidmore has thus established that Mary Jacob cannot be the 'Mysterious Visitor'. He also establishes that the governess was in the nursery at the time when she called. As a matter of fact, Lowder is not saying that Mary Jacob is the 'Mysterious Visitor', because he knows that Edith would be thought to be able to recognise her, however disguised. Lowder's inability to link the governess with the 'Mysterious Visitor', going along as he does most seriously with the whole farrago, actually weakens his case.

After the court rose Scidmore proceeded to the judge in chambers — who was Judge Mowat — and obtained bail for his client in her own recognisances, with two sureties, W. Till and F.S. James.

The hearing was adjourned until the following day, January 13th, but it did not come on, because Lowder quietly obtained a remand until January 25th. In the judge's trial court on the 13th there was a large attendance, 'chiefly of loafers from the purlieus of Chinatown'.

Harry Vansittart Dickinson was called by the Crown — a wretched Youth, and, like Adelaide Bartlett's Revd George Dyson,[21] when the crunch came, a swain without loyalty. By now, passion had fled on both sides. There never was any real suspicion that Dickinson had been implicated, that he had egged Edith on while safely cricketing in Kobe, there to await tidings of death by telegram, but for a moment he must have felt terror whose assuagement made almost bearable the scandal and shame.

For the first time in court, openly and explicitly, coxcomb Dickinson was going to deny Edith — not their love but her truthfulness, and the effect was of a total betrayal of her. The Crown was determined to push to the hilt the point that Dickinson had been duped as to the true state of her marriage, and he eagerly jumped at every opportunity to repudiate her. In his state of outrage it was as if she had committed a crime against him. But to what end? No reason for such a masquerade was ever put forward.

The judge decided that Dickinson should read out his own stitched letters. It was a kind of punishment. Faltering and stumbling over the sewn-up joins, with the aid of a magnifying glass, he cut a sorry figure, but he was unrelenting in his disavowal of just about everything that Edith had told him about Walter:

'Mrs Carew told me that she was exceedingly unhappy, that her husband had ill-treated her in a great many different ways. I know it now to be all untrue.'

The day in court drew to a close, with Dickinson still floundering through his letters. Meanwhile the Minister, Sir Ernest Satow, was so concerned about the way that things were going in the lower court that, at midnight on the 13th he despatched to the Foreign Office from Tokyo an urgent telegram, which, deciphered, read:

Counsel for prisoner Edith Carew, while her trial is proceeding, has preferred before Troup charge of murder of Walter Raymond Hallowell Carew, against Mary Esther Jacob, an essential witness for the Crown, and has obtained remand till after trial of Edith Carew, rendering the giving of Jacob's evidence impossible. In order to prevent miscarriage, Crown Advocate recommends free pardon to Jacob, whom he believes entirely innocent. I concur in his recommendation. The matter is urgent. Patent of pardon of 1866 to Minister cannot be found.

John Lowder's motivation for proceeding against the governess had, with the remand, turned out to be more devious than a mere shifting of the blame. His actions raise the question of what exactly it was that Mary Jacob knew and could say — the presumption is that there was something new, and very incriminating.

The Foreign Office asked the Home Office to advise, and there was a frantic exchange of memoranda. The idea of Mary Jacob's having a free pardon 'in order to give her a free mouth' seemed to the Home Office to be 'a most dangerous expedient'. It was suggested that 'if such a course be adopted, H.O. should have nothing to do with it, and that it should not be adopted before other alternatives are exhausted'.

For example, 'Could not Mrs Carew's trial be postponed till after the charge against Miss Jacob is disposed of?' or, 'Could not a *nolle prosequi* be entered as regards the latter charge or would this prevent subsequent proceedings against Miss Jacob as effectually as a free pardon?'

Anyway, 'The course to be pursued depends on the procedure obligatory in Japan, of which H.O. knows nothing'. Therefore, 'Say to F.O. that it appears to Secretary of State impossible under the circumstances stated to advise the grant of a free pardon to Miss Jacob'.

The Foreign Office had managed to unearth the original draft of the lost Letters Patent of 1866, preserved in the office of the Clerk of the Crown in Chancery, but it showed that the sole power thereby conferred on Her Majesty's Minister and Consul General was that of pardoning offenders *actually convicted* in the Supreme Consular Court.

There the matter rested for the time being, and on January 14th Dickinson's ordeal continued. A good hour was spent on the comical topic of the telegram and the Minister of Ways and Communications. On October 21st Edith had sent a telegram to Dickinson in Kobe, which he had not kept. The Crown attached huge importance to it, because if Dickinson's memory of it was correct it caught Edith out in a dastardly lie. That at any rate was the allegation.

According to Dickinson, it read: *'When do you return Baelz says most serious'*. Dr. Baelz, of course, had *not* been to see Walter. According to Lowder, it read, or should have read, *'When do you return have sent Baelz most serious.'*

The Crown had made strenuous diplomatic efforts to obtain a copy of the telegram, but the Japanese Minister of Ways had refused to release it, and there was no power to serve a subpoena on him.

Then there was the embarrassing admission through Wilkinson, at Lowder's request, that Edith had never applied to Charles Litchfield upon the subject of divorce, although she had led Dickinson, as his letters show, to believe that she had so consulted him. In this way the jury did not have to see Litchfield in the witness-box, solemnly exposing another dastardly lie. What then is the significance of *'Saw Mr L.'* in the diary, on October 8th? Is it possible that Edith let Dickinson see her diary? Or did she go to Litchfield, who *was* her lawyer, on other business?

Lowder forced Dickinson to spell out his position as to marriage:

'Was that advice [on divorce] given with the ultimate view of a marriage between yourself and Mrs Carew?'

'No, it was given because I thought, or had been led to believe by Mrs Carew, of the existence of such cruelty that it was positively unsafe to leave her with him.'

Counsel: 'You have stated that already. A marriage between you and herself was never alluded to in any way, shape or form?'

'No.'

'You were not, I believe, in a position to marry?'

'No.'

The Judge: 'Pecuniarily?'

Counsel: 'I mean in reference to his position in the bank. You would lose your position in the bank?'

Dickinson: 'Not necessarily. It is an understood thing. No one under the rank of an accountant can marry without permission.'

'And that permission is only given in the event of your having sufficient means to marry on?'

'Yes; permission would certainly be refused unless that was the case.'

Counsel: 'Was that known to Mrs Carew? Had you informed her of that at any time?'

Dickinson: 'It is not in my recollection, but I presume it was known to her. It is generally known.'

Dickinson's evidence confirmed that Edith had spoken of the 'Mysterious Visitor' on the actual day of her supposed visit. She had mentioned the caller to him at the boathouse on Regatta Day, October 10th. Further, on October 12th Dickinson had written to Edith, 'I should think you might ask for the letter. I should do so without hesitation. Ask L. if you like, but I should go and do it. I see the usual signal. I could also look in after tiffin perhaps, though I am not certain *re* this. I should go and ask for the letter taking care however no strangers are near you.'

Dickinson explained that Edith had told him that Walter had written to someone care of the Post Office. He had addressed his letter to 'A.L. and M.J.' Edith had said that she wanted to get hold of that letter, and she wanted to know if she *could* get it. She did not say why she wanted it. By 'strangers' Dickinson meant the addressees, 'A.L. and M.J.'

It was left to Lowder to elicit that Edith had told Dickinson that she had not obtained the letter. There was a letter in evidence — 'I feel greatly distressed about you, and ever since I got your card last Saturday have been endeavouring to find you' — but it was dated October 14th, and it was addressed to 'Miss Annie Luke'. Finally, Edith had seemed quite dazed when he saw her on his return from Kobe, the day after Walter's death.

Dickinson shambled off, and Elsa Christoffel took his place. When Wilkinson asked her, 'Have you been a friend of Miss Jacob?' she burst into tears. Lowder in cross-examination was not going to be very nice to her. Why had she held on to some Dickinson letters before giving them up? *'Because I thought they were too incriminating'.'*

Suddenly Lowder produced yet another anonymous letter, which by some process had reached his hands, and got Elsa to admit that it was all her own work. Labile after her tears, her face was wreathed in inappropriate smiles as she obediently read it out:

> *'Why o why will you go down that hill tonight ** for your own sake ** keep away from that place **laugh** call this the produce of a madwoman I daresay she has gone mad or she would not humiliate herself down to the very dust before a man I was alone my friend shall never know anything about this.*
>
> *Sunday night.'*

It emerged that Elsa had written this peculiar piece of gibberish on October 25th. One would have thought that the fright of Walter's death would have inhibited this sort of thing. It was sent to a 'gentleman, a member of this community', at the Yokohama United Club, and the friend was Mary Jacob.

Although the judge hoped and supposed that nothing turned on the contents of the letter, it is strange that the climate of the community had thrown up another anonymous letter-writer. The words are more deranged than cryptic. Clearly, frustrated Eros is at work somewhere. Lowder had a special use for the letter. 'I am not suggesting that this witness wrote the "A.L." letters; that is not the object.' How can he, when everyone knows that in another place he has named Mary Jacob as 'A.L.'?

'I show the witness,' he went on, 'an exhibit which is one of the Annie Luke letters, the letter addressed to Mr Hall, and ask you to look at the capital letter 'I' throughout that letter. Do you think it is a good imitation of your handwriting?'

'Yes,' Elsa replied, artlessly, perhaps. 'I think it is a very good imitation of my handwriting, but mine was written on October 25th'. [As against October 29th].

Judge: 'It need not be an imitation of that letter because it was written first.'

Into what fantastic realm was John Lowder straying: that Mary Jacob deliberately imitated her good friend's handwriting while perpetrating the 'A.L.' letters? Odder, really, is the similarity of *style* between Elsa's letter and the 'A.L.' letters. Elsa's words: '...call this the produce of a madwoman', may be compared with the 'A.L.' letter to the coroner: 'The world will call me mad'.

On the ninth day of the trial, January 15th, Lowder was still cross-examining Elsa Christoffel, thoroughly but gingerly since she was obviously unpredictable:

'Did Mary Jacob then conceive an admiration for the gentleman to whom you wrote this letter?'

'The contrary; she greatly disliked him.' [But did *Elsa* greatly like him?]

'And why,' asked Lowder, 'did you think it necessary to tell him that your friend should never know?'

Elsa's marked hesitation in replying seems to indicate a complex of emotions: 'That refers more to myself. I did not want to let my friend know that I had written to a man I did not know, of whom I did not know his past or present or anything about him.'

Counsel: 'Were you in the habit of writing anonymous letters?'

'No, this was the first one.'

Hiram Wilkinson, re-examining, and asking to see the letter, decided to rehabilitate his witness by asking a few plain questions. To whom was it written? *To Mr Norman Walter* — who figures quite frequently in the diary.

The hill that he was not to go down was, of course, the Bluff. Elsa had seen Norman Walter going down to No. 169 at 10pm on October 25th, when she was herself delivering a note from Mary Jacob to Mrs Carew. Did Elsa feel as if she were indeed going mad at that time, Counsel asked, rather as if he had abandoned her.

'I felt that I was doing a thing I hardly could believe I could do.'

And there they left the Swiss governess, who had certainly made an impression of mental disturbance.

On Monday, January 18th, the tenth day of the trial, even after the weekend's rest, Edith's face was drawn and haggard, and once or twice she shed quiet tears, but she was not too upset to pass frequent notes to her Counsel.

John Lowder introduced a tone of dissent. He objected very strongly to the Crown's proposed calling of additional witnesses without full notice, and complained that the case was being unnecessarily expanded. He could talk, with his own Mary Jacob case! In this way he kept out some evidence by Mrs Tocque, who must have been missing her spooning trips with Walter Carew, and thwarted the calling of Norman Walter. This is a pity. He might have had some interesting things to say. The judge became restive, 'Is there much more of this?' as Counsel cited cases about additional evidence.

The Crown particularly wished to call the late evidence of a very substantial witness, the most important personage in the courtroom, who had been sitting beside the judge. This was Sir Ernest Mason Satow (1843-1929) Envoy Extraordinary and Minister Plenipotentiary in Japan, who had already taken a secret part in the proceedings against Edith Carew.

Satow was an extremely distinguished diplomat, Japanologist and linguist. He was a man of adventure, stern-faced, had seen horrors, and feared the sharp sword of the assassin. In later years he brought back to Ottery St Mary a Japanese wife.

Lowder objected to the proposal that Satow should testify about a certain letter which he had received, and under pressure the judge allowed Sir Ernest to prove only formal receipt of the letter. It was an embarrassing débacle, entirely the fault of the prosecution, who had held the letter for some time without putting the defence on notice. Hopefully, Wilkinson called William Benjamin Mason, deputed by the Crown as their handwriting expert. Lowder was committed to resisting the proposition that the 'A.L.' letters were in his client's handwriting, and he objected that he had had no notice of such evidence, nor had it been opened.

Feigning, perhaps, innocent surprise, Wilkinson argued that he *had* intimated that the handwriting would be examined: 'Do you *really* object?' By now a fully engaged and delving judge, Mowat put in:

'It didn't imply that you would call an expert.'

Wilkinson: 'It *would* imply that I would call witnesses, my Lord.'

Judge: 'Not necessarily. It might mean that you would leave the jury to make the comparison. Is he an expert?'

Wilkinson: 'He is an expert.'

The judge, in spite of this assurance, was determined to examine the competency of the submitted expert. He seemed to be opposed to the whole idea: 'In the absence of any professional experts, I think the jury is as able to form an opinion as anyone.'

Wilkinson, struggling: 'I hope to satisfy your lordship of his right to be called an expert.'

Lowder: 'It is not just and fair that I should be stopped in the middle of a case with this question to be decided.'

Mason was called. The atmosphere in the courtroom was jagged with contention, and he could expect to have a bad experience, which was a shame, because he was actually a very nice man. It so happens that he has another place in Anglo-Japanese history: he was a close friend of Lafcadio Hearn. He lived in Yokohama with his Japanese wife and their two sons, and he will not have been on visiting terms with any of the protagonists in the Carew case, but they knew who he was, never fear!

Wilkinson extracted his credentials. A British subject, Mason had been employed for seven years in the British Postal Telegraph Department, and for 16 years he had been employed by the Japanese Government in the same capacity. He was at present an instructor in English at the Japanese Higher Middle School, and for three to four years he had taught handwriting to Japanese students. For many years he had made a private study of the peculiarities of handwriting, and was practised in making comparisons. So far so good, but Lowder was waiting. If he genuinely had not expected Mason to be put up, his extempore cross-examination was clever, funny, unconventional and rather bad form:

'You are Chess Editor of the *Japan Mail*, are you not?'

'Not at present.'

Undeterred, a minor setback, Lowder rode on:

'You have been?'

'I have been.'

'Do you remember during a whole year when you were Chess Editor, receiving correct solutions of problems that were published weekly, from a certain person signing himself Scacchi? You told me, did you not, that the handwriting puzzled you, and that until I denied it you thought *I* was the solver of those problems?'

Wilkinson, amusingly, when he asked Mason if he had ever found out who Scacchi was, got the reply: '*His lordship now sitting on the Bench!*'

15 Sir Ernest Mason Satow, British Government Minister in Japan.

16 British Consulate, Yokohama, where the trial took place.

163

1896 31 Days **10 SATURDAY** [284-82] [10] **October**

Oxford Michaelmas Term begins

Got up at 5. I find it pouring. So went to bed again. It rained hard until 3. o'c. Most disappointing weather for the Regatta, which was held however in spite of the rain. As I never take any interest in it myself, it didn't upset me very much. Had a curious & mysterious visitor shortly after tiffin. Who called to see Walter. I went down to the Boat House about 3. & walked home about 5. as it cleared. Walter doesn't seem too well, & I wish he could get a thoro' change. I suppose it is the damp. I saw Dr. Wheeler at the Boat House. He gave me a prescription for my malaria.

17 Diary, October 10th: the 'Mysterious Visitor'.

I *must* see you. why have you done nothing
since you got my two cards. or perhaps
she never let you get them. I cannot meet
her again. she makes me mad. when
I think of what I might have done for you.
I cannot give you any address. I am living
wherever I can find shelter. but you can find
and help me if you will. as I know you
will for the sake of old times. "*Annie*"

18 Letter from 'Annie' to Walter Carew.

I feel greatly distressed
about you & ever since I got
your card last Saturday have
been endeavouring to find you.
I *wish* to & *will* help you if I
can only find you. Meet me
this evening at *5.30 p.m.* on the
Bund opposite the Club Hotel –
Wednesday 14th Oct W.

19 Letter said to be from Walter to 'Miss Annie Luke'.

us electrify Japan. (2)
I have never professed to be a good woman, but for the sake of a few lines I do not see why I should let a silly innocent woman be condemned for what she knows nothing about. and for what she never will know anything about and for which when you get this no one on this earth could enlighten her. She is a silly fool otherwise she would not have treated the last 2 weeks as she has done. By the time you get this I shall be well on my "way" (?) to join him. my twin soul. You may call this what you like. but I think deep-down in my heart I write

20 Letter (*extract*) from 'A. L.' to John Lowder, Edith's Counsel.

to C
Exhibit: Jany 11. 1897 A.W.W.
No 3 1/4 No 2 1897 15.1. com.

Bluff.
Sunday Oct 25.

Dear Mrs Carew -
In reply to the
note I received through
Mr Lowder this evening -
I regard my engagement
in your employ to be at
an end - If you have
any questions to ask me -
please do so through Mr
Lowder, your lawyer -
In respect to the message
you sent me by Mr Lowder
this afternoon - asking
me to take your children

21 Mary Jacob's handwriting.

22 Edith, chastened.

23 Strathalbyn, Baltonsborough: Mary Jacob's home.

24 Robert Bagehot Porch, schoolmaster at Malvern: one of Edith's brothers.

25 Penfeidr, later Troed-y-Rhiw, Edith's last home.

26 Edith at the cove.

27 Walter's grave, Tennysonian in Yokohama.

The judge ruled that Mason *was* competent to give expert testimony. The admissibility of his evidence was still an issue, but a compromise was reached; Mason would not opine as to new matters not yet before the court. Lowder claimed that that had been the meaning of his objection all along.

With trepidation, certainly, for Wilkinson complained that, 'It is impossible for my learned friend and I to agree in this case', the Crown put in Edith's diary. Lowder raised no objection at all; indeed, the diary bears a note, written and signed by J.F. Lowder: 'This Diary was obtained through Mr Porch from Mrs Carew's house on Saturday, the 28th November, and handed to me on the same day.' Having studied the entries minutely, Lowder will have surrendered the diary to the prosecution, and extracts would be read out in open court later.

Mason was brought back to give his evidence proper, but the judge still held a fixed belief that the jury were just as competent as the deputed expert, and inelegant exchanges with Counsel were creeping in:

'Don't you think the jury might be left to find similarities for themselves?'

Wilkinson: 'I think not, my Lord.'

Judge Mowat, petulant: 'Then I don't see when this will end.'

Wilkinson: 'I am sorry, my Lord. It is not any particular pleasure to me to pursue this course, but it is necessary. The process may be slow, but I shall not consider that I have done my duty unless I continue in this way.'

The judge, climbing down: 'I am not complaining about the slowness.'

Photographs of the 'A.L.' letters were handed to the jury, and William Mason delivered his opinions. Edith Carew's handwriting showed characteristic capitals, particularly C,P,D,M,R,H, and T, and characteristic small letters, particularly a,b,d,f,h, and e. Her punctuation was very distinctive, with periods or marks scarcely distinguishable from full stops and short dashes.

Mary Jacob's handwriting had few special characteristics. The letter f was abnormally formed. She was not the writer of the 'A.L.' letters. Elsa Christoffel's handwriting was characterised by its badness, and she was certainly not the writer of the 'A.L.' letters.

The 'A.L.' letters were not intended as imitations; they were simply disguised. There were more of the characteristics of Edith Carew's handwriting in the 'A.L.' letters. The punctuation in the diary and the 'A.L.' letters was similar.

The long afternoon was ending, and, safely tucked away in Miss Britain's house on the Bluff, not venturing out, Mary Jacob was waiting anxiously for news.

Chapter 14
LIGHTER THAN DUST

Mere pawns can only play the game if they are made of ivory. Mary Jacob was flesh and blood indeed, and she had taken to her bed, with outward symptoms which revealed her state of inner distress. It is most unlikely that anyone in real authority had told her that she was going to be all right. Miss Britain had called in an American doctor, a medical missionary of the Methodist Episcopal Church, graduate of the Syracuse University, New York. This was Dr Whiting Sweeting Worden, who had been concerned about the governess, and had seen her six times between January 15th and 19th. The worst symptoms were a very severe headache and a pulse rate of 110.

The illness had not been anticipated, and it changed things subtly. On the morning of Tuesday, January 19th, the eleventh day of the trial, Hiram Wilkinson, proceeding as if there were no other impediment than disability upon Mary Jacob's attendance, made an application for her depositions taken at the lower court to be read out under Rule 294 of the appropriate Order in Council. To that end, he called Dr Worden to testify that she was unfit to give evidence.

John Lowder was taken by surprise. Wilkinson had not warned him that he was going to make such an application, which is an indication of how strained relations had become. However Lowder knew that, even if he had by guile prevented the governess from testifying (as was the Establishment view of his actions), he would be quite unable to keep out her depositions. Anyway, the jury had already read every word of her previous evidence in the newspapers. It was what she might say in the future that he feared, so he kept quiet.

Judge Mowat: 'I am a little embarrassed, Mr Lowder, by your

not putting any question. I do not know the ground you mean to take if you take any ground. Do you resist the application that her evidence should be read? '

Lowder: 'I have had no notice of the application and I am just reading the Order in Council. I have had no time to consider it.'

Bluffing (for he knew their content only too well), Lowder complained that he had not had time to consider the depositions, and that he should have had written notice. Wilkinson was irritated: 'I protest against such an assertion. I intended to call the witness if possible and I had to take the other alternative. There was no necessity for any notice whatever.'

The judge temporised — the witness might be able to attend on a later day. A second independent medical opinion should be sought. Her evidence was material to both sides, and Defence Counsel would no doubt like to cross-examine her.

Lowder: *'My Lord, if you ask me, I am in a peculiar position with regard to this witness.'*

Judge: *'Then perhaps I had better not ask you.'*

Lowder: 'It is for that reason that I am not speaking at all, but leave the matter to the Court. It is for this reason that I shall not insist upon any right that I may have.'

Judge: 'It seems to me she should be called in the interests of both sides, and she may be called during the case for the defence.'

Lowder: 'I make no answer upon that point.'

After that interesting exchange of veiled threat and manipulation, upon strong representation by Wilkinson the judge reversed his decision, and allowed him to call Mrs Tocque, wife of Captain Charles Henry Stuart Tocque, to prove receipt of an entry in her chit-book: 'Very many thanks. Much about the same. *Dr Baelz comes again this evening.* E.H.C.' Lowder did not cross-examine.

William Mason was back in court after tiffin, by special permission of the Japanese Government. He caused a mild furore by innocently referring to the letter to Sir Ernest Satow, which had not been admitted, obviously considering it as an anonymous letter from Edith Carew. Lowder was very angry.

Judge: 'I think he went on without knowing he was wrong.'

Lowder: 'He should be taught.'

On the twelfth day of trial Dr Whiting Sweeting Worden was back to report that in the interim he had seen Mary Jacob three times, and that she was still too ill to attend court, with a severe headache and a pulse rate of 118.

Dr William Bryce Orme, London qualified and surgeon of the P&O steamship *Formosa,* had been prevailed upon to give a second opinion, and he had found the pulse to be 116, while the heart was beating at 132. He would infer, he said, that the heart was in a very weak condition, because 16 beats to the minute were not reaching the pulse.

In fact, then, the governess will have been feeling very unwell, and the abnormal heartbeat and pulse probably indicate the presence of the frightening symptom known as atrial flutter, when a bird with wingbeats seems to burst from the chest. Dehydration from vomiting, which was soon to occur, would have exacerbated the condition. It is also quite probable that there was an underlying cardiac or thyroid pathology.

Encouraged by his success in changing the judge's mind over Mrs Tocque, Wilkinson now came back at him about the disallowed letter to Sir Ernest Satow, and caused him to reverse his ruling, against bitter protest from John Lowder. It read:

Dear Sir,

I wish to call your attention to the very scandalous way in which our Consul Mr Hall has conducted the inquest of the late Mr Carew. Had he any right to sum up in face of evidence produced as he has done?

Faithfully yours,

6th November *A.L. Price.*

The point was that there was, according to the Crown, no such person resident in Yokohama. Robert Cecil Day Guinness, of the Hong Kong and Shanghai Bank was used to prove that only two Prices had business at the bank: Alexander Price of Hankow, and the Hon. J.F. Price of Bombay. William Mason, a little prickly, was brought back to opine that Mrs Carew, with scarcely any attempt at disguise, was the writer of the Satow letter and its envelope. 'Mr

Price' in the diary for July 16th was — said Mason — in similar handwriting.

Unexpectedly, after all the fuss that he had made, Lowder conceded: 'I may say I do not contend it is not in the handwriting of the accused if it will save the time of the Court.'

Mrs Priscilla Ellis, a British subject, who lived at Miss Britain's house with her husband, Harcourt Whipple Ellis, had two picturesque anecdotes to contribute to the proceedings.

On November 10th, she had been sitting on the front verandah at No. 2, the Bluff with Mary Jacob when Reginald Porch had come to deliver to the governess the letter from Edith which began — 'I hope for the sake of Edgarley.' Then, 'Miss Jacob stepped inside the hall, opened the note and read it, and Mr Porch and she proceeded to the sitting-room, where they had a conversation....I passed into the hall, and saw Mr Porch sitting in a chair with his head in his hands and his elbows on his knees.'

For some time Mary Jacob had been sleeping in Mrs Ellis' room, which was directly underneath Mary's room. On the night of November 12th, when she was due to give evidence the next day at the magisterial hearing, she had retired early at about eight o'clock. At around ten o'clock she started up and said, 'Oh! someone has gone up to my room.'

Mrs Ellis herself heard someone pass quickly up the stairs into Mary's room. It would seem therefore that the governess had very good reason for fearing the darkness of her own room. No one had any right or purpose to go there at that hour, and upon later enquiry the intruder was not found. It was another 'Mysterious Visitor'.

At Wilkinson's request, the Clerk of the Court read out the uncompleted evidence given by Edith Carew during the adjourned Jacob case, and also the complete diary entries for the dates October 10th to 21st. The names and incidents will have been greatly enjoyed by the British community. On the thirteenth day of the trial, January 21st, Mary Jacob was still conspicuously absent, and Dr Worden was called upon again. His patient was decidedly worse. Her pulse was 130, and vomiting had supervened. He thought that it would be weeks, possibly months, before she would be well enough to leave the house. It was a disordered mental and nervous condition. Lowder, unsympathetic, asked if the symptoms were hysterical (and he intended the clinical meaning).

Dr Worden: 'The symptoms might indicate hysteria, or they might indicate something worse.' Dr Orme had steamed away out of port, so that no second opinion was available, and Wilkinson tried again to get in Mary Jacob's depositions. Lowder did some more bluffing and bargaining, but he could not prevail, and the governess' evidence at the inquest was also read. Copies of all her evidence were printed and distributed to the jury, and thus impressed deeply into their minds.

The case for the Crown was closed, and Lowder was allowed the next day off, to prepare his opening speech. He was an embattled man. None involved in court was ignorant of what he had set on against the governess, and there was disapproval.

He had indeed for the sake of his friend placed himself in a peculiar position: while still committed as a private individual to the proposition that Mary Jacob was Annie Luke, and thus by definition the killer — in itself an unsafe presumption — he was professionally bound in the higher court upon his client's own assertions to explore the possibilities of the 'Maybrick defence' of arsenic-eating.

His powerful speech, ornamented with the rhetoric of the time, was brave and confident. He had worked long hours at the preparation of the medical part of his case, and he was going to use to full advantage the three doctors whom he had rallied to refute Dr Divers' opinions. Leaning by implication rather than direct imputation towards Mary Jacob's guilt, he was seeking to establish that there could have been one single fatal dose of solid white arsenic. The sugar of lead, he argued, was always, clearly, for Walter Carew's own needs.

As for his client's conduct, could she not if guilty have slipped down to town and sent the first urchin she met into Maruya's with an order for arsenic under an assumed name? Indeed, if the prosecution were right in thinking that she was the writer of the 'A.L.' letters, would she not have used the same disguised hand? Was she really such a bungler that not one of the array of bottles was without an order in her own handwriting? (Always a risky sort of point, this!)

He regretted his resistance to the Satow letter. He had not been instructed. Driven to distraction by the coroner's partial summing-up, and thinking that a complaint from a disinterested party would carry more weight, his client had chosen for the signature to her letter the name of a great friend of hers, who did not happen to be in Japan at that time. Anyway, her disguised hand was so poor as to show that it was impossible for her to have written the 'A.L.' letters.

Unwisely, he read to the jury the coroner's summing-up, to demonstrate the unfair bias. Perhaps the word 'again' was inadvertently put into the Tocque chit-book. No husband was more complaisant than Walter Carew. Harry Dickinson was merely one of a series. The letters from Miyanoshita showed that affection had not died. And here Counsel permitted himself some masculine chauvinistic characterisation:

> *Quid levior pluma? Pulvis.*
> *Quid pulvere? Ventus.*
> *Quid vento? Mulier.*
> *Quid muliere? Nihil.*

With exquisite lack of tact, he explained for the benefit of those who had left school before him that these lines meant:

> *What is lighter than a feather? Dust.*
> *What lighter than dust? Wind.*
> *What lighter than wind? Woman.*
> *What lighter than woman? Nothing.*

How could an affectionate wife pass all at once from October 10th — as seemed to be the theory of the Crown — into the appalling wickedness of a Borgia? Such a thing was not possible.

The *Epsilon* letter was a document which had been stolen from her, and in repossessing it she was thinking only of her own shame. Until the production of the Dickinson letters her name, so far as the public were concerned, was untarnished. Her shame was to be read one day perhaps by the children in whose name she had so pathetically appealed, and appealed in vain, to the cruel Mary Jacob.

All the letters addressed by his client to Mary Jacob, as well as her own and her brother's visits to that person, were with reference to the suppression of those letters alone. If she had been a calculating murderer she would not have acted so impulsively. The real reason, Lowder suggested, why the 'two pilfering thieves, Jacob and Christoffel', stitched together the Dickinson letters was to use them against Mrs Carew: to serve as a weapon of defence *if and when she should discover the true relations between Jacob and Walter Carew.* That was why, to injure Mrs Carew, Jacob had falsely alleged that her mistress had been down town on October 19th. Counsel would show (but he did not) that Jacob paid Ah Kwong to raid the wastepaper-basket.

Lowder's speech occupied the entire Saturday morning. In the afternoon the jury toured No. 169 the Bluff, and inspected the various shelves and cabinets which had held medicine bottles. A bed, a washstand, and a chair or two had been taken down to the gaol for Edith, but the matrimonial bed was still in its place.

On Sunday, January 24th, Miss Harriet Britain wrote a letter to Mary's aunt, at home in Baltonsborough:

Dear Madam,

Your dear niece, Miss Mary E. Jacob, wishes me to write to you, but it is a most difficult task, for how can I explain to you what both she, poor girl, and all who take an interest in her have suffered in her behalf. First let me explain who I am. For many years I have been a missionary in Africa, India and Japan, and at last, feeling too old for any more such active service, I opened a boarding-house for missionaries and other Christians in this city, and my house is well known as a Christian home. My health not being very good, I do not go out much, therefore do not mingle at all with the so-called society people here, my home duties sufficiently occupying my time.

Therefore, till the account of Mr Carew's death with all the attendant circumstances came out in newspapers, I had never heard the name either of Mrs Carew or of Miss Jacob. Then Miss Jacob came to board here pending the trial as her evidence was supposed to be of the greatest importance. All in the home came to like her and to take the greatest interest in her, but never dreaming that there could be the slightest suspicion against her until we were all startled by her arrest.

The whole city was thunderstruck and everyone believes that it was to prevent Miss Jacob giving her evidence, which she was to have done the very next day. As soon as it was known in the city, several gentlemen who had never seen or known Miss Jacob before immediately came forward and offered any amount of bail, and she was brought back to my house, but, I am sorry to say, poor girl, so broken down that she has been ill ever since, having two doctors to attend her.

She has the interest, the pity and sympathy of the whole community. The house is besieged by enquiries about her health, gifts of flowers, fruit, etc., etc. But it is such a pity that at present she cannot rally sufficiently to be able to give her evidence, as that is felt to be so very important. She has felt so terribly concerned about the trouble and grief that this will have inflicted upon you and her uncle and I think the greatest help you can give her now is for you and her uncle and any of her friends to write her kind, loving letters.

She will want for nothing that money can supply for I have never seen a whole community roused as this has been and money has been subscribed for everything she may need, and after this trial is over if a prosecution can be brought for false imprisonment it will be done and money will be raised in her behalf. Rest assured that everything that can be will be for her health, comfort and happiness.

Yours in Christian sympathy,

Harriet G. Britain.

P.S. Tuesday 26th. A telegram came to Mr Dunlop the other day. How we have not found out, nor exactly who from, only from her friends we heard, saying to get her the best counsel and everything she needed. She is very anxious to know who it is from.'

On the Monday morning, January 25th, before he finished his elaborate speech, John Lowder had a prior engagement in the other court — the set date for the remanded Jacob hearing. The governess was still absent, and Dr Worden testified again to her incapacity. Her Counsel asked for the charge to be dismissed.

Lowder: 'I only wish to say that the application seems to be very premature, considering that the evidence to be placed before your Honour is not yet before you, and you are hardly in a position to say what it will be.'

James Troup: 'I presume you propose to call evidence to connect the accused with the circumstances of the death. Otherwise I should have to rule that Mr Scidmore's application was correct. You cannot connect her by those letters alone.'

Lowder: 'I have other evidence besides that.'

The assistant judge could not resist Lowder, and adjourned the hearing until Friday, February 5th.

Back at the trial court, after a few final flourishes to his speech, Lowder began to call his witnesses. Louis Jephson, who was sworn in the Jewish manner, wearing his hat, was the forerunner of a train of 'Maybrick defence' supporters. Over tiffin at the Club, Walter Carew had boasted, 'Arsenic? Why, I have taken tons of it.'

Dr Stuart Eldridge, Lowder's principal medical adviser, stated that he was an American citizen, previously Associate Professor of Anatomy at the University of Georgetown, Washington. He thought that Walter's symptoms, considered as a whole, might have been due to almost any form of irritant poisoning, even that caused by bad food such as oysters. The kidneys should have been microscopically examined. He himself had prescribed 90 drops of Fowler's per day.

Dr Eldridge disapproved strongly of Dr Divers' estimate of lead present in the organs; it should have been weighed. It was almost impossible to say if arsenic or lead or both had caused death. Determined suicides *do* often choose a painful form of dying. He himself knew of an educated druggist who killed himself by means of strychnine. Death from one dose of white arsenic was possible. So also from lead.

Lowder: 'Dr Divers has stated that the absence of gastritis pointed to death being due to arsenical poisoning?'

Dr Eldridge: 'I cannot agree with that. Gastritis occurs in a large proportion of cases of arsenical poisoning.'

Judge (on the ball, and with his nose in a book): 'I see that it was so stated in the Maybrick case. The defence there was that the death was due to gastritis, and not arsenical poisoning.'

Lowder: 'These questions are taken from that case, my Lord.'

Dr Eldridge made a very important point about the specks of white arsenic: if there had been crystallization from Fowler's Solution *it would probably have been in another form of arsenic, not solid white arsenic.* Dr Divers had been made to appear too rigid, too definite, and the prosecution was slightly dented.

Edith looked very fragile on January 26th, having grown strikingly thinner during the previous few days. Dr George Robert Moore Graham had been brought from Kobe to attest that he was the surgeon on the SS *Portosi* in 1880 who had treated Walter for congestion of the liver, jaundice and malaria: he had refused quinine, and called arsenic his stock remedy. It was not a heavy dose.

The learned judge was beginning to get plaintive again. He did not, he said, want the trial to degenerate into a contest between doctors on small points. Wilkinson, preparing to have a go at Dr Eldridge: 'I will bear that in mind, my Lord.'

Dr Eldridge, unshaken, was replaced by Dr Baelz, who was notably more forthcoming than when called by the Crown, and he too said that the symptoms as a whole were not so distinctly specific as to indicate arsenical poisoning. The kidneys should have been examined. In acute arsenical poisoning it was impossible to determine the number of doses. The symptoms could have been caused by one dose of white arsenic.

According to Dr Wheeler, Walter's stools had been darkish green. Dr Baelz informed the Court that the stools in arsenic poisoning were often like the rice-water stools of cholera. There was no characteristic colour. In a drawn point Wilkinson, however, extracted the concession that the stools in arsenic poisoning might be greenish, due to bile.

Dr Neil Gordon Munro, stricture specialist, caused a burst of childish laughter in a generally grim-faced courtroom by saying that it would be impossible to disguise the taste of lead unless it was taken in a bucketful of liquid. He still knew of no medical authority for prescribing arsenic for stricture, he told Wilkinson. In calling Dr Munro, Lowder had decided to risk this important question for the sake of Dr Munro's endorsement of Dr Baelz's opinions.

By way of a small triumph, on January 27th Lowder produced Robert John Ward, who had actually given Walter Carew some Fowler's Solution. It had been at either the spring or autumn race meeting in 1895, when Walter had called him to one side and said that he had heard he was a good hand at doctoring dogs. Some days after, Ward had prescribed for the ailing dog, giving some Fowler's out of his own stock bottle, which he had brought to court. Invited, Lowder did not want it put in as an exhibit: of course not, the amount missing (for only Walter had taken any of its contents) was not significant enough for the jury to ruminate upon! The dog got better.

Mrs Harriet Louise Walter, wife of James Walter (both of whom appear in the diary) was a nervous, flustered witness, but Lowder managed to winkle from her the memory that she was with Edith at No. 169 for about one hour in the region of 10.30 to 11.30am on the disputed October 19th. This was fairly helpful.

Mrs Madelaine Rede Guinness remembered dining with the Carews on about October 9th, 1896. (There is no such record in the diary). Walter told her then that he had been dosed with all sorts of things, and arsenic into the bargain.

Mrs Emma Mary Hutchison was a confident witness about October 19th. On her return from a country house at Zushi that day, she had spent some time shopping in Yokohama, and at about 10.45am, she had seen Mary Jacob, with the two children, passing Kuhn's window in the Main Street. Edith Carew was not with them, or anywhere about.

Richard Durant Robinson's evidence throws a little light on Edith's long trip home in 1893. She had asked him to look after Walter a bit while she was away. Walter had harped on to him about his health, and had confided in him about his stricture, saying, 'I have not consulted Wheeler, and I specially don't want him to know about it.'

Walter had also told him that he had been cured or rescued from malaria in the Straits through taking enormous doses of arsenic. In 1893, when he felt ill, he used to say, 'It's my old trouble, malaria.'

One day in 1895, while at the Carews' house for luncheon, Robinson had gone to the sideboard to take a glass of sherry and bitters. He saw there a small white bottle about one-third full of an amber-coloured liquid, and went to pick it up out of curiosity. One of the Carews said, 'Don't take that! It is poison — arsenic.' Then Edith said, 'It is Walter's drops.'

Ambrose Berry Walford, Lowder's junior until the *Epsilon* letter incident upset his equilibrium, must have attended most unwillingly. His task now was to substantiate the fact that when sent to Maruya's on November 26th to make enquiries he was clearly told by Hayashi Schichiro (who made reference to two books of record), that October 19th was the day of the purchase of arsenic by the foreign woman.

The defence witnesses were beginning to peter out, and Wilkinson pointedly was not bothering to cross-examine much, or at all. They were not, frankly, so good as Lowder's own opening speech. Loyal friends swearing to the Carews' marital harmony were of no use in the rather sophisticated forum of the Yokohama court, but at least few could reasonably doubt that Walter had *in the past* taken more arsenic than was wise.

Chapter 15
THE BIRTHDAY BOOK

John Lowder, not the Crown, had decided to call Edward Owen of the P&O office, but as before at the inquest his evidence did not take the case beyond Walter's *belief* in the 'Mysterious Visitor'. Since Lowder could not propose that Mary Jacob was the 'Woman in Black', and he never went so far as to suggest that the 'Visitor' and the governess were accomplices, there was little advantage in Owen for the defence, except for a partial corroboration of Edith's account of the 'Visitor'.

Hiram Wilkinson watched closely for discrepancies, and picked up his changing of the day when Walter called at his office. The new date of October 13th was certainly more apposite than the 15th, because this was the occasion when after dinner Walter told Kauffman, 'Le moment est arrivé'.

Owen still did not provide, nor was he asked for, the name of the woman enquired about by Walter. One would have thought that Walter would have offered the name of the person he had been engaged to in England. Conceivably, it was a gallantry to withhold it. This time Owen added the information that Walter had also wondered if the 'Visitor' could have been a woman whom he had known in the Straits.

Dr Piers James Hatton, practising in Yokohama, was a defence witness who went wrong. He had called as a friend at the Carews on October 21st, and somehow, by asking the doctor if Edith Carew had mentioned getting a second opinion, Lowder led him into the unwelcome evidence that 'She said she was expecting Dr Baelz at five o'clock that afternoon.'

James Stewart, who was on the Committee of the Club, had lunch at the Carews' on October 19th. Edith had complained that Walter refused to take his medicine. 'I am sure', Stewart had said,

'he will take all the medicines he wants, if you will give him a kiss with it.'

'Then she took his hand and whispered something in his ear, which I stepped back not to hear, but it was done in a very affectionate manner.'

Takayama Sadakichi, who had a jinrikisha stand opposite No.169, was brought to refute the implication of Hayashi Schichiro's revised statement that the foreign woman had bought arsenic from him on October 20th, not the 19th. He remembered taking Mrs Carew down town, before midday, on the 20th. He remembered especially because it was the festival in honour of the god Ehisu. He took her to the Post Office, to Omiya's in Sakai-cho, to a Chinese tailor, and then back to the Bluff. He did not take her anywhere else.

It would be fair to say that his evidence was not well received. Wilkinson cross-examined fiercely and asked him who or what had made him come to court ('I...', said Lowder, '...I asked him to attend.') and the judge commented that he seemed to be more of an authority on distances than on anything else.

Asa, the amah, was brought to explain why the fender bore the stain of urine, not spilt arsenic; before it was taken away from the house she had wiped it with a damp cloth which was kept in the bathroom and used to clean the water-closets.

Then the promised dark, dirty evidence as to an improper relationship between the governess and her employer. On two occasions, at about 3 or 4 o'clock in the afternoon, Asa had seen Mary Jacob enter her master's bedroom, (which he shared with Edith), when her mistress was not there. One of those times turned out to be on Sunday, October 18th, when Walter was ill. One time was before.

Lowder: 'How long did Miss Jacob remain in the bedroom?'

Asa: 'I don't know.'

'Did you go downstairs in the meantime?'

'Because I went downstairs in the meantime that is the reason I cannot say when she came out.'

Wilkinson asked where Rachel Greer had been at the time, and the judge caused Rachel (who was present) to be conducted out of court. Lowder suggested that there should be an adjournment, and that there should be no communication between the two amahs. If the cross-examination went on further there might be a particular point in their talking together.

Judge: 'How can you secure it?'

Both girls still lived at No.169, and objected to any proposal to separate them overnight. Finally Reginald Porch gave an undertaking that he would see to it that there was no communication. When the newspaper reporters left the court, however, they were amused to see the two amahs — cousins — engaged outside the consulate in animated conversation!

During that day, January 27th, the Pastor of the Union Church, Yokohama, wrote to the governess' uncle, William Jacob, at Baltonsborough:

Your niece Miss Mary Esther Jacob has requested me through Miss Britain, with whom she is boarding, to write you concerning this unhappy affair. I would like to assure you in the strongest possible manner that the sympathies of the public are almost wholly with your niece and that great indignation has been felt at her arrest. It is regarded as a device to avert suspicion from the guilty party. I myself felt that I never met one who seemed more incapable than your niece of such a crime as that with which she is charged. It is probable that when it has served its temporary purpose it will never be heard of again.

I am told that her friends are advising her to claim damages for false imprisonment from her prosecutor, and am assured that she has good grounds for claiming damages from the cable company. [Distress had been caused by a Dalziel's cablegram which had wrongly reported on January 11th that Mary Jacob had confessed in court that she had administered the poison and written the anonymous letters. Reuters had modified the report on the same day by making it clear that she was alleged to be the author of the letters, and that there was no confession.]

At present Miss Jacob is suffering from nervous prostration and but few are allowed to see her, but I think you need be under no apprehension as to her health or the result of her trial. The trial of Mrs Carew is drawing towards its close. It is watched with keenest interest by the foreign community and probably no case before the courts of Yokohama has ever evoked such unanimity of feeling as this has done. Miss Jacob has friends among the married men here, who, quickly as possible, bailed her out of gaol and are looking after her interests.

Very Respectfully Yours,
B.M. Meecham.

Asa, who arrived late at court on January 28th, had to face Wilkinson again; had she talked to anyone about Mary Jacob's going into her master's room? To everyone's surprise, Asa had a sharp reply ready. She had never said a word to Rachel about it, but it was Mrs Hutchison who had asked her about it! This was Mrs Emma Mary Hutchison, Lowder's earlier witness, who had seen the governess down town on October 19th, without Edith Carew.

The judge insisted on a proper account of this unexpected interposition. Apparently at some time in that month of January Mrs Hutchison, who was in the dining-room at No.169, had sent Rachel to fetch Asa, and had questioned her: had Miss Jacob ever gone into Mr Carew's room, and did she know anything about it?

Judge: 'Has she spoken to Rachel since yesterday?'

And Asa brazenly denied it!

Kitamura Kichiro, servant at No.169 for two years, and still so employed, stated that he too had seen and heard the governess in the bedroom with his master. That is, once he saw her and once he heard her. Personally, he did not go upstairs very often.

Wilkinson, however, elicited the information that on both occasions the children were in the bedroom with their father. Nor was Kichiro consistent about whether or not his mistress was there.

Wilkinson: 'Well, I think that will do.'

After tiffin Lowder's confident attack had gone, following the embarrassing failure of his last witness to come up to proof, and he indicated that he had been seriously considering the fact that the only other evidence on the point of Mary Jacob's being in the bedroom on which he could depend was the evidence of the two Japanese cousins. 'I therefore unhesitatingly withdraw all I have said that may have been based upon my ability to adduce such proof.'

Counsel was also most anxious to make it clear that the

suggestion of impropriety had not come from his client. Rachel Greer was brought back. Edith had not noted in her diary that she was expecting a baby. Lowder explained to the court that she tended to become hysterical about her baby, when being sent in and out, and kept disappearing. She was allowed to sit.

Rachel insisted that she saw Mary Jacob in the act of sewing together some torn-up letters — ie, not Elsa Christoffel alone. 'Miss Jacob', Rachel said, 'was in the habit of getting Japanese paper from the privy, and sewing the fragments on it, but she was also in the habit of getting some pieces and merely sewing them together.'

Rachel had thought she was doing something very wrong and had told her mistress, but she had scolded her, and said it was nonsense. The governess used to dance about, rejoicing, and read bits of the letters to her. Wilkinson asked her about Mary Jacob's character; it was *bad,* Rachel said.

The amah kept to her previous evidence that Walter Carew had told her to send a jinrikisha man to Maruya's on Sunday, October 18th, for sugar of lead. Her mistress was definitely out — probably at church with the children, although she did not generally take them (as the diary shows). Wilkinson cross-examined closely: she did not actually see her mistress go out.

Then Lowder tried to get in his evidence about Ah Kwong's having been asked by Mary Jacob to rifle the wastepaper-basket, but he was blocked by hearsay and gave up.

As his last-ditch witness, Lowder put up Reggie Porch, who was always reliable. Walter did not take sugar in anything (and therefore would have noticed sugar of lead). His sister definitely did take the children to church on Sunday, October 18th, (and indeed the diary says so).

Did Walter give himself the same freedom in the selection of friends of the opposite sex, Lowder asked him. *'Yes, I should think so.'*

The court-day was over, and all the evidence was in, and on the nineteenth day, January 29th, John Lowder rose to make his closing speech. It was only a shadow of his opening, and indeed the fight seemed to have gone out of him round about the time of Kichiro's defection. He held to his contention that Mary Jacob had written the 'A.L.' letters, but he laid more stress on their contents than on

their handwriting. They were 'altogether too nonsensical, too idiotic' to have emanated from Edith Carew's pen.

He still clung to the notion that a single dose of white arsenic had caused the death, and neither purchase nor possession of that poison could be traced to his client. He relied upon what he had said previously to convince the jury that the prisoner was not the 'incarnate fiend' the prosecution had made her out to be (a striking phrase to inflame the jury, which would have come better from the Crown.) In fact, Lowder said very little, in a speech unbalanced by a long consideration of R. *v* Dyson on full intent to kill.

Hiram Wilkinson's closing speech was of a different standard. A gloomy Lowder had to sit by as he remarked that the charge which he had laid against Mary Jacob had made his learned friend's position very difficult. It was not the duty of the Crown to take advantage of any mistake, misunderstanding or want of judgement that affected the defence.

The charge against the governess might be considered as narrowing it to the question of whether Mary Jacob or Mrs Carew were guilty. The Crown did not ask the jury to try it that way. Nor did the Crown ask the jury to take the view that whoever wrote the A.L. letters was guilty by her own confession.

If the jury found that Edith Carew had written the letters, they had an important bearing, although not conclusive of guilt.

'You are not here', Wilkinson went on, 'to try Mary Jacob, but *the character of Mary Jacob as a witness, her conduct and motives, are matters of importance as far as they may be considered to affect her credibility* and they become of much greater importance when you are asked to attribute to her acts which the prosecution allege were committed by the accused.'

If any of the jury had been brought up in a quiet country place he would understand the impact made by the free Carew family life upon an unsophisticated girl. She would be further confused by the kindness which she received, and her own semi-feudal sense of allegiance to the Carews. 'To Elsa Christoffel, matters would present themselves in a colder and more unsympathetic light. The speaking of actions savouring of impropriety is apt often to produce on the hearer a stronger impression than that originally received by the speaker.'

A careful attention to those considerations would supply a true and consistent explanation of the two girls' activities, and the advice given by Elsa Christoffel to her friend — to fortify her own position against contamination and tarnishment — *received its justification from subsequent events.*

'I shall ask you,' Counsel continued, 'to treat Rachel, who seems to have been the manager of the household, as a most untrustworthy witness [as to Mary Jacob's unchastity]. My learned friend could not rely on her evidence, and very properly he withdrew the charge. Gentlemen, you saw the history of the beginning of this cruel slander. You have watched its growth, and you were present at its death, and if there was one pleasant moment which I have experienced during this most painful trial, it was while I was listening to its funeral oration.'

Counsel turned now to Mrs Hutchison and her nasty incitement of gossip. It was his cross-examination of Asa which had drawn forth this incident, and he seemed to be embarrassed to meet Mrs Hutchison on the Bund again: 'In this small community, I will take a liberty I would not take if speaking elsewhere. I am sure it is the feeling of you all, and it is my own feeling, that however it came about that she interfered in the matter, her action was honest and well-intentioned.'

Everyone realised, of course, that Mrs Hutchison was a person committed to helping Edith in any way she could, but Counsel blundered on, making things worse: 'I am sure she will ever deeply regret having been the means of casting suspicion upon one of her own sex.'

With relief, Wilkinson moved to the target of young Reggie Porch, whom he seemed quite happy to meet afterwards on the Bund, even though he had reduced him in men's eyes by saying that he had not seemed to comprehend anything that was going on around him, and had shown a complete absence of apprehension in just about everything. Counsel nearly, but not quite, imputed a deliberate closing of the eyes.

His learned friend had said that the governess had shown no signs of any merciful motives, but the Dickinson letters and the bedpan note were not produced until the Preliminary Examination, when they came out in the natural course of events and could no longer practically be kept back. Counsel now read out Mary Jacob's inquest evidence, to show how discreet and merciful she had been.

It was not at all likely, though, Counsel argued, that Mary Jacob had written the 'A.L.' letters to help Mrs Carew, to exonerate her. There was no evidence that she had been working hard to save the prisoner.

The jury might dismiss from their minds the idea that Annie Luke had ever been in Yokohama. 'There never was an Annie...the same mind that conceived the 'Mysterious Visitor' conceived the letters.' There was no real 'Mysterious Visitor'.

If Mary Jacob was supposed by the defence to be the author of the card presented by the 'Mysterious Visitor', as the paper allegedly found in the birthday book by Reginald Porch suggested, 'Then she must have employed someone to come up with a thick veil and appear and go through that farce.'

Wilkinson asked the jury to believe that the paper was put fraudulently and surreptitiously into the birthday book 'between the time Mr Porch looked into it on January 2nd, and the time it was handed to Mr Lowder'. (As a matter of fact, Reggie's evidence, at the Mary Jacob proceedings, had been that after finding the book on January 1st and 2nd he had not opened it until January 8th.) 'That piece of evidence', Wilkinson argued, 'was prepared afterwards. It became necessary to connect Mary Jacob with this tissue of falsehoods, and that was resorted to.'

A century later the birthday book survives, bound in plum-coloured leather, with gilt-edged pages, and it is quite small, being three inches wide and four inches long. At the time, a shrewd member of the press noted that the half-sheet of paper actually protruded from the book — so that it was unlikely that Reggie would not have noticed it immediately. Edith herself could not have done any tinkering, because she had been in custody since November 16th, but Wilkinson plainly considered that there had been a conspiracy here to pervert the course of justice.

He said with some sarcasm that Mary Jacob must have learnt a great deal about Walter's past if she were able to write a letter which so effectively 'fetched' him as that Annie Luke letter did. (Counsel could say this boldly, since the defence had relinquished their suggestion of pillow-talk!)

On the twentieth day of the trial Wilkinson focused on Edith Carew: 'The motive for the commission of crime is often obscure and generally inadequate.'

Judge: 'Always.'

Counsel: 'And always inadequate in the highest sense of the term.'

He so understated the matrimonial fault of Walter Carew as yet again to demonstrate the condition of women in the 1890s: 'The accused has been shown to have been systematically representing him as guilty of acts which would stamp him as a brute and a villain.' Referring to Lowder's poetic flight (which had been the cause of some derision), he commented that whatever might be said of the lightness and frailty of female human nature, poisoning one's husband was not the form that it took! The position was that behind the action of the prisoner there lay strong motives not revealed to the world.

It might be that she had not contemplated the *whole* of what happened. She did not mention the 'Mysterious Visitor' in her first statement at the inquest (although the *family* had accepted what she had told them about the caller) and invented Annie Luke when she found that suspicion was directed against herself.

Referring to the diary, Counsel stated that it was his duty to point to ambiguities, by which he meant, 'Not that it will do him much good, I am thinking' and 'I wonder how long it will last.' The abstraction of *Epsilon* showed 'boldness and daring' which might attach to some of her other actions.

The purchases of arsenic must have been the subject most feared by the defence, and Wilkinson's points hurt to the bone. Even a Styrian peasant, he said, could not have got through the amount of arsenic traced to the house. That, of course, is the core of the case. The accused had been inconsistent in first saying that her husband took small quantities of arsenic, and later saying that they were large quantities.

Hayashi Schichiro's failure to identify Mrs Carew was natural enough, because to many Japanese, all foreigners were much alike. Wilkinson held to Schichiro's second version — that Fowler's and chloral had been bought by a foreign woman on the 20th, not the 19th, even though Mary Jacob's evidence went towards the 19th.

The jinrikisha man of the 20th had in some way or other acquired the *opinion* (and Wilkinson said that he chose that word carefully, without going so far as to impute a wrong intention to anyone) that it was necessary to say one thing and nothing else, and his credibility was quite demolished by his denying that Counsel for the defence had ever seen him because of course Mr Lowder had seen him, quite naturally, during the preparation of the case.

This is an interesting observation. It is the first overt suggestion that perjury and pressure had been at work around the subsidiary witnesses. If there is once perjury in a trial, it is reasonable to look for it elsewhere.

The truth of the boathouse prescription, Wilkinson argued, was a matter of simple arithmetic. The bottle of half an ounce of Fowler's was exhausted within six days, and it should have lasted for at least 12 days.

Finally, there was the 'very serious' and 'very terrible' fact that the accused had offered no satisfactory explanation as to what was done with the arsenic purchased by her, or as to where the husband had obtained the arsenic for the alleged self-administration.

If there had been perjury it had not been of a heroic nature; wisely, no back-street drug pedlar had been suborned with false records. Wilkinson would have taken him to pieces.

Chapter 16
THE EMPEROR'S AMNESTY

Judge Mowat had caught a bad cold, and at times he was scarcely audible during his summing-up on Monday, February 1st, 1897, the last day of the trial. Outside the hushed courtroom, the weather in the streets was horrendous, with a howling northerly wind and driving, slatted rain.

The judge ruled that it was to the evidence as a whole, and not merely to the medical part, that the jury had to look in order to decide if arsenic had conduced to the death. All the medical evidence went one way — that the circumstances were not inconsistent with arsenical poisoning.

In the matter of the Hayashi Schichiro inconsistency, the judge was obviously not convinced by his revised version of the sale on October *20th*. He took a very poor view of Edith's not mentioning arsenic and sugar of lead to Dr Wheeler until she had learnt that there was to be a post-mortem. He called this one of the important facts in the case. Her explanation that she had wished to conceal from the doctor the nature of Walter's complaint was inadequate. She could just have said that he took arsenic, for whatever reason.

Was it an innocent act for her to go to two separate druggists? The suggestion was that she might not have able to get so much as one and a half ounces of Fowler's Solution from Schedel's, and therefore she divided the order. Entire concealment there was not, of course. In her statements she had stepped up the amount of arsenic which she said that Walter Carew was in the habit of taking, but the evidence of *recent* intake was unsatisfactory. If he was a constant consumer, it could not have been a secret. There was no evidence of the purchase of a single phial of arsenic by himself.

The judge directed the jury to disregard the *Epsilon* incident. Although it was a wrong act, and extremely foolish, its connection

with the case was exiguous. The ambiguous entries in the diary seemed to him to be perfectly innocent and natural remarks to make, and should be entirely disregarded. 'A diary is not the book into which one would put incriminating evidence.'

The fender was a very long story, and the jury would not derive much light from it, and the finding of arsenic in Dr Baelz's bottle went either way. The finding of falsehood over whether or not Dr Baelz was coming ought not to be pressed too hard, because some allowance had to be made for the circumstances which the accused was under at the time.

The Dickinson letters were only a reflex of her own. Hers were undoubtedly couched in terms sufficient to elicit the sympathy and affection which she seemed to desire, but they were probably not couched in the same strong terms of endearment as his. It would induce him to paint things in stronger colours. The jury could take it that what she said about her husband's bad treatment was untrue.

The defence used that untruthfulness to argue that no greater untruth could for a moment be imagined than the maligning of an affectionate and tender husband, *and therefore very little weight could be placed on anything that the accused said.* The judge advised the jury to scrutinise the statements which she had made to Dickinson about her husband very carefully before attaching any weight to them.

The Annie Luke letters could not be left out of the jury's consideration of the case. The deceased did write to Annie Luke in the belief that she really was in Yokohama at the time. There were several reasons for the jury to believe that she was never there. The handwriting of the first letter was disguised and it was clear that the real Annie Luke would never have used a disguised hand. If she had come to see Walter Carew, she would not have wished to disguise her identity. It was impossible for any stranger to have stayed in the community from October 10th to November 11th without leaving some trace.

'The real Annie Luke would have furnished an address; the sham Annie Luke would not.' The lack of an address was an insuperable difficulty in the way of the fictitious Annie Luke, because if the address had been given Walter Carew would have gone there and found there was no such person and the hoax would have been disclosed. The whole story was a transparent trick.

Only the deceased and the prisoner knew of the existence of someone named Annie Luke. The judge thought it very likely that Mary Jacob did not hear of her until later in the case. If the jury came to the conclusion that it was not Mary Jacob who wrote the letters, they were to decide that the prisoner was the perpetrator. To that end they should consider the handwriting, the subject-matter, and something of the style.

The judge had been very much struck by the way in which Mr Mason had given his opinion on the handwriting: he was guarded and impartial, and candid when there was a doubt in his mind.

The jury should remember that the 'A.L.' letter to Defence Counsel, according to the prosecution, was an imitation by the prisoner of Mary Jacob's handwriting. She had letters of the governess in her possession to copy from, in an attempt to connect her with the previous letters.

If the jury were to look at the photographs of the letters they would see that the prisoner's handwriting sloped from right to left, whereas Miss Jacob's was almost perfectly upright. They would then see that the letter to Mr Lowder was in a more upright hand than any previous 'A.L.' letters. That bore out the prosecution's suggestion.

That letter to Mr Lowder was intended to 'screen' the accused, but, as the Crown had pointed out, Miss Jacob had not been accused at that time, and there was no reason why she should screen the prisoner. There was no point then in her, notionally, attempting to exonerate herself.

The judge described the style of the letters as that of mystification and desperation, 'such as you find, I think, in the Dickinson letters.' (A curious point.) The 'A.L.' letters were not to be taken as a confession of crime, because they were not written over a true signature.

The motive was impossible to discover.

Judge Mowat drew to a close. He had summed up against Edith Carew, although he had made a number of scrupulous reservations. He had not tried to cover all the evidence, but he had a sore throat and what he said was quite enough.

The jury retired at 2.35pm and a great silence fell over the courtroom. For the first time during the case Edith drooped over the edge of the dock and buried her face in her hands. It was some minutes before she lifted her head and wiped her eyes with a handkerchief. At 3.03pm the jury returned with the unanimous verdict of guilty. The *Japan Gazette* reported:

> *There was a silence that could be felt, an awful hush, as the next question followed, and the prisoner with blanched cheeks and quivering mouth stood once again at the bar.*
>
> *Had she anything to say why sentence should not be passed upon her?*
>
> *A faint 'No' escaped from the prisoner's trembling lips.*

There was no plea in mitigation.

Judge: 'Mr Lowder, as you are aware, the penalty which follows upon such a sentence in England can in this country only be carried into effect under direction of the British Minister [Sir Ernest Satow].'

'Yes, my Lord' — a shaken Lowder.

'The sentence cannot be carried into execution without instructions under his directions, signed and by writing under his hand [the judge was reading the Order aloud] and if he should think fit to direct that the sentence be not carried into execution, he then directs or instructs what punishment shall be inflicted upon the prisoner in lieu of punishment of death.'

Then Judge Mowat placed the black cap on his head, and in a voice broken with emotion pronounced the death sentence. Edith managed to listen in a manner fit and becoming, but she was ghastly pale and her lips turned noticeably blue. Perhaps her heart faltered, like Mary Jacob's.

At home in Glastonbury, on that Monday, a telegram was received from London: *Yokohama wires 'Advise Porch Edith convicted. Sentence requires confirmation of the British Minister.'* By the next available train Harry Swayne, an intimate friend of the Mayor of Glastonbury and son of W. T. Swayne, his legal adviser, proceeded at once to Bournemouth, where Edith's parents were staying, to break the news to them that their only daughter had been sentenced to death by hanging. The Porch family were 'crushed' and Walter's parents in Exmouth were greatly distressed.

The purloining of *Epsilon* was said in Yokohama to have sealed Edith's fate. It was widely believed that Sir Ernest Satow would exercise what was in effect his prerogative of mercy. However, he had so far in the case shown a stern and unrelenting disposition towards her, and in fact Home Office papers indicate that she was lucky to escape by an 'accident'.

In view of the Imperial Proclamation of H.M. the Emperor, dated January 31st, 1897, granting to all subjects under sentence on that day a remission of punishment — this general amnesty being to mark the death of the Dowager Empress — it appeared proper that a similar measure of grace should be extended to Edith Carew, whose trial in a court sitting in the Emperor's dominions had been proceeding for some days before and was about to be brought to a conclusion at the time of the proclamation.

It does sound as if the coincidence of date was grasped at to save a genteel neck, but that is *not* the way which the Home Office viewed the reprieve. Sir Ernest Satow decided to commute the sentence to life imprisonment with hard labour. If the case had came up three years later Edith would have found herself in the even more frightening position of being tried by a Japanese court. On January 31st, 1900, the Consular Court in Japan was to stand formally adjourned for ever. Under the system of extraterritoriality, foreigners in Japan had been exempt from the jurisdiction of the Japanese courts. The Japanese law was backward and feudal, enforced with torture and other barbarisms, but by the turn of the century there was such an improvement that the treaties were revised and all foreigners became amenable to Japanese law.

The result of the Carew trial was printed in the Japanese newspapers, which had been prone to comment during the proceedings on the immorality of the foreigners in their midst. The Yokohama *Mainchi Shinbun* reported on February 4th, that Mrs Carew was devoting herself to God, in the consular gaol, and reading the Bible daily.

On the set date of February 5th the Jacob hearing was reconvened, and lo! the governess was there in court, wonderfully recovered and vindicated. John Lowder was also intent on vindication of his diminished reputation:

I had taken this decision [to offer no further evidence against Mary Jacob] *before the conclusion of the recent trial, in consequence of the withdrawal of his evidence by one witness, and the failure of another under cross-examination, thus leaving me with the statements of two Japanese maid-servants only, who turn out to be cousins, and who were in the pay of Mrs Carew* [What *does* he mean?] *to establish a point which I considered of vital importance to the success of the prosecution, namely, that the relations that had existed between the accused and the deceased were such as to make it probable that she knew of Annie Luke.*

By the weakening of that link, he conceded, the chain of evidence had become so attenuated that he had sent a note to George Scidmore to tell him of his withdrawal.

Scidmore asked James Troup for a certificate to state that the charge had been heard, and dismissed; his client would soon be going home to England, and such a certificate was important to her. The Assistant Judge however, ruled that such a certificate applied only to summary trial and refused the application.

Nor was Counsel successful when he applied for an order against John Lowder to compel him to pay the costs incident to the proceedings. He referred to the Vexatious Indictments Act of 1859, and, heedless of future relations with Lowder, put it that the charge against Mary Jacob had been brought hastily, inconsiderately and heartlessly, and had been withdrawn coldly, formally and without one word of regret. She, a young girl, had been subjected to mental and almost physical torture. Her character had been traduced and a charge made against her which to any virtuous woman was worse than a charge of murder, and yet this man stood and withdrew his allegations without apology.

In spite of these strong words, James Troup ruled that on precedent the application for costs was dismissed. Lowder challenged Scidmore's attack: if he had indeed brought a false charge, that certainly implied malice, and the accused was entitled to far more than her costs, for she had a remedy by action for malicious prosecution. Scidmore had nothing to say at that time about such a move.

Counsel went on to complain about a coincidence which had greatly upset his client. When Mary Jacob had been released on bail, and had gone to the gaol to remove her personal effects, she had found in her cell a copy of a book with unfortunate associations — Marie Corelli's *A Romance of Two Worlds.*

The Assistant Judge, in his capacity as governor of the gaol, had made enquiries and found the subordinate who had been responsible. He felt that it was an accident. Perhaps.

James Troup then made a commitment to John Lowder which must surely have been political: 'I am satisfied that the prosecutor at the time he made his charge was convinced of the truth of the charge.'

Lowder: 'I am much obliged to your Honour.'

Mary Jacob was left in an unsatisfactory position. Perhaps the Assistant Judge, not sure of his ground, consulted Judge Mowat, because later that day he did issue a certificate along the lines that Scidmore had pleaded for, and it included the statement that 'No imputation whatever in connection with this matter rests on Mary Esther Jacob.'

Worried, as well he might be, that the governess would take proceedings in tort, especially since she was no friendless lady, Lowder, on February 13th, wrote a curt and grudging lawyer's apology to her:

> *Madam,*
>
> *I am this moment, and for the first time, in receipt of proof which is conclusive to my mind that you were not the writer of the A.L. letters; and I now hasten to ask you to accept that apology which I have heretofore been unable conscientiously to offer you for the pain and mental suffering to which you have been put in consequence of the charge I considered it my duty to prefer against you, and which I am now convinced was unfounded.*

Anxious to evade the charge of malice, he wrote a further, more contrite letter to George Scidmore:

> *Sir,*
>
> *The publication of the letter to Miss Jacob (on the 13th*

inst.) has resulted in the communication to me of facts which indicate the existence of a depth of duplicity and deceit which is to my mind unimaginable; and of which I, among others, have been the unconscious dupe, and Miss Jacob the victim.

Words fail me to express the regret with which the hearing of the story has filled me; for I feel that an act of injustice has been committed, for which, had it been intentional on my part, no reparation in my power could be adequate.

Believe me, my single desire and sole concern is to satisfy your client by doing what lies in my power to restore her character to the extent that I have been instrumental in impeaching it; and, to that end, I now explicitly withdraw every word I have said imputing the existence of questionable relations between her and the late Mr Carew.

One may infer that there had been a complete breakdown of the bond between Lowder and his convicted client, with recriminations on both sides. He was lucky, because the governess, not vengeful, left quietly for home. Soon Edith too left Japan for ever. On May 3rd, 1897, she was transferred to Victoria Gaol, in Hong Kong.

Reggie, with the help of friends, but not Harry Dickinson, will have closed up No. 169 the Bluff, which must, as the murder house, have proved difficult to re-let. The rented furniture will have been quietly returned, and some remaining effects were shipped home.

The children were taken to the family in England, and Reggie, unable to settle at an office job, began to wander the world. Did someone take on Babel, who had like an angel transported her mistress to the Plains of Heaven? Or was she regarded as unlucky, and did she fall on hard times? The Porch family never lost their belief in Edith's innocence. More remarkably, Walter's parents felt the same way.

The Porchs' family solicitors, Gould and Swayne, instructed their agents, Bridges Sawtell and Co., of 23 Red Lion Square, London, to brief Counsel to appear before the Privy Council on Edith's behalf.[22] The hearing took place on July 17th, 1897, before the Lord Chancellor, Lords Hobhouse and Morris, Sir Richard Couch, Sir Samuel Henry Strong and Sir John Henry de Villiers. It took the form of a petition for *leave* to appeal against conviction and sentence. Sir Frank Lockwood QC and Mr Malcolm MacNaughten appeared for Edith Carew, but the weak petition was doomed from the onset, and it has always, anyway, been difficult to make any headway against the restricted catalogues of the Privy Council.

Lockwood argued that there had been no jurisdiction in the court at Yokohama to try the case, and that there had been improper reception of evidence. He submitted that the order which created the Yokohama court was *ultra vires,* in so far as it enabled that court to try felonies with a jury of only five persons. The original Foreign Jurisdiction Act (41 and 42 Victoria) gave Her Majesty no power to alter the laws of England.

Lord Chancellor: 'Do you contend that the result of the trial is contrary to natural justice?'

Lockwood: 'No, I don't say that.'

Leave to appeal was refused. The Privy Council had no doubt whatever that Her Majesty had ample powers and full jurisdiction to act in the way that Counsel had complained of, and their lordships did not review criminal proceedings in the absence of such factors as a grave and serious failure of justice.

Affidavits which had been carefully prepared were thus of no use at that time. It was particularly disappointing for a certain chemist named William Thomas Mignot Tucker, formerly of Glastonbury, latterly of Kingsbridge, Devon. For some months he had been writing to the newspapers in a state of high excitement, armed with information which he fondly imagined to be of the gravest importance. In Glastonbury in 1889 he had supplied Walter Carew with solution of arsenic as a 'pick-me-up', and on one such occasion Walter had informed him that he had been in the habit of taking arsenic for years. It was easy to tell from his conversation that he was well acquainted with the nature of the drug. Tucker had not come forward before because he had expected that the case against Mrs Carew would be easily refuted. He said that unless she had become insane, she was a young lady totally incapable of such conduct. This was still a popular sentiment.

Edward Faithful Thomas, of St Brelade's Bay, Jersey, swore that in about the year 1883 he had been introduced in Singapore to Walter Carew, who was the Sheriff of that place. Thomas was told on more than one occasion, and believed that it was a matter of current report, that Walter took arsenic habitually.

Mrs Emma Marjoribanks, of Longwood, Langholm, Dumfriesshire, swore her affidavit too late for the Privy Council, but it was used later. What she had to say was really very interesting:

> *I was in Japan on a visit to that country, touring about in the month of April to June, 1893. On the occasion of such visit I saw the late Mr Walter Carew on several occasions. He informed me that he was not feeling well and had taken large doses of arsenic. I told him he should be careful over taking such a medicine, but he replied that he was accustomed to it.*
>
> *From the manner, appearance and conversation of the said Walter Carew I came to the conclusion that he was careless over taking arsenic and thought lightly of it.*
>
> *He seemed despondent having no good appointment and at his wife's absence in England, she having just left Japan, each day saying he had dosed himself with arsenic and felt no better and did not think he could last much longer. When warned about arsenic and advised to see a doctor, he refused, saying he was accustomed to it and just 'tipped it in the glass' (suiting the action to the words). He was nonchalant in manner.*

The absolutely startling new information, however, related not to Walter Carew but to the character of Mary Jacob. She had a shady past.

Chapter 17
THE GOVERNESS

Rachel had said that her character was bad. John Lowder, when he began his proceedings against Mary Jacob on January 11th, had a telegram in his possession which told him that she was not quite as she appeared, but the opportunity never arose for him to substantiate its purport by bringing witnesses all the way from England.

Until the telegram, she had seemed an innocent abroad, and indeed in her state of vindication she had become something of a heroine in Yokohama. This she will have enjoyed, but at what cost? One of the factors which had made her so ill must have been great fear of Lowder's discoveries, and later it will have been difficult to stave off the pressure of well-meaning sympathisers with money in their hands who wanted her to sue Lowder.

It was not that she had a criminal record, although she had risked a conviction. The short point is that she had a history of dishonesty, but the more relevantly (if ultimately irrelevantly) her trouble arose from her disturbed, fantasizing imagination, which could dredge up lies potent enough to deceive those people who wished her well. She was a great deceiver, but prone to flee, and to confess.

Edith was particularly vague about her governess' past. It seems unlikely that Mrs Porch would have selected someone with a dubious history to care for her two grandchildren in a foreign land. The Carew household turned out to be the worst possible place for her continuing moral rehabilitation and it was the governess herself who was harmed. Being held in a prison cell must have been catastrophic, and indeed precipitated the illness.

It was especially unfair that the disgrace had come about in 1884, twelve years earlier, when Mary was only 18, and that the

chance to work under powerful protection in Japan had promised a new beginning.

Her closest relatives at Baltonsborough had kept quiet, but a relative by marriage, John Harry Miller, of Street, in Somerset, felt it his duty to produce to the Privy Council a series of documents which proved her 'by her own confession to have been at one time a heartless thief and an ingenious and unscrupulous liar.'

Previously, on March 10th, 1897, Miller had sent the original papers to John Lowder in Yokohama, 'to assist him in his defence in proceedings which Miss Jacob was at that time threatening to take against him.' There it is — Miller felt a greater duty to a stranger, but some people are like that!

Miller's bombshell was as follows: in about 1883, Mary Jacob had gone to work as a shop assistant at a Berlin wool repository in Bowdon, Cheshire, kept by a Miss Sophia Okell. In August 1884 she ran away, having stolen money from the till as well as articles of clothing and other items. Several days after her flight, Miller received a letter from her:

Miss Morris,
Ivy House,
Carnarvon.

Dear Mr Miller,

I am sure I can trust you.

You have given me every proof of your trustworthiness. I am going to make a confession to begin with, perhaps before this you will have heard of my marriage. If not I will tell you. I was married last February — in secret of course, no one knew save my husband — myself, the Verger and the Clergyman — I left Bowdon about the 12th August and have been travelling about N. Wales with my husband.

We were at Carnarvon and were in a boat on the Channel. My husband had been rowing and had taken off his jacket. We were in deep water and he was cold he asked one of the men for the jacket, he threw it and in so doing, it hitched in one of the oars and the contents of the pockets fell into the water.

I heard my husband say 'Good God'. But that was all — when we reached home he told me he only had £5 in the world his purse had gone overboard — I was very cheerful and laughed, and said never mind we can work — he seemed better then but was rather gloomy all the evening.

I had some coffee for supper, and there was something in it, for I slept till noon next day when he was gone and I have sent you a copy of the note pinned to the pillow — I can't go to Emily — for I ran away as you may say from them, where can I go.

The clergyman's wife here has been most kind, and answered advertisements for me. She has had me there all day, but they are leaving for Carnarvon, and so I shall lose my only friend. They are willing to help me to get a situation, but I must live meanwhile. The clergyman is a Canon of the Church of England and his name stands high. I hope with his help to get a home as mother's help or nursery governess — but meanwhile as I said before I must have a roof over my head — Canon Evans has been an invalid for five years — and is now leaving the Church, and is retiring to Hastings, to live as a private gentleman, on his wife's means — they will of course be greatly altered in circumstances. Could you have me for a little while to stay with you — I should be so thankful to you.

Neither Manchester nor Baltonsborough people knew about his Ernest's leaving they know I am married the last time I wrote I told them I was going to Germany — and so we would if that incident had not occurred. Of course I hope he may come for me soon but I know he did all for the best, I have no notion where he has gone. All this I write in secrecy to you and Lucy. Heaven knows how and what I suffer mentally, myself so much in the wrong — God is indeed punishing me for my deceit.

I love him (Ernest) and ever shall love him dearly. All of my friends are sure to be so angry with me for deceiving my kind brother and sisters — and also Miss Okell — that I cannot ask them to take me back at present at any rate, and I hope in a short time to have a situation — I would do all in my power to repay you by helping in the house and School.

Could you let me know what you think soon, as I am fearfully anxious — and my little money is running short. Please don't let any of the Baltonsborough people know — or Manchester, for the present I would keep it secret.

My address is
Mrs Mentz
c/of Miss Morris
Ivy House
Llanberrig Road
Carnarvon
and you know me as
Mary Jacob

The supposed note pinned to the pillow was enclosed:

My dear little Elsie,

I am leaving you — go back to your friends for a time, I will make my fortune and come for you (if you trust me).

From your own
Ernest

Elsie, she added, was his pet name for her. Greatly concerned by this woeful letter, Miller despatched a telegram on August 29th: '*Glad to receive yours come immediately if you can arrive tonight wire time of arrival and I will meet you.*'

Mary stayed with the Millers for several months. On her arrival, she wrote out for them a voluntary confession, addressed partly to them, and partly to Miss Okell, in which she admitted that the story of the marriage was false and had been concocted to account for her sudden departure from Miss Okell's. She had bought jewellery with the stolen money, some of which she had pawned in the name of Miss Mary Morgan (the pawn ticket was attached).

The confession shows a worrying state of mind, but also a surprising amount of insight:

To begin

Bowdon

Love. I took money from Miss Okell's till. Ernest Okell never made love to me. I bought all the jewellery with money stolen from Miss Okell. The ring in Exford Road on the afternoon (a Saturday) when I met Flo going to Miss Barret's the bracelet on Whit-Tuesday when I went alone to Exford Road — I bought it in

Stretford Road. The chain on the morning I went to Glastonbury to change Mr Miller's cheque. The silver brooch at Goodwill's The Downs Bowdon.

Hugh Elson never made love to me — or gave me anything — in fact no one ever did to mean anything — I have never seen Robert Colmer since last summer, when he came up with the children, and he has never made any sort of love to me. I used to fancy myself in love with him but he never took notice of me. I can give no reason of any sort for my proceedings — I have acted like an idiot — while I was at school it was the same, I deceived constantly.

Proofs

On Sunday previous to my leaving Bowdon, I wore the bracelet Miss Okell questioned concerning it and I having told so many lies about was afraid, I have no excuse. I believe I did fancy I loved Percy Okell, but I fancied myself in love with everybody. Miss Okell hardly spoke all Monday. She knew I had told a lie, and treated me accordingly — I wanted to do something romantic and so I told a heap of stories about going to Mrs Barrow's with my dirty clothes, I went to the Station and booked for Exford Road Station, and then took a hansom to the Victoria — I then went to Criccieth, where I told the people I had run away from home because of my lover — I walked to Port Madoc, and on my way I was caught in a storm, I went into a cottage for shelter and told the old man and woman a story of running away from home. I think his name was Roberts, he advised me to go to a Miss Thomas, who had taken Emily's place at Hendrigedryfd. I went back and asked to see her. Emily lived with a Mrs Walker at Port Madoc and I remembered being desperate I went and saw Miss Thomas — she advised me to return to my friends or go to the Clergyman at Criccieth and offered me two shillings which I refused — I never told her my name, and only told her I had left home. Then I came to Carnarvon — the people I slept with at Criccieth their name was Jones I think and they kept a taylor's shop — had been kind, and took a pair of gloves for the bed, and gave me my breakfast, they advised me to go to Carnarvon to try to get work of some kind — when in the train or on the road a thought came into my head, and the plan formed, to say I was a widow, but then how to account for death, no I must say I was married and my husband had left me. I made up the tale as I went along.

When I got out of the train at Carnarvon I asked a lady the way to the town, and told her my lies — She was very sorry for me, told me where to go for tea and told me to go to Mrs Evans, The Vicarage — I went to Mrs Owen's, Bangor Street to tea, and then to the Vicarage. I told Mrs Evans — she told the Canon and he told me to write home, and to my Clergyman. I did — I wrote to Grandma telling her I was married and to Mr Perkins telling him I was married, and my husband had deserted me, and all the rest of it. The Owens in Bangor Street were kind. I met a Miss Wood, address 120 Ashford Road, Denton, Manchester who I told the story to, she believed every word, and kept me for two days. Then she went and the letter came from Mr Perkins. Mr Evans answered advertisements for me and believed me.

I told them I was married in February, had run away from Grandma who I said was very cruel and had been married in Manchester at St Bride's had travelled through S. Wales with Mr Mentz who never existed and while at Criccieth he had left me — Mr Perkins sent me ten shillings Mrs Evans had me to work for her — at first I stayed with a Mrs Mills, Secundum Terrace, Carnarvon. She kept me and then I went to Miss Morris, Ivy House.

I went to Mrs Evans every day and worked, no answers to advertisements and the Canon became uneasy — was going to write himself to Mr Perkins — I had written two letters to Katie, one to Emily, and one to Grandma all of which said I was married and was with my husband — I was desperate wrote to you — N.B. I bought a photo at Humphrey's the Photographers and sent to Katie as a likeness of him — who? — nobody —

I told the Evans you were my Godparents and would receive me — had your telegram a letter from Katie through the Police Agency — started for Shrewsbury 3.30 — Slept there sent an impudent and false telegram to Katie from Shrewsbury — came on to you today —

Mrs Evans gave me fifteen shillings and I had one pound before from the bracelet ring charm etc. I pawned, I have the ticket, I bought the ring wedding [sic] at Carnarvon a few doors from pawn shop — gave four and sixpence — told the man I had lost mine while bathing. I can remember no more now — I think I feel sorry — I have prayed now, and I think God helped me to do this the address will be proofs for you can follow me from the day of leaving Bowdon till today — if I am asleep don't wake me. God help me and bless you I pray I mean it. Question me now not tonight and I beg of you write to all the addresses and see that this is true I have written this while you were downstairs after I prayed — I meant to deceive you and when you mentioned poor Robert I jumped at the chance. Mr Miller you have saved me by telling me to pray. God made me do this.

Shall I write to Mrs Evan, Grandma and Mrs Perkins, if it is really necessary I will do my best and show you the letters. I can more easily write down things because I have time and I am not so afraid and therefore can tell the truth, so if I have things to tell you I shall write them and not trust myself to tell them, don't ask me things because I feel frightened and then tell — [she means lies]. If you would, I hardly can trouble you would you mind when you want to ask me things, writing them down. Indeed it would help me for being asked point blank I feel frightened and hurried and so make fearful mistakes....It is my own fault.

On a separate sheet she wrote out a sum which showed that ten pounds and eight shillings was to be paid to Miss Okell by Mary Esther Jacob, of her own earnings. Only a person of the calibre of Miss Britain would knowingly take in such a girl as governess. The passage of time might by 1896 have caused some amelioration of a disordered personality, especially since her insight was good, if glib. In Yokohama her public face will have been one of frozen rectitude, while in Baltonsborough she will have been permanently under silent punishment by her family, and watched for further outbreaks of wild behaviour.

Although people believed her, the 'confession' does not show a really practised plausibility. Her picaresque flight, her small odyssey, almost a kind of fugue, has the quality of nightmare with the fear of destitution. There is a passivity in her constitution which makes her appeal to others to help her out of self-dug holes and throw herself upon the mercy of authority figures.

She views her life as a moving psycho-drama, and weaves her lies out of the stuff of romantic fiction. The obvious sexual need seems to render Elsa Christoffel as a particularly compatible bosom friend. The dishonest appropriation of finery, the jackdaw eye for jewellery, have a relation to that unfulfilled condition.

To Miss Okell, Mary wrote a letter of formal self-abasement:

I have no right whatever to ask a favour of you. But I can ask you to forgive me the sin of the deed. I am truly sorry and by God's help my future life shall show my sorrow and repentance. May I beg you to give a few thoughts to that which I am going to ask you. Mr Miller will help me to get work and please can you, will you wait till I earn it, I could pay by littles I may be years earning it for I am not clever and may be I may not succeed in my work. I see and know how thankful I should be not to find myself in prison. It is a great thing even to ask forgiveness but I do so because I am really sorry. Thank you again and again for your goodness to me, my ungratefulness only shows up the more because of it.

The trouble I have brought on my friends will by the help of heaven aid me in trying to live as they would have me so as to make some small amends.

Only moderately touched by these sentiments, Sophia Okell wrote on September 27th to Mr Miller:

I received your letter and Mary's on Tuesday, her box was sent off on Wednesday by Midland Rail....Can Mary give any satisfactory account of the corsets two or three pairs which she had with her at Baltonsborough, the suède gloves and the music which she had brought back with her and said had been given to her and of her journey to Baltonsborough in June of which she gave two quite different accounts. Of course it is immaterial to me whether she answers, but an explanation that does not include everything is not satisfactory and as I have been obliged by her own doings to make enquiries which under different circumstances would never have been thought of and her best response to them

is the simple truth. If you should come north at any time I shall be glad to see you.

Mary's 'doings' had the power to outrage, and to wound. Feeling sorry for her was one thing, but realising that she had still been partial with the truth was difficult to accept. Alfred Simon, of 139 Shrewsbury Street, Brooks Bar, Stretford, wrote to Miller in sceptical and punitive terms:

I saw Miss Okell before I left but of course I could not get from her a promise and indeed would not try, that it should not go any further — naturally she will keep it within the narrowest limits, for her own reputation and poor Kate's sake but one thing you may be sure is certain and that is that Miss Okell will not be satisfied with what she has heard, she is a great deal too full of commonsense to know that if Mary has taken one pound she has much nearer taken six pounds or perhaps ten pounds and I should not be surprised if she takes the most rigid course possible in regard to Mary. It is simply idle for Mary to make such pretences. I am positively sure that she is at present deceiving you.

To tell me that she is repentant and at the same time treating the matter in the way she is doing is simply impossible. Let us hear from her with a detailed account of the money she stole. The only money she got besides what she stole from her uncle, we can easily tell what that was, and if we run up the things she was constantly buying it will show at a glance that the one pound that she speaks of is simply one more lie added to the many. Why has she not sent the finery she bought back to us or Miss Okell? She surely cannot think that by simply confessing that they are stolen property, she can continue to use them.

I tell you, Mr Miller, that I believe so little in her sincerity that if she had robbed me I think I should as a Christian duty (the only Christian course a man can take) prosecute her. I would go to seventy times seven if I saw any sign of true repentance but I am not moved by merely canting. I think Mr Jacob should have seen her, no one has a greater right and if she feels what she says she does, she will gladly speak with him. If things cannot be more satisfactorily explained I think I shall try to come and see Mary.

While I write like this think not friend that I esteem lightly your kindness. You are more than kind and this is felt keenly by all of us.

And on September 29th Simon wrote again to Miller:

I am sorry if I appear to you unduly hard upon Mary, it is far from my intention, but I cannot feel otherwise than I have written until I am persuaded that she feels the wrong of what she has done, still I am persuaded that she has not felt it yet. Did you see the letter she wrote us? What the many excuses are I cannot imagine. No one could have had less excuses to justify such wickedness. She had a delightful home surrounded by people most perfectly refined in soul and as true as the sunlight — were more than kind — really highly indulgent — not one girl in a thousand had such home advantages.

She never wanted for anything, money she had as much and more than was good for her and I am sure that wherever she goes a more perfect house she will never be privileged to enter. She was noticed and treated with great kindness by all our friends and I think that say what she likes our home was as open to her as to our own children and our interest in her not less. So what excuses there are I cannot understand. I have not seen Miss Okell and cannot say what her feelings are at present. But to punish for spite she never would, it would be more intense pain to her to punish than it would be to Mary to be punished.

The scandal was hushed up, and Mary must have been 'placed' regularly until the ultimate, crowning post in Yokohama, with the pattern repeated over and over, she the odd one out in a household of man and wife and their children, with sexual congress going on and on in the aired connubial bedroom, with kindness lavished on the spinster governess, an orphan, as a Christian duty, as if she were a member of the family — which she was not. How much indeed she sought to be 'noticed', but learnt to check her stronger impulses.

The revealing documents arrived too late on John Lowder's desk for him to use against her in the defence of Edith Carew, but had they come earlier they would have fallen upon him like manna in the wilderness of his lonely Counsel. Here for him to wing and impale was a girl who had lied from her schooldays, who could not stop herself, who made up a tale as she went along, who spoke of 'something' in her coffee, who fancied herself in love with everybody, who wanted to do something romantic, who invented a person called Ernest Mentz, who wrote a fictive note from that man, who sent a false telegram and a false likeness of him, who made a kind of suicide threat — 'If I am asleep don't wake me' — who told only half the truth even when the chips were down, and with mock modesty (surely not self-knowledge) confessed herself as not clever.

Chapter 18
A GLEAM OF MERCURY

The last time that Edith had sailed home it was to the cheers and garlands of Glastonbury. Now, one year after Walter's remains had been laid in the cemetery on the Bluff, the captain of the P&O steamer *Sumatra,* in whose custody she had travelled, handed her over to the grip of warders from Holloway Prison, who were waiting at the docks to receive her. Once, she had flirted with officers over tea and music from the ship's band, but all she had left was a distant hope of release when her youth was gone.

It was not the policy for convicted British subjects to serve long sentences abroad. In due time the Governor of Hong Kong had made representations to the Colonial Office, and the Home Office had authorised the removal to Holloway, to arrive on November 26th or 27th, 1897. Within a month they transferred her to Aylesbury Prison, in Buckinghamshire, where Florence Maybrick was also serving her term. The two women will undoubtedly have been acquainted, but Edith will probably have considered American-born Florence socially inferior, and too fluffy — not a robust outdoor type. One may also suspect that Edith calculated that a friendship with another convicted husband-murderer would have been a contamination. She knew that her behaviour would be watched.

Settled, if such could be the expression, at Aylesbury, with her strong family and English lawyers conferring and planning, Edith bethought her of her financial affairs. Walter had died intestate, and she (well, her solicitors) had the effrontery to petition the Home Office for permission to take out Letters of Administration and to appoint her brother-in-law, Robert George Hallowell Carew, or her brother, Robert Bagehot Porch, as Administrator.

It is of course a well-known precept of British law that a convict

shall not profit from his crime, but in the Carew case a curious anomaly arose. By Section 6 of the Felony Act 1870, the word 'convict' was stated to mean a person condemned by any court of competent jurisdiction in England, Wales or Ireland. Not Japan! The Law Officers of the Home Office agonised, and finally *allowed* the petition.

There was still plenty of support for Edith in the world at large. Many residents in Yokohama still believed in her, as did just about the whole of Glastonbury. On October 2nd, 1897, the *Saturday Review* was sure that 'a more lamentable exhibition of bemuddlement and imbecility on the part of all concerned....has never disgraced English legislation.' The closing speech for the defence was 'absurd' and the prosecution speech and the summing-up were 'simply indistinguishable'. The case called aloud for reconsideration.

After the failure of the petition to the Privy Council the only avenue of appeal left open from the Court for Japan was a petition to the Queen for a free pardon, and documents were duly lodged in January 1898. Edith's petition was meticulously and voluminously prepared, and caused the Home Office a nearly commensurate amount of work. In effect, this was a fresh look at all the evidence by new minds under less pressure. The names of the petitioners — relatives and dignitaries — were headed by Walter Carew's parents. For the petitioners, Counsel had prepared a lengthy analysis of the whole evidence, which was submitted to Dr Washington Isaac for resettling, to exclude any medical contention that was not sound. The submission was that there had been a miscarriage of justice, that the verdict was contrary to the evidence, and that Edith Carew had not obtained a fair trial.

Dr Divers, a kind of bearded scapegoat in his particular Japanese wilderness of a hostile laboratory, was of course criticised for his omissions. It was argued that it might have been that every trace of arsenic found was taken in *solid* form, and it was merely a matter of speculation whether Walter Carew had in fact taken *any* Fowler's Solution.

The case being one of circumstantial evidence, the judge ought to have told the jury that they could not find the prisoner guilty unless they were satisfied that the circumstances were not only consistent with her guilt but were also inconsistent with any other rational explanation.

Mrs Carew did not obtain a fair trial: its excessive length of four weeks was the fault of the prosecution, in calling a mass of evidence which, although wholly irrelevant with regard to the issues in the case, was calculated to excite prejudice. In itself the length of the trial prevented the jury from grasping the true issues.

The charge against Mary Jacob had caused the question put to the jury to be changed to: 'Admitting murder was done, is it more probable that Mrs Carew or Miss Jacob is the guilty party?'

The jury of only five residents in Yokohama must have been familiar with all the details of the case, and primed with scandal, gossip and rumour. The trial should have taken place in Hong Kong or England. The evidence of Mary Jacob was admitted without cross-examination (because the defence had excluded her and made her ill!). She went to the jury as a perfectly honest and truthful witness, but it was very probable that knowledge of her past life and character would have had great influence on the verdict.

The Law Officers of the Crown called on Dr Thomas Stevenson to advise on the medical and chemical evidence. Stevenson, later knighted, was Senior Scientific Analyst to the Home Office from 1881 to 1908. Born in 1838, he died in 1908 from diabetic coma. He was expert witness in many notable murder trials, including those of Florence Maybrick and Dr Thomas Neill Cream. From his chemical laboratory at Guy's Hospital he wrote on May 20th, 1898, to the Secretary of State in terms which entirely supported the conviction of Edith Carew.

The specks of white arsenic, he said, could well be accounted for by the fact that Fowler's Solution had been freshly and hurriedly prepared. In the preparation of Fowler's, the white arsenic employed dissolves in the alkaline solution of potash slowly and with difficulty, and particles of white arsenic may remain suspended in the finished solution.

He did not doubt the legend of the Styrian peasants, but knew of only one case of large dosage of arsenic. Habituation to Fowler's Solution was non-existent in England. The symptoms were not consistent with poisoning by sugar of lead.

On May 25th a Home Office official noted that the defence had only themselves to blame for Mary Jacob's non-appearance in person, for: 'There is grave reason for thinking that the charge against her was trumped up by Mrs Carew's Counsel solely in order to confuse the case.' The affidavits did seem to establish the point that in 1884 Mary Jacob was both dishonest and untruthful. 'Of this the jury knew nothing, and of course the new facts damage the case for the prosecution.'

However, although the governess' statement undoubtedly told against Mrs Carew, 'it seems to me that if the whole of her evidence is rejected, Mrs Carew's own actions and letters are fatal.' Some of these matters, it was urged by the petitioners, were irrelevant, but 'they prove that she is a woman of doubtful moral character, capable of forging or lying or stealing to accomplish her end.'

The petitioners admitted that the charge against Mary Jacob was most unwise, and that there was no ground whatever. The trial had been exhaustive, and every point that could be made was taken by Defence Counsel. There was no moral doubt of the guilt.

Characteristically ingenious, Edith wished to make her own contribution to the deliberations of the Secretary of State, by means of a 'Statement' dated July 29th, 1898:

Dr Divers of Tokyo stated in his evidence that he had discovered some white particles in the throat, and which he suggested were white arsenic.

I use the word suggested, as Dr Divers did not make any positive assertion: he only drew a conclusion. As on enquiry no purchase of white arsenic could be traced, the above evidence did not excite much comment.

I now wish to state that the white particles found by Dr Divers were white precipitate, and that the poison as stated on the packet was purchased by my late husband in the summer of 1893, during my absence in England.

Evidence was given at my trial to prove my giving an emetic. I call upon Messrs.Brett & Co., Chemists, in 60 Main Street, Yokohama, to verify the purchase. I am willing to answer any questions with reference to the above statement, but refrain from doing so now, as I have no witness to corroborate my word as to the details.

The Home Office was not at all impressed: 'Now Mrs Carew says (or implies) she gave the hot water because her husband had been taking white precipitate. If so, why did she keep it a secret at the time? Assuming for the moment that Mr Carew did buy white precipitate in 1893, she does not even now say positively that he used it shortly before his death. Her 'statement' seems extremely weak.'

The Under Secretary of State, Sir Kenelm Digby, commented: 'I fear this statement now that it has come does not help us much. If she could have shown that her husband had white arsenic in his possession shortly before his illness, it might have been material. The statement appears to throw no real light on the question and this of itself is unfavourable to her.'

At this late stage, Edith has introduced yet another poison — mercury — into the case. White precipitate, hydrargyrum ammoniatum, or mercuric ammonium chloride, *can* be a formidable poison, according to Taylor.[23] The word 'packet' would signify the powder, not the more usual ointment or lotion, and Edith indicated that the contents of the supposed packet resembled Dr Divers' white specks. White precipitate was used, and still has a use, in skin complaints, including eczema, impetigo, herpes, scabies and other parasitic skin diseases such as pediculosis (lice).

The implication would be that Walter had a skin problem of some kind in 1893. A far-fetched alternative would be that he had bought the powder as a stand-by for suicide, while lonely and depressed.

No packet of white precipitate was put in at the trial, or recorded as confiscated from the house. Edith's 'weak statement' is curiously oblique: rather than implying that Walter *had been* taking the powder, Edith must have been implying that in despair Walter had clutched at the old packet — conveniently close to the sick-bed — and swallowed down, perhaps in a handy glass of liquid, a lethal, suicidal dose of mercury.

He was, however, by then far too weak to attempt such an act, and moreover on caution from Dr Wheeler, Reginald Porch was watching over him. No mercury was found post-mortem. Dr Divers did state that the process which he adopted was calculated to enable him to find arsenic, antimony, lead, copper, tin, bismuth 'and others', but he never mentioned mercury.

Theoretically only, Edith could have kept quiet about the mercury because of the shame of suicide. If she had been less positive in her statement, offered the mercury as a mere suggestion, she would not have made so poor a show of credibility.

The nearest that Convict No. X19, Edith Carew, ever came to a pardon was in the matter of the summing-up. The Law Officers had noted that some words of the judge — 'It is not necessary that death should be shown to be actually *due* to a particular poison; it is sufficient if it is shown that such poison *conduced* to the death' — were not happily chosen, but they did not actually mislead the jury.

The Under Secretary of State allowed that Judge Mowat had been inaccurate and defective in his address, (which seems rather hard), but took it into account that the Privy Council had not thought that a substantial injustice had been done by the judge's summing-up. That seemed to be the right tribunal to deal with the point.

On August 10th, 1898, letters were written to Edith's solicitors, and to the Foreign Office, to say that the Secretary of State saw no ground for interference until the case came up for reconsideration at the end of 15 years under the Hong Kong prison rules. Again, in August 1902, a petition praying for a free pardon was presented, with no success. On January 29th, 1904, the Governor's routine report to the Secretary of State on a convict who had completed seven years of sentence described Edith's mental and physical health as good.

The comparison with Florence Maybrick was always vividly present in the collective mind of the Home Office, just as it had pervaded the court in Yokohama. An obdurate official comment was that: 'The case is to be reviewed after fifteen years, but *without any presumption in favour of release.* Her case was worse than Mrs Maybrick's because she tried to put the guilt on an innocent person.'

In this way the ill-considered charge against the governess lived on as a nail in Edith's cell door. The Establishment viewed a legal device as a moral fault. Suppose that Lowder himself and alone, on receipt of the telegram with its intimation of Mary Jacob's past, had decided to proceed in person against her, it would then have taken a good deal of moral courage for a client on a capital charge, relying entirely on that Counsel to save her, to question his judgement and countermand absolutely his action.

In 1905, as Walter's grave grew lichened (for no Carews still lived in Yokohama), Convict X19 was transferred to the Long Sentence Division. In November 1906 Edith was admitted to the prison hospital, suffering from debility, and still continued to lose weight. The Medical Officer found no organic disease, and attributed her condition to external factors. In an unimaginable tragedy, Edith and Walter's only son, Benjamin, who had kept her awake at night with his riding competitions, had died on May 16th, 1906, at the age of 13. The death certificate gives the cause of death as 'Otitis Media 3 days, 12 hours acute meningitis Cerebral, 3 days Coma'. He was being educated in the Carew tradition at the Royal Naval College, Osborne, and the place of death was Park House, York Avenue, East Cowes, Isle of Wight. The informant was his uncle, Robert Hallowell Carew, of Raleigh Villas, Exmouth.

Nearly as devastating a cause of grief — for she loved him dearly — was the death of Reggie Porch. He was 29. Unsettled, he had ranched in Colorado, served for some years with the Mounties and been a fur-trader and trapper for the Hudson Bay Company. He was variously reported killed or disappeared in the San Francisco earthquake of April 1906, in which the city was almost destroyed. A fire, in the Japanese fashion, followed the tremors, and some 1500 lives were lost.

In 1907, after ten years of sentence, Messrs Bridges Sawtell and Co.asked for a reconsideration of the petitions, but the view of the Home Office was that ten years was inadequate punishment for a poisoning in which considerable skill and determination was shown in the endeavour to divert suspicion. The absence of any agitation on the convict's behalf was in her favour, and her petitions showed a much better tone than was usually found in female convicts.

It was felt that Edith ought not to be released earlier than Florence Maybrick, even though she was now a specially good and well-behaved convict. (In 1905 Edith had forfeited 384 marks for misconduct.) Both women had some excuse in the character of the husband. (This is the first such admission during the entire case.) If Mrs Carew's husband was not all she could have wished, at any rate he did not interfere in her compromising correspondence with other men.

The worst feature (and still the mistake returns in vengeance) was the charge against the innocent governess, who was nearly killed by the shock. It could not have been done without her consent. She should serve at least 15 years, as Mrs Maybrick did. For the time being the reply had to be that, taking into account the character of the crime, it was too soon to consider any reduction of sentence.

Still in the hospital in March 1907, Edith was steadily losing weight, eating a great deal without any benefit. Dr H.B.Donkin, of the Prison Commissioners, examined her on April 8th, in consultation with the Medical Officer, and found hers to be a case of considerable gravity. The emaciation was by then extreme. Eventually, however, the authorities discovered that Edith had been deliberately starving herself and secretly disposing of the food set before her, in order to be released. This perverse act was so cunning, and so in character, that it told against her as another moral fault to be taken into consideration.

She endured, and gained weight, until March 1910, when her solicitors asked for an indication of the prospects of release, since her father was a very old man (nearly 77). As it happened, the Secretary of State at that time was Winston Churchill, who in 1918 was to become a kind of relative. The supporting letter from the Porchs' Glastonbury solicitors pleaded that:

> *Neither her own family, nor the family of the late Mr Carew have ever lost their faith in Mrs Carew's innocence. If released, she would not be homeless or unprovided for. It is, we believe, Mrs Carew's desire when the time for her release comes, to enter some Roman Catholic establishment, and this course would have the approval of her parents. Mr Porch and her brother, Captain Cecil Porch, who has recently visited her, fear that the long imprisonment is telling on her mental capacity.*

The Home Office debated whether the claims of justice had been satisfied, and obtained a medical report, dated March 26th:

Her general bodily health is fair and her mind is in my judgment sound. She is thin, weighing 108 lbs. She expresses herself as being quite well and I believe she is. She is engaged in active and apparently congenial work in the kitchen. Imprisonment has not in my judgment impaired her in body or mind and further imprisonment is unlikely to do so.

Thus satisfied, the Home Office noted: 'Mrs Carew, apart from her crime, is I believe a most charming person who wins the heart of all her gaolers. On one occasion, by her personal influence, she prevented a mutiny among the Roman Catholic prisoners, which should count in her favour.' An official, however, did add the qualification that Mary Jacob, he had been told, never got over the shock of the false accusation.

Another official argued that 'There is good reason to hope that if released she will lead a quiet, useful and honourable life.' Unfortunately for Edith, though, an implacable, unforgiving personage at that time walked the corridors at the Home Office: this was the Assistant Under-Secretary, Ernley Robertson Hay Blackwell (1868-1941), knighted in 1916, who was active behind the scenes in many important criminal causes. His opinion was that:

Her crime was murder of the worst sort and she escaped hanging by an accident. Whatever may be her present disposition and character — and her petitions show no signs of penitence — she certainly was a criminal who stopped at nothing to attain her end.

She nearly achieved the ruin of a wardress whom she persuaded to post a letter for her. The fact that she is of gentle birth and good education and has a home ready for her is scarcely relevant.

Gradually, however, a softening of attitude began to show up in further comments at the Home Office which questioned the background of the crime:

The motive for the murder may have been derived from her intrigues with other men; her own husband had also not been very faithful to her and was clearly by no means impeccable. There may have been circumstances of their life together of which we can know nothing but which might furnish some excuse for the crime.

Having taken life, she might properly have been hanged, but as she is neither brutal, criminal, nor dangerous by instinct, society does not need to be protected and she is herself unlikely to benefit by a few years more in prison.

On October 26th 1910, Edith May Hallowell Carew was released on licence from Aylesbury Prison. She was only 42. She had never embraced Roman Catholicism in the outside world, nor had she been particularly pious in her adult life, and there was no question of her entering a nunnery, whatever the expectations of the world at large. She was going to enjoy the many years left to her, quietly indeed, but not as a recluse, and surrounded by the animals which she had missed. Perhaps she had not lost the taste for flirtation, but she hid away that part of herself.

Just before her first Christmas at home, her father effected a release of her obligation to report to the police, and she was as free as air. For a time she attempted to brazen it out at Glastonbury, but the gossip was terrible. There is a story told in the town that a Mrs Barbara Dunston was informed by her mother that when she was a servant at Somerset House, in Magdalena Street, (which can still be seen) Edith was a guest at dinner, soon after her release, and it was noticed that her hands were coarse and gnarled. They thought that sewing mail-bags must have caused this condition, but it was more probably due to her work in the prison kitchens.

Eventually she moved to Wiltshire, where she lived for some years with her daughter Marjorie, who never married. She did not change her name. One day, it is said, in 1934 a book [24] which covered the Carew case appeared in the local library. Mother and daughter simply abandoned their house and much of its contents, leaving a deserted maidservant to sell up for them.

The shutters were closed, and 'hundreds' of angora rabbits were taken away in wheelbarrows.

Chapter 19
INCARNATE FIEND?

The mysteries of the Carew case, (and they interlock), are the 'Woman in Black', the 'Annie Luke' letters, and the precise stage at which Edith formed her murderous intent, as manifest in the diary. As to her guilt, there is no getting away from the fact that she was instrumental in bringing into the house large quantities of arsenic during the week of Walter's dying, whatever the ins and outs of precisely who was the carrier, and when.

If one could imagine that she had laid out a table of the poisons (see page 201) introduced to No.169 she would by her reckoning have rationalised the total intake of eighteen grains of arsenic by the following computation: six grains were for her own undoubted malaria, four grains were bought by some stranger, and the remaining eight were got in by Walter's request. Walter must have taken longer to expire than she had anticipated, and the necessity, under pressure, for more 'plenty deadly poison' wrecked her. He was no stranger to injury by arsenic, and his body seems to have had an abnormal resistance. It would have been more fiendish if supplies of poison previously and discreetly acquired and hoarded had been drawn upon.

No one, except Lowder's expert witness Dr Eldridge, seriously believed that the fatal illness was consonant with a single dose of arsenic. Even the defence abandoned the fantasy of a 'Woman in Black' sneaking into Walter's bedroom and administering one killing draught, in favour of Mary Jacob and her opportunity for repeated doses. The specks of white arsenic, a useful gift to the defence and peddled for all they were worth, were almost certainly deposits from improperly prepared Fowler's Solution. Sugar of lead was not intended to kill, but, sinisterly linked with arsenic in its acquisition, was used in an attempt to control the purging of

Poison introduced to 169, the Bluff, prior to Walter Carew's death

Date	*Description*	*Arsenic*	*Chemist*	*Carrier*
Saturday October 10, 1896	Day of the visit of the 'Woman in Black' and the 'boathouse prescription' Half-ounce of Fowler's Solution prescribed for Edith by Dr Wheeler			
Sunday October 11	Above obtained	2 grains	Schedel's	Messenger
Thursday October 15	Walter sent home to bed			
Saturday October 17	Repeated half-ounce of Fowler's solution	2 grains	Schedel's	Messenger
Sunday October 18	One bottle (one-third of an ounce) sugar of lead		Maruya's	Messenger
Monday October 19	One ounce of Fowler's solution. One bottle (at least one-third of an ounce) sugar of lead	4 grains	Maruya's	Unidentified 'foreign woman'
Tuesday October 20	One ounce of Fowler's solution [and a bedpan.]	4 grains	Maruya's	Messenger
Wednesday October 21	One ounce of Fowler's solution One bottle (half to three-quarters of an ounce) sugar of lead Half-ounce of Fowler's solution	4 grains 2 grains	Maruya's Schedel's	Mary Jacob Mary Jacob
Thursday October 22	Walter Carew dies	18 grains		

arsenical poisoning. The purpose of such binding would have been to keep the arsenic in the system for as long as possible, to seal it, to kill more effectively, and also to disguise the fatal illness as a blander alimentary upset.

Hopeful of success, Edith would not have expected a chemical analysis of the organs. She did manage to delay the diarrhoea until the day before Walter's death. How did she know about this property of sugar of lead? It could scarcely have been common knowledge, even if the effects of arsenic itself were well understood at that time.

Edith was accustomed to doctoring her own animals. Probably there was some kind of medical or even poisons book in the household, and it might have had the tell-tell underlinings which so often occur in murder cases, but of course no such book was to be found by the time that enquiry reached No. 169.

As to motive, there is absolutely no difficulty in analysing the components of a particularly strong reason to be without Walter Carew: her gallant husband had been retaining her money. Willingly at the inquest she revealed the financial rift, perhaps as a double-bluff. True, she had sorted it out, but no doubt Walter still schemed, and an awkward situation had prevailed, with a resentful, carping husband watching her expenditure. His status and career prospects were not so good as they had appeared to be at marriage. Any improvement would have had to come from an invasion of Porch family funds.

He had chronic ill-health; years of decline lay ahead. He had gonorrhoea, which was incurable. She was only 28. Her predicament was unfair. Although once she must have loved him physically — or she would not have married him without her parents' approval — he must have become repugnant to her. After only a few years of marriage Edith found herself needing to chase other men. Walter let her, but he could be nasty about it. Where was it all going to end? He drank, who knows how often? His symptoms of liver damage were probably not all due to malaria. He was bad-tempered.

The 15-year age difference, in combination with his lesser energy, had led to different interests, or rather, they had shown up in Yokohama. In short, the Glastonbury bride now neither loved

nor liked her fallen husband. The desire to marry Dickinson, who was not in a position to take a wife anyway, was not paramount. Edith had not yet met the new lover of her romantic imaginings.

Divorce or separation, which would have meant a return in ignominy to the town where flags had flown for her, was unthinkable in that social setting. Even if late-Victorian prejudice still prevailed, it is ironical that the Queen herself (vide: her *Journal*, May 10th, 1887) was by now taking a more enlightened view. She saw no reason why wronged divorced women should suffer social eclipse, and held a 'drawing-room' at Buckingham Palace which included certain 'poor divorced ladies'.

Anyway, Edith was short of evidence for divorce, which required strong proof in 1896. She told Dickinson about threats of brutality, but she had no bruises to exhibit. In spite of Walter's flirtation with Miss Bolitho, his spooning Mrs Tocque, there was no evidence of *his* adultery, and she would certainly have had every reason to fear a cross-petition and frightful scandal. By staying with him she had technically condoned a great deal of what she had to complain of, and, all in all, it is no wonder that she failed to consult Counsel about divorce. Widowhood was Edith's best solution. And like a girl she toyed on paper with her name annexed to other men's.

The only mystery attaching to the motive is how she developed the force to leap that volitional gap between dreaming of the deed and its actual commission, which leaves most people trapped in hopeless situations. For the explanation here we must look to Edith's morbid mental state, which was not at issue in the trial, because of her plea of not guilty. Her exogenous circumstances were enough to make any woman significantly depressed, to turn on the wheel in her cage.

The diary, cryptic though it may be, reveals an underlying depression which marches with the round of activity. The stresses with Walter show. She has headaches. The rain keeps her indoors and she broods. Very importantly, she has chronic malaria. The parasites were not all killed off by quinine — the drug of choice then — and relapses were the rule, not the exception. Mental disturbance ranks with slight fever, wasting, secondary anaemia, enlarged spleen and liver, palpitations, dizziness, digestive troubles and general lassitude. At the very least, Edith's malaria will have

had the effect of causing an episodic clinical depression. The diary also reveals a tendency to mood-swings. She certainly was feverish, which may have affected her judgment and contributed to some of the murderer's mistakes which otherwise appear to be 'stupid'.

The diary, which is the best available evidence on the point, suggests that the washed-out holiday at Miyanoshita in September was the time when Edith plotted the broad design of the murder. The uncharacteristic patterning of the two stark entries on grumbling at the rain indicates an extreme reaction in Edith's mind. Edith's two letters to Walter from Fujiya's Hotel are also enlightening, where they are not false. She is seedy and depressed, and they parted badly. He has written a carping letter about her failure to enclose a note with his slippers. She resents his tone.

The business talk about buying a house with her money worries her. She thinks something is the matter with her, she feels so awfully wretched. It is tempting to interpret these words as a 'cry for help' or an appeal for release from her darker self, but Edith was not made like that, and Walter was not the man to save her from herself.

If a woman intends to murder her husband by slow poison, she must retain a stance of dutiful docility, and so she signs herself 'Your loving little wife Edith'. If she is really fiendish, she tells him she wants him. And the Miyanoshita letters are to be set against the contemporaneous Dickinson correspondence, which delivers a different message.

Let us examine the veiled apparition, the 'Woman in Black', who materialised from nowhere like an extraterrestrial on the rainy afternoon of October 10th. The Crown argued that she never existed, and that probably is the best view. It means that the diary entry is a lie, as are all the last entries. By the same token, Edith's letter to 'Dearest Walter — A most mysterious lady came here just now...' must also be a lie.

The indications are that she did send this letter to Walter at the boathouse, although it is always a bad sign when, as here, she professed to have found a letter amongst Walter's papers after his death. It *must* be more than a coincidence that the 'Woman in Black' makes her entry on the same day as Edith's first acquisition of arsenic. There must be a connection. It must be the start of the mischief. Once set upon murder she will not have been coetaneously pursuing another device. She was in no mood or state for a jape, even a vicious or resentful one. The 'Woman in Black' was an invention calculated to affect Walter, to work upon and poison his mind.

As, knowing him, she had anticipated, the apparition put him into such a paroxysm of anxiety and guilt (which does him credit) that outsiders would notice, and that he would take to drink and to his bed. Then the family doctor would diagnose and treat him for over-indulgence, liver and digestive disorder. If, as is argued, there was no veiled woman in the hallway, then Edith could not have been trying to push Walter into adultery, because there was no real person for him to pursue! Crown Counsel at one stage canvassed the idea that she had been playing upon Walter's mind to drive him to suicide, but that is not suggested here.

Bluff and hearty as he may have appeared to acquaintances, Walter was not in fact a man with everything to live for. His marriage was in tatters, although he would not admit it, and his health was unlikely to improve. His secret disease shamed him. His stricture hurt like the devil. His little wife had stopped at source that useful supply of readies which had made life bearable.

His job was not up to much. No independent evidence was ever brought by Lowder to prove that his business prospects were more than a pipedream. Edith had the name of the firm handed to the jury for them to read privately. The late affidavit of Mrs Emma Marjoribanks — sworn for another reason, and therefore all the more convincing — shows that Walter, at least in 1893, when Edith had left him, had the potential for profound depression. Edith, however, was locked into a course much more positive than a mere vague hope that Walter, stressed, might end it all.

It is quite natural, at first thought, to dismiss the 'Mysterious Visitor' as any ordinary woman with whom Walter had been dallying in Yokohama — impregnated, even — and rejected. In that case, though, if she were indeed a 'lady' with a calling card, Edith would have known her. *And Walter did not react as if this were the situation: his instinct was to look to the past.*

Why, if she were a genuine woman in distress, would she have been veiled? She was asking for Walter, who could have been at home, and she would have let him see her face, wouldn't she? There was a conversation, so that Edith would have recognised her voice, if she knew her. If Edith did not know her, why bother to conceal her face? The implication was that all was about to be revealed. There was no explanation that she was bereaved, and therefore in mourning.

The veiling exonerated Edith from exactitude. It rendered the visitant more mysterious, amorphous, with more scope for perplexing Walter.

Since Ah Kwong, according to Edith, opened her door to the 'Woman in Black', should he not have been able to attest to that incident? The coroner made a wretched mistake at the inquest, when the Chinese boy was fresh, and terrified — but might have been pinned down. 'Gentlemen of the jury,' the coroner said, 'it is unlikely that any evidence we get from this boy will throw any light', and they let him go, unquestioned.

At the magisterial proceedings the assistant judge too peered down at the 12-year-old boy, and undervalued and silenced him. Later, at the same tribunal, Litchfield called him about other matters and missed the real question. Ah Kwong showed here that he was as bright as a brass button, and might well have been brought to remember Regatta Day, when it rained. He was clever enough about other 'foreigners' dates.' He was not called at the trial.

Edward Owen, of P&O, as has been remarked previously, was a very important witness. No one was brought to corroborate the scene in the hallway, but Owen's testimony, if it were true, proved that Walter believed what Edith had told him about the 'Mysterious Visitor'. It does seem most unlikely that Edith had suborned him, although there is a whiff of perjury elsewhere in the case.

There is some indication too, that on Sunday, October 11th, the day after the apparition, she was a subject of banter over the luncheon table. Mary Jacob, who had no reason to lie about her, would have testified, if she had been well enough, at the trial, according to Wilkinson, that 'there was a good deal of chaff about the strange visitor but that Annie Luke was never mentioned.'

Reggie Porch, called by Lowder at the inquest, remembered perfectly well the joking about the visitor on that same occasion. He offered no name. It was he who, on 20th October, heard Edith telling Walter, to reassure him, that Annie Luke had called and that she would do her best to help her. *(That would indicate that Annie Luke was the right name.)* Dickinson did say grudgingly, at the trial, that Edith mentioned the mysterious woman at the boathouse on October 10th.

According to Owen, testifying at the trial, Walter thought that the visitor was either the jilted Englishwoman *or* a woman from the Straits (who might, theoretically, have been the mother of his children). At the lower court, however, Owen said only that Walter had mentioned the Englishwoman. Walter must be presumed to have known both their names. It seems beyond belief that Edith would not have known the name of the woman whose child she was (if it were true) helping to support. She already knew Annie Luke's name, if her testimony that Walter had confessed his relationship with her shortly after their marriage was genuine.

The card produced by the visitor should have borne her own initials, or else there was no point in wanting Walter to see it. Disguised initials would have defeated her purpose of an appeal or a showdown.

Wilkinson said that when the time came to call Mary Jacob at the trial she would testify that when she first saw the card it was inscribed only with 'M.J.1888'. That was, of course, the year before the Carew marriage. The inference was that Edith had added the 'A.L.' later, as an improvement.

It seems curious that Walter was so drawn by the initials M.J. They do not appear to have been the initials of the Straits woman, because Walter was mystified. Owen, however, can shed some light, in that he was the only witness to Walter's speaking of having received *two* cards; the second one, he said, had made things clearer. The second card certainly looks like second thoughts unless Edith had orchestrated a pattern of mystification and suspense. M.J., her governess' initials, might have been a random choice subconsciously selected. Reginald Porch, it must be said, testified that he saw the card with the full inscription on Saturday, October 10th.

If the 'Woman in Black' was so desperate for a rendezvous with Walter that she would cross oceans to get to him, why would Walter go to the P&O office to enquire about a lady who wanted to book a passage *out* of Yokohama? Owen provides a kind of explanation:

Walter said that Edith had told him that she had seen the 'Woman in Black' outside the P&O gates. The assumption was Walter's.

Edith's lies formed a web: at the same time that she was telling admitted lies to Dickinson about her steps towards getting a divorce, she was also, between the 12th and 14th October, telling him that Walter had written a letter to 'A.L. and M.J.' at the Post Office, and Dickinson was telling her to ask for it there. There is no evidence of a letter so addressed.

It was adversely remarked that Edith did not mention the 'Woman in Black' when she *first* testified at the inquest. The reason is not that she was keeping her powder dry, or that she was improvising as she went along, but that she was not going to reveal part of her stratagem at a time when she was hoping to get away with her crime. The visitant was not originally a segment of Edith's defence, but became so as she used every available means to divert suspicion, and she did turn to improvisation.

We come now to the Annie Luke correspondence: that is, the letter from 'Annie' to Walter at his club, postmarked October 13th, (see plate 18) and his letter of October 14th to 'Miss Annie Luke, Post Office' (see plate 19). The first was, ominously, found by Edith after Walter's death, in his papers. Possession of the second was more difficult to justify, but conveniently it was sent 'anonymously' to Edith on 16th or 17th, was it not?

There is every reason to believe that both these letters were written by Edith. The similarity to her handwriting is remarkable. Any wife worth her salt can have a stab at imitating her husband's hand. No independent evidence was ever brought that the letter to Miss Annie Luke was in Walter's handwriting. There is anyway a striking discrepancy which was not picked up at the proceedings. The alleged letter from Walter — 'Meet me this evening at 5.30 pm on the Bund', clearly indicates that he would *be there,* anxiously pacing with flicked cigar. Edith's diary for October 14th, however, shows a different state of affairs: 'Walter came home at 4 o'clock and went to bed. The result of last night's dissipation.'

The later, anonymous 'A.L.' letters, in a totally different handwriting, sent to the coroner and to Lowder (see plate 20), and 'found' on Edith's doorstep, form a different series of mystification. They are essentially *false* in tone. No one could pretend to believe

that they are the outpourings of a real person. The perfervid style exactly matches that of the 'Annie' letter of October 13th. Their handwriting is peculiar, and obviously disguised.

As she improvised, Edith must have realised that the handwriting of the Annie Luke exchange was too like her own, and devised a gross variation signed 'A.L.' which was sufficiently like Annie Luke to sustain the charade without commitment, to confuse. This was one of Edith's mistakes, because an Annie Luke with two separate handwritings was a weakened figure.

The Home Office thought that the uniformity and consistency of the writing of the 'A.L.' letters indicated the genuineness of the hand, and worryingly set them apart from Edith's hand, but this need not be a problem; the 'A.L.' letters are so fault-free that they must have been copied from a draft.

What is the intended force of the 'A.L.' letters? It is of course to exonerate Edith. Who would do that? Edith herself, in a disguised hand? A kind of amanuensis, writing from Edith's draft, using a natural hand, or a disguised one? Who would do such a thing? Dickinson showed no particular animus to save Edith, did he? Rachel could scarcely read or write. Reggie? Possibly. It was he who acted suspiciously by first missing but later spotting the sheet of paper protruding from Mary Jacob's birthday book.

How about Mary Jacob? The difficulty here is that she was not hand-in-glove with Edith — that is, before relations were severed — in the way that Florence Bravo and her companion Jane Cox were close.

It *was* widely thought and commented upon that Mary's handwriting (see plate 21) matched the 'A.L.' letters, and certainly melodrama was her style, but she left 169 the Bluff on October 24th, well before their flowering, and steadfastly refused to see Edith again. No one else was close enough to Edith to try to save her. The letters could not have come from some wandering lunatic, some freelance confessor, because of their inside information such as 'Do you know what waiting means for eight long weary years.' *Edith wrote them.*

If there really were a jilted woman of Devonshire, called Annie Luke, was there not a risk that upon reading the case so freely reported in the newspapers, with copy telegraphed from day to day to England, she would feel a duty to say that she had never been to Yokohama in her life? Or would she be too embarrassed to speak out?

If the case had been investigated by English police in Yokohama they would have called on their counterparts at home to seek out Annie Luke by interviewing Walter's family and associates. There is no record in the Home Office papers of any official contact with Annie Luke, even or especially at the time when the whole case was being reviewed.

The local newspapers in the West Country did not dare to speculate, because of the heinous libel of suggesting a relationship between Walter Carew and a young woman. However, it has long been believed in Glastonbury that Annie Luke existed. 'Captain and Mrs Luke' were listed as giving a wedding present (an electro bread scoop) at the Carews' wedding, and it has been thought that they were related to her.

By modern research it has been possible to find an Annie Luke, connected to the Carews' wedding, and connected to Walter's home town of Exmouth. There is full documentary evidence that between 1889 and 1891 Captain William Stephen Luke, J.P., R.N., was living with his family in a house called Springfield, at Exmouth, Devonshire. His eldest, unmarried daughter, aged 22 at the time of Walter's marriage, was *Annie Georgiana Louisa Luke*. Her mother was Georgiana, and she had two younger sisters, Ada and Mabel.

Supposing that she were indeed the jilted one, Walter Carew did not ruin Annie's life, because after some nine years — during which her nautical father died — she married Philip Gordon Nicholson, bachelor and gentleman, son of John Stuart Nicholson, gentleman. Both parties were aged 31. The marriage took place at St Philip's Church, Kensington, on July 18th, 1900. Annie's residence was 34 Pembroke Road, and her groom's was 10 Lisgar Terrace, West Kensington. Her mother was a witness.

Annie Luke lived, but she was not the 'Woman in Black'.

Chapter 20
THE COVE

Even today it is easy to miss the narrow lane, once a rutted cart-track, which drops for a long Welsh mile to the hidden cove of Cwm-yr-Eglwys. The main highway runs through the village of Dinas Cross, which lies above the wooded cliffs that guard the sea, and a traveller on horseback would only have picked his route down for a purpose, and if he knew the hamlet was there. This was the hideaway on the remote North Pembrokeshire coast in which Edith spent the last years of her life. The few cottages, gathered closely together around the head of a perfect sandy cove off the wider saucer of Newport Bay, were isolated from civilisation, but not lonely in themselves.

It is said that Edith knew of the place because she had spent holidays there with a friend. Dinas Cross, called 'The Village of Thirty Captains', has some splendid white houses built by those sea captains in their prosperity, but there were no such big houses down by the shore, and so, in 1934, Edith bought two cottages and converted them into one modest beamed white house named Penfeidr, and filled it with antique furniture. The house now is far from gloomy, with a walled and terraced garden at the back, over which a particularly verdant deep moss spills like rampant seaweed, and a beech tree spreads its boughs over the wall to the lane which climbs upwards to the wider world. At that time Edith had an unobstructed view of the sea, and in microcosm the shaped bay with fishing boats below the guarding bluff was a memory of Yokohama. She would never have liked the greater obscurity of hiding away in a city.

The cove has a history and an atmosphere created by the Celtic pattern of the ruined belfry and arch of the twelfth-century church of St Brynach, which stands with old gravestones at the centre of

the sea-wall, right out by the beach. The great storm of October 1859 destroyed the church and wrecked the *Royal Charter* and 113 other ships along the coast. In the Dinas cemetery aloft, in the consecrated field which grows lush across the lane from the new Church of St Brynach, sleep the departed master mariners and their families.

Here Edith and Marjorie (the daughter who never married) lived their private remembering lives, and in spite of village gossip their secret was safe until the day they died. They had neighbours, and were not entirely unapproachable, but were respected as keeping themselves to themselves. Edith did not venture up the 'gorge' as they called it, on foot, nor was she, once an admired Sunday school teacher, any longer a churchgoer.

Even so she *was* conspicuous, and wondered at, in the community. To start with, she was an Englishwoman, and, quite bizarrely, she kept a liveried chauffeur-gardener, her 'houseboy'. First there was Charlie Carew, as he was known locally, with his big cap, and then there was Harold Massey, a cockney.

The 'servants' quarters' were in the small, bothy-like attachment to the side of the house which can be seen on the photograph (see plate 25). A well-remembered focus of resentment was the fact that the 'houseboy' was made to fend for himself for meals. The car, at one time a Standard, stood in a barn across the lane. Edith and Marjorie were driven in some style on shopping trips to Fishguard and Haverfordwest, but the old life of social calls was over.

The two thin, dignified women with their fluting voices and formal manners, dressed very much alike in long, dark clothes, were always out with the dogs (which must be why there was a permanent hot-pot on the stove!) The horses had gone, but the love of animals was there as strongly as ever, and indeed provided a reason for living.

Bedlington terriers — those lamb-like yet varminty little dogs — were Edith's fancy. The National Bedlington Terrier Club had been founded in 1875, but the breed had made slow progress, and Edith became an early and known breeder of quality dogs. If she sold you a puppy it was a good one. The house and garden were crowded out with litters of Bedlingtons, corgis, and ducks.

Mother and daughter were not to live alone for ever: a whole

new family structure grew around them. They were joined by a girl, Pansy Porch, actually Marjorie's adopted daughter, who was believed throughout Dinas to be Marjorie's *illegitimate* daughter, and the family did not actively discourage the rumour. In fact, Pansy's birth certificate shows that her father was Colonel (retired) Cecil Porch Porch, and her mother was Constance Edwards, formerly Robinson, of no occupation. She was born on August 17th, 1920, at 239 Selhurst Road, South Norwood. Cecil was Edith's eldest brother, educated at Charterhouse and the Royal Military College, Lieutenant Colonel of the East Surrey Regiment, DSO and Bar. He died on November 29th, 1933.

Pansy Porch was an unconventional, scatterbrained girl, a character, who loved all animals and was well-liked and appreciated for her use of picturesque language. She married Joseph Dilwyn Mills, a shoe shop manager, and they lived for a time at 6 Sapphire Street, Cardiff. Two children were born to them, a boy and a girl. They all returned later to live at Penfeidr with Edith and Marjorie.

Edith died at home, aged 90, on June 27th, 1958. The cause of death was congestive heart failure and arteriosclerosis, and she had been bedridden for some time. Harold Massey, present at the death, was the informant. Marjorie arranged for her mother to be cremated at Swansea Crematorium on July 1st, 1958, and her remains were scattered on the Garden of Remembrance. No application was made for an entry in the Book of Remembrance.

Marjorie, known in the hamlet as 'Mardie', lived on to February 9th, 1978, dying as Edith had done before her, of congestive cardiac failure and disseminated atherosclerosis. Pansy was present at the death.

Between 1965 and 1967, when Edith was no longer alive, the name of the house was changed from Penfeidr to Troed-y-Rhiw. Pansy died of cancer on February 1st, 1985, at Withybush General Hospital, North Prendergast, Dyfed, and Joseph followed her on December 3rd, 1987. Both, after a service at St Brynach's Church, were cremated at Parc Gwyn Crematorium, Narberth. The villagers were saddened by their passing.

Towards the end it was thought that the money had begun to run out,[25] and it was noticed that a large portrait of the Admiral of which Edith was inordinately proud had quietly disappeared

from the walls of Troed-y-Rhiw.

Of the 'old people at Edgarley', Edith's father, John Albert, died on May 27th, 1914, aged 81, whereupon Edgarley House was sold, and Edith's mother, Margaret, died at Chippenham on August 11th, 1930, in her ninetieth year. Edith attended both funerals. Edward Albert Porch, Edith's youngest brother, educated at Clifton, had a successful military career, MC, Colonel, Indian Army. He married twice, first Maud Cecil Palmes, of Naburn Hall, and secondly, Esther Florence Lund. He died on November 11th, 1937, without issue.

Robert Bagehot Porch, the second-eldest brother, was the academic member of the family. Educated at Malvern and Trinity College, Oxford, he was for 35 years Assistant Master and Housemaster at Malvern College. A great character, he was a master of the old school, devoted to the College. Known as 'Judy' Porch, he never spoke of the family tragedy, which was not guessed at in college. One of the few things that made him angry was denigration of the past. He was an accomplished letter-writer. He married Kathleen Mitchell Hector, and they had two sons and two daughters. Reaching the age of 87 in Malvern's ozoniferous clime, he lived on to 1962, when a memorial service was held on November 28th at Christ Church, Down Street, London.

John Frederic Lowder did not long survive his most difficult case, and died on January 27th, 1902, in his fifty-ninth year, having continued to practise in Yokohama. Ambrose Berry Walford, however, took the other course, and returned to England in 1900, to practise on the Oxford Circuit. He married, on October 30th, 1907, Edith Mary Louisa Walford, daughter of Dr Edward Walford of Cardiff, and appears to have died in 1940.

It is pleasant to be able to report that Mary Jacob, after long ordeal, found happiness and stability at last. Safely back in Baltonsborough, she rode out the gossip, and, on November 14th, 1899, she married Richard Palmer, bachelor. Her husband was a farmer, son of Richard Hicknell Palmer, also a farmer. Her bridegroom came from Hinton St George, a village some 16 miles from Baltonsborough. He was 37 and she was 33. The marriage took place in the Parish Church of Baltonsborough, which is dedicated to St Dunstan, and Mary's brother William was one of the witnesses. No Porch or Hallowell Carew will have been a jovial wedding guest.

Nearly a century after the deed, Walter's large black gravestone in the foreigners' cemetery in Yokohama still proclaims blankly to the disinterested visitor:

WALTER RAYMOND HALLOWELL CAREW
In Loving Memory
of
My Husband

Who died October 22nd 1896 aged 43 years

Sunset and evening star
And one clear call for me!
And may there be no moaning of the bar,
When I put out to sea.

FOOTNOTES

1 The classic murder mystery. Did Florence Bravo poison her husband, Charles, or was it her companion, Jane Cox or her 'ancient lover' Dr Gully?

2 Sturdy realism, perhaps. The Somerset and Dorset Railway, which served Glastonbury, was known as the 'Slow and Dirty'!

3 *V. Walter Bagehot*. William Irving. Longmans, Green & Co. 1939.

4 For more details of the Porch-Churchill marriage see *Jennie. Lady Randolph Churchill*. Peregrine Churchill and Julian Mitchell. Collins. 1974.

5 'What a country of greenery and shade, this Japan, what an unexpected Eden.'

6 'And it was raining, raining: falling so thickly that it nearly turned day into night ... And with it there was a wind, too: one could hear its deep, profound voice howling in the ravines.'

7 Cubebs: the dried berry of Piper cubeba, a Sumatran climbing pepper shrub.

8 Copaiba: The balsam obtained from South American trees and shrubs of the genus Copaifera.

9 From *Guinevere: Idylls of the King*. Arthur reproaches his Queen for her adultery with Lancelot.

10 A variety of the game, played with seven instead of five cards, and with two disclosed.

11 The ** represent tears in the paper.

12 In this case, and elsewhere, the omissions were deliberately made by official hands to protect named persons from publicity.

13 Samuel Rutherford Crockett (1860-1914). Scottish minister and prolific novelist, member of the kailyard school of fiction (from the cabbage patch kept outside cottages) in which, with much

use of the vernacular, rustic life in Scotland was portrayed in a frankly sentimental manner.

14 Presumably Thomas Hardy's *Jude the Obscure* which had just came out in novel form in 1895.

15 Edith's punctuation in the diary, not in anticipation of publication, is perfunctory, and relies on points and dashes. Therefore, it has been lightly standardised, for clarity.

16 'The moment has come when the thing ought to be done.' Or — 'It's time to do it.'

17 The horse mutilation crimes which were investigated by Conan Doyle.

18 Four grains of arsenic = one ounce of Fowler's solution. One grain of arsenic = 100-120 minims of Fowler's, depending on the way it is made up. One minim = one drop (roughly). Thus 200-240 drops would be needed to constitute the fatal dose of two grains.

19 The peasants of Styria, a former province of Austria, were avid arsenic eaters and had developed a tolerance. They were always invoked in these poisoning cases to illustrate how much arsenic a person could safely consume.

20 The sex disqualification, naturally, followed the law in England, where it was not removed until 1919.

21 The Pimlico mystery of 1886. Dyson procured some chloroform. Adelaide Bartlett allegedly used it to eliminate her husband. Neither was convicted.

22 No record has been found of an appeal to Shanghai.

23 Although Taylor also states that of 14 cases of ingestion of doses varying from a few grains to 40, only two proved fatal. *Principles and Practice of Medical Jurisprudence*, Alfred Swaine Taylor, 1865.

24 Short accounts had been included in *Woman and Crime*, Hargrave L. Adam, 1912; *Noted Murder Mysteries*, Philip Curtin, 1914; and *Feminine Frailty*, Horace Wyndham, 1929.

25 Edith's estate was valued at £442.7.11d, and Marjorie's was £26,775.

INDEX